Elizabeth L. MacNabb
Mary Jane Cherry
Susan L. Popham
René Perri Prys
Editors

Transforming the Disciplines
A Women's Studies Primer

Pre-publication
REVIEWS,
COMMENTARIES,
EVALUATIONS . . .

"Women's studies is distinct from other interdisciplinary fields (such as film studies) in that its introductory-level books are less about women's studies as an academic field of study than about feminism as a sociopolitical movement. *Transforming the Disciplines* fills this gap admirably, presenting an exhaustive collection of essays describing how women's studies affects the various disciplines, in both substance and method. Contributors focus not simply on women as subjects of study in disciplines or as academic participants, but on the kinds of questions disciplines ask, and how the rise of women's studies has offered new kinds of questions and challenged the primacy of the old questions.

The inclusion of bibliographies at the end of most essays makes it a valuable reference tool. Most welcome is the section on natural sciences. Given that most women's studies faculty tend to come from the humanities and the social sciences, faculty teaching women's studies courses will benefit from the attention paid to the effect women's studies has had on the natural sciences. Additionally, the book can help broaden women's studies as a discipline by showing faculty from all disciplines how women's studies has changed not just who works in their fields, but how they do."

Dr. Karen Adkins
Director of Women's Studies,
Regis University,
Denver, CO

More pre-publication
REVIEWS, COMMENTARIES, EVALUATIONS . . .

"*Transforming the Disciplines* truly reflects upon the interdisciplinary nature of women's studies. Teachers and students alike will appreciate its broad scope, clear language, and lively analysis of how feminist inquiry has shaped and continues to shape diverse scholarly fields and professions.

The book's final section, which focuses on the professions, provides a welcome complement to the preceding ones on the humanities, social sciences, and natural sciences. Here readers can learn how feminist theory and practice inform one another in real-world settings."

Allison Kimmich, PhD
Director of Pre-College Programs,
Barnard College,
New York, NY

"What a great book! *Transforming the Disciplines* is intelligent, informative, and readable. This book breaks new feminist ground by assembling in one volume a wide array of essays that explain feminisms' impact on disciplinary ways of thinking.

This expansive collection demonstrates the transformative influence of feminisms across the disciplines. Exquisitely written to communicate both to undergraduates and to women's studies scholars, the book provides a concrete example of the ways in which feminist thought has made an indelible mark on the academy. The bibliographies themselves are worth the price of the text! This is a book I will use in an unlimited number of ways: with upper-division undergraduate students, with freshman seminar students, with graduate students, and as a valuable scholarly guide to feminist work outside my field."

Heather E. Bruce, PhD
Department of English,
University of Montana,
Missoula

"*Transforming the Disciplines* maps the extensive terrain of women's studies across the disciplines. In lucid prose, contributors detail just how and why women's studies has radically changed disciplinary practices in the humanities, social sciences, physical sciences, and professions. The editors have assembled a rich collection of essays that are free of jargon, yet profoundly informed. Over and over, you will encounter fine examples of feminist recovery work that revises disciplines and makes it possible to consider women's lives, hear women's voices, and use gender as a category of analysis. But most significant, *Transforming the Disciplines* reminds us how women's studies not only changes how we study, but also how we live the personal as political. This comprehensive primer is a perfect introduction for the beginning women's studies student and an excellent sourcebook for more seasoned scholars."

Gioia Woods, PhD
Assistant Professor,
Humanities, Arts, and Religion,
Northern Arizona University,
Flagstaff

NOTES FOR PROFESSIONAL LIBRARIANS AND LIBRARY USERS

This is an original book title published by The Haworth Press, Inc. Unless otherwise noted in specific chapters with attribution, materials in this book have not been previously published elsewhere in any format or language.

CONSERVATION AND PRESERVATION NOTES

All books published by The Haworth Press, Inc. and its imprints are printed on certified pH neutral, acid free book grade paper. This paper meets the minimum requirements of American National Standard for Information Sciences-Permanence of Paper for Printed Material, ANSI Z39.48-1984.

Transforming the Disciplines
A Women's Studies Primer

HAWORTH Innovations in Feminist Studies
J. Dianne Garner
Senior Editor

New, Recent, and Forthcoming Titles:

Anorexia Nervosa and Recovery: A Hunger for Meaning by Karen Way
Women Murdered by the Men They Loved by Constance A. Bean
Reproductive Hazards in the Workplace: Mending Jobs, Managing Pregnancies by Regina Kenen
Our Choices: Women's Personal Decisions About Abortion by Sumi Hoshiko
Tending Inner Gardens: The Healing Art of Feminist Psychotherapy by Lesley Irene Shore
The Way of the Woman Writer by Janet Lynn Roseman
Racism in the Lives of Women: Testimony, Theory, and Guides to Anti-Racist Practice by Jeanne Adleman and Gloria Enguídanos
Advocating for Self: Women's Decisions Concerning Contraception by Peggy Matteson
Feminist Visions of Gender Similarities and Differences by Meredith M. Kimball
Experiencing Abortion: A Weaving of Women's Words by Eve Kushner
Menopause, Me and You: The Sound of Women Pausing by Ann M. Voda
Fat—A Fate Worse Than Death?: Women, Weight, and Appearance by Ruth Raymond Thone
Feminist Theories and Feminist Psychotherapies: Origins, Themes, and Variations by Carolyn Zerbe Enns
Celebrating the Lives of Jewish Women: Patterns in a Feminist Sampler edited by Rachel Josefowitz Siegel and Ellen Cole
Women and AIDS: Negotiating Safer Practices, Care, and Representation edited by Nancy L. Roth and Linda K. Fuller
A Menopausal Memoir: Letters from Another Climate by Anne Herrmann
Women in the Antarctic edited by Esther D. Rothblum, Jacqueline S. Weinstock, and Jessica F. Morris
Breasts: The Women's Perspective on an American Obsession by Carolyn Latteier
Lesbian Stepfamilies: An Ethnography of Love by Janet M. Wright
Women, Families, and Feminist Politics: A Global Exploration by Kate Conway-Turner and Suzanne Cherrin
Women's Work: A Survey of Scholarship By and About Women edited by Donna Musialowski Ashcraft
Love Matters: A Book of Lesbian Romance and Relationships by Linda Sutton
Birth As a Healing Experience: The Emotional Journey of Pregnancy Through Postpartum by Lois Halzel Freedman
Unbroken Homes: Single-Parent Mothers Tell Their Stories by Wendy Anne Paterson
Transforming the Disciplines: A Women's Studies Primer edited by Elizabeth L. MacNabb, Mary Jane Cherry, Susan L. Popham, and René Perry Prys

Transforming the Disciplines
A Women's Studies Primer

Elizabeth L. MacNabb
Mary Jane Cherry
Susan L. Popham
René Perri Prys
Editors

The Haworth Press®
New York • London • Oxford

The Haworth Press, Inc., 10 Alice Street, Binghamton, NY 13904-1580

Cover design by Marylouise E. Doyle.

Library of Congress Cataloging-in-Publication Data

Transforming the disciplines : a women's studies primer / Elizabeth L. MacNabb . . . [et al.].
p. cm.
Includes bibliographical references and index.
ISBN 1-56023-959-X (hard : alk. paper) — ISBN 1-56023-960-3 (soft : alk. paper)
1. Women's studies. 2. Feminism and education. 3. Feminism and literature. 4. Feminism and science. I. MacNabb, Elizabeth L., 1952-

HQ1180 .T73 2000
305.4'07—dc21

00-040739

CONTENTS

ABOUT THE EDITORS

Elizabeth MacNabb, PhD, teaches at the University of Richmond in Virginia. She holds a PhD in comparative literature from the State University of New York at Stony Brook. She studied writing pedagogy as a postdoctoral fellow at Illinois State University and has taught numerous women's studies courses, including two versions of "Introduction to Women's Studies." Her book *The Fractured Family: The Second Sex and Its (Dis)Connected Daughters* was published in 1993.

Mary Jane Cherry is a doctoral candidate and instructor in the rhetoric and composition program at the University of Louisville in Kentucky, where she has taught intermediate and advanced composition and women's literature. An assistant coordinator with the university's Writing Across the Curriculum program from 1999-2000, she also received fellowships in 1998 and 1999 with the *Henry James Review,* where she served as an editorial assistant. In 1997, she received the expository writing award for graduate research from Kentuckiana Metroversity, a consortium of regional colleges and universities. Between 1995 and 1997, she was program assistant to the chair of the University of Louisville's women's studies program.

Susan L. Popham is an assistant director of the Writing Center at the University of Louisville in Kentucky. In addition to her administrative duties, she teaches composition while pursuing her PhD in rhetoric and composition. Her research interests include the rhetoric of science, medicine, and technology, as well as feminist theories of pedagogy.

René Perri Prys received her MA degree in English from the University of Louisville in 1997. She teaches freshman, intermediate, and advanced composition, and business/professional writing at the University of Louisville and Spalding University in Kentucky.

Contributors

Haithe Anderson is an assistant professor in the School of Leadership and Policy in the College of Education and Human Development at Bowling Green State University. She has published in the *Harvard Educational Review*, the *Journal of Higher Education* and in *Philosophical Studies in Education*. Her work focuses on cultural studies, history, and education.

Robert Bambic is an art historian, critic, and curator who writes, lectures, and teaches in the fields of nineteenth- and twentieth-century art. He is currently completing a dissertation in contemporary art at Bryn Mawr College.

Amy Sue Bix received her PhD in the history of science, medicine, and technology from Johns Hopkins University in 1994. Since 1993, she has been an assistant professor in the history department at Iowa State University. As part of ISU's program in the history of technology and science, she regularly teaches undergraduate and graduate courses on the history of women in science, technology, and medicine. She has published articles on breast cancer and AIDS activism, on the history of women as eugenic fieldworkers, and on the postwar development of physics and engineering at Princeton University. Her book, *Inventing Ourselves Out of Jobs?: America's Depression-Era Debate Over Technological Unemployment,* was published by Johns Hopkins University Press in 1999. Currently, she is researching the history of American women's engineering education.

Lyndie Brimstone graduated from the University of North London in 1985, with a first-class honors degree in English literature. She earned her MA in twentieth-century literature from the University of Sussex in 1986. She has taught courses on arts and humanities and feminist theory, and in 1993 she joined the Women's Studies Multidisciplinary Team at Roehampton Institute London. In addition to teaching, she has contributed to several international reference works and published articles in the areas of women's studies, women's literature, and lesbian studies, including "Taking the Next Step" in the *Introduction to Women's Studies* (1995) and "Out of the Margins and into the Soup: Some Thoughts on Incorporation" in *Out of the Margins: Women's Studies in the Nineties* (1991).

Juan R. Burciaga is a lecturer/laboratory coordinator in the physics department at Bryn Mawr College. He received a BS and MA in physics from the University of Texas at Arlington and a PhD in physics from Texas A&M University. As a graduate student at Texas A&M, Burciaga first became interested in discerning the reasons students have trouble learning physics, mathematics, and other academic disciplines. His research interests include molecular physics, meso-scale phenomena, and astrophysics.

Barbara S. Burnell is a professor of economics and coordinator of the Women's Studies program at the College of Wooster, in Wooster, Ohio. In addition to teaching courses such as Macroeconomics, Public Finance, and History and Philosophy of Economic Thought, she teaches several courses in the Women's Studies program, including Economics of Gender, Women and Work, Feminist Research Methods, and introductory and seminar courses in women's studies. Her research interests focus on occupational sex segregation, with particular emphasis on the roles that workplace technology and the construction of urban space play in this process. As her essay demonstrates, this research has fostered feminist critique of mainstream economic methods.

Kimberly Burton began her public career in art at five, exhibiting extensively on the walls (literally) of her kindergarten. She has since completed degrees in English, Medieval Renaissance studies, and Fine Art with a focus on live figure drawing. Her work as an artist is inspired by classical art history, archetypes in myth and dream, and, frequently, by her favorite stories and texts. Currently, she is completing an MA in English at the University of Louisville and exhibiting her art in Indiana and Kentucky.

Karen Chandler is an assistant professor of English at the University of Louisville, where she teaches courses in African-American and

American literature, women's studies, and film. She has published essays on Hollywood and independent films, melodrama, and women's literature. Her study of melodramatic formulas in narratives about women's transgressions is currently under review by a university press, and she has begun work on a study of intersections between the African-American vernacular and film.

Mary Childs is a lecturer in the Faculty of Law at the University of Manchester. She worked as a law clerk to the British Columbia Court of Appeal before qualifying as a lawyer in Canada, then moved to the United Kingdom to pursue postgraduate studies at Oxford University. Her teaching and research interests lie in the areas of criminal law, evidence, and gender and the law.

Dayna Beth Daniels had a dream of playing first base for the New York Yankees. When she was eight years old, she was denied access to little league baseball because she was a girl. This event set her on the path of studying sport and honed her personal feminist convictions. Always active in a variety of sports, Dayna majored in physical education at Ithaca College, received an MA in Kinesiology from Indiana University, and earned a PhD in biomechanics at the University of Alberta. Over the years, her research interests have changed from skill analysis to issues of gender and sexuality in sport and physical activity. Dayna has been a professor of kinesiology at the University of Lethbridge, Canada, since 1980. She is currently the chair of the Department of Kinesiology and is also the coordinator of Women's Studies, a position she has held since 1987. Dayna teaches courses in the sociology of sport and in women's studies. Her favorite course is Women and Sport.

Amy Begg DeGroff is a senior librarian with Progressive Technology Federal Systems, Incorporated (PTFS, Inc.), a Maryland-based systems integration firm that specializes in document management and information system solutions for government agencies and commercial corporations. Amy provides PTFS clients with professional services including end-user training, digital library development, imaging and library consulting, World Wide Web system development, and needs analysis. In 1996 she was recognized by the American Libraries Association as one of 25 emerging leaders in the library and information science profession. Amy received her MSLS from the

Catholic University of America in 1994. Her BA in history was awarded in 1990 from Westhampton College at the University of Richmond in Richmond, Virginia. She currently resides in Rockville, Maryland, with her husband Tom.

Helen J. Forgasz, PhD, is a senior research fellow at Monash University, Australia. Her research and teaching interests include mathematics and science education, gender issues, mature (nontraditional) students, learning environments, and learning settings. Helen has published widely in books and scholarly and professional journals and is a regular presenter at scientific and professional meetings. She is a former executive member of the Mathematical Association of Victoria, and is currently vice-president (conferences) of the Mathematics Education Research Group of Australia.

Janet L. Gream is an accomplished Kentucky artist who captures much of the state's heritage in her work. She works comfortably in a variety of media but concentrates on pen and ink drawings, watercolor, and oil. She received a BA in fine art from the University of Kentucky and an MA at Western Kentucky University, and continued her studies during extensive travel and a ten-month stay in Germany. Since 1996, Janet has participated in the Art Teacher's Forum at Savannah School of Art and Design. She has also studied with nationally known artists Tony Van Haselt, Arleta Pech, and William Scott Jennings. Janet also has an interest in creating handmade baskets, and she belongs to the Kentucky Basket Association and other state basket guilds. She resides in Hodgenville, Kentucky, with her husband, Larry, and daughter, Heather.

Mara R. Greengrass received a BA in anthropology from the University of Maryland, College Park, in 1993, and an MA in applied anthropology from the American University in 1996. She has worked as an archaeologist for a variety of employers, including the National Conference of State Historic Preservation Officers (as a consultant to the National Park Service). She has excavated in two countries (Israel and the United States), and enjoys artifact analysis and giving site tours. Mara's true love in archaeology is public outreach—teaching others how archaeologists work and think. Currently, she works for the American Anthropological Association as a program assistant in Government and Media Relations, where she writes press releases, talks to the press, helps monitor the federal budget, and encourages conversations between policymakers and anthropologists.

Gwyneth Hughes taught science in schools and colleges for a number of years after earning a degree in chemistry. She then completed an MA in women's studies and became increasingly interested in feminism and science. As a consequence, she left science teaching and the narrow curriculum that she was expected to deliver, and now lectures in women's studies and science and technology studies at the University of East London, UK. She also does research on gender in science and technology education and has recently completed a doctorate.

Eileen John teaches philosophy at the University of Louisville. Her area of research is aesthetics, or philosophy of the arts. She is especially interested in philosophical questions about literature, such as the kinds of knowledge we can gain from literary fiction. Her publications include "Reading Fiction and Conceptual Knowledge: Philosophical Thought in Literary Context" in the *Journal of Aesthetics and Art Criticism* and "Subtlety and Moral Vision in Fiction" in *Philosophy and Literature*.

Jeanne Halgren Kilde is a visiting assistant professor at Macalester College in Saint Paul, Minnesota, where she teaches courses on American religious history and women and religion. She received her PhD in American Studies from the University of Minnesota in 1991 and has taught at Cleveland State University and the University of Notre Dame. Interested in religious architecture and sacred space, she is currently completing a book on nineteenth-century Protestant churches. She is also working on a book on women and sacred space and an article from this project, titled "The 'Predominance of the Feminine' at Chautauqua: Rethinking the Gender-Space Relationship in Victorian America," was published in the February 1999 issue of *Signs: Journal of Women in Culture and Society*.

Kathleen M. Kirby, PhD, is an associate professor and licensed psychologist. In addition to her work as the clinical training director of the Educational and Counseling Psychology Department at the University of Louisville, and clinical supervisor of the Learning Improvement Center at the University of Louisville, she maintains a small private practice in Louisville, Kentucky. Her areas of specialization include treating traumatized children and adults, individuals with sexual-orientation issues, children adopted after infancy, women of all ages, and individuals with mood problems. Her research areas include parenting stress, identity development issues of adolescents who are members of multiple marginalized groups, gender issues in job satisfaction, and cultural historical theory and treatment intervention. In her work as a counselor and researcher, she draws from her life experiences, from twenty years in social work, and from her feminist colleagues and foremothers.

Gilah C. Leder, MEd, PhD, is a professor in the Graduate School of Education and director of the Institute for Advanced Study at La Trobe University, Australia. Her teaching and research interests embrace the interaction between the teaching, learning, and assessment of mathematics. She has published widely in the areas of mathematics education and gender-related issues. Gilah serves on various editorial boards and educational and scientific committees and is a frequent presenter at scientific and professional meetings. She is past president of the Mathematics Research Group of Australasia and is the current president of the International Group for the Psychology of Mathematics Education.

Julianne Lynch, MA, is a PhD student in the Graduate School of Education, La Trobe University, Australia. The proposed title of her thesis is "Introducing Internet Technologies: A Study in Four Victorian State Secondary Schools." Before returning to study, Julianne worked as a research assistant on a three-year investigation into images of women and mathematics in the popular press and how these images contribute to the broader context of mathematics education. Her research interests include gender and education, educational technology, and research methodology. Julianne serves on the Electronic Communications Committee of the Mathematical Association of Victoria and the Human Ethics Committee of the Graduate School of Education, La Trobe University. She is the editor of a student-run online journal: *The Weaver: A Forum for New Ideas in Educational Research.*

Debian Marty earned her PhD in 1996 from Ohio State University. She is now an assistant professor with the Institute for Human Communication at California State University, Monterey Bay. Her areas of specialization include rhetoric, communication ethics, and women's studies.

Marilyn Matthews, a Kentucky native, is an accomplished artist who has had much of her work exhibited in galleries throughout the state. She worked for several years as a graphic artist before raising her family; two of her children have now also become accomplished visual artists. She recently completed an MA in art therapy at the University of Louisville and has worked with a state educational grant to teach arts and humanities to young, rural Kentucky schoolchildren. She is highly interested in feminist theories of psychology, spirituality, and personal expression. She and her husband live in a log cabin, where she practices her artistry and finds interest and solace in watching the change of the seasons reflected in the woods around her home.

Hildy Miller is director of writing and associate professor of English at Portland State University. Her PhD in English is from the University of Minnesota. She has taught graduate and undergraduate courses in feminist rhetorics and has published articles and presented papers in the area of epistemology, feminism, and writing. Currently she is working with Lillian Bridwell-Bowles on a collection exploring contemporary theories of feminist rhetorics.

Cynthia Negrey is an associate professor of sociology at the University of Louisville. She is the author of *Gender, Time, and Reduced Work* and articles on industrial restructuring, employment trends, and income in U.S. metropolitan areas. She continues to be interested in work-time issues, urban economic and social change, and welfare reform. Recently she has taught courses on "Diversity and Inequality," "Women and Work," and "Industrial Sociology."

Ursula M. Rempel is an associate professor at the School of Music, University of Manitoba, where she teaches courses in music history, women in music, and recorder ensemble techniques. She has published articles, presented papers, and contributed essays on various aspects of late-eighteenth- and early-nineteenth-century women composers, many of which focus on the harp. Her work appears in *The American Harp Journal*, *Man and Nature/L'homme et Nature*, *Mosaic*, *French Women and the Age of Enlightenment*, *The New Grove Dictionary of Women Composers*, and *The New Grove Dictionary of*

Music and Musicians (revised edition). Her current research focuses on music as social accomplishment, as evidenced in eighteenth- and nineteenth-century conduct/education manuals, and in the novels of Jane Austen.

Georgia Rhoades, a member of the English department at Appalachian State University in Boone, North Carolina, teaches women's studies and coordinates the Composition program. She also often teaches Irish and English feminist literature in Appalachian State's Study Abroad program. As a member of Black Sheep Theatre, she writes and performs feminist theatre. She is currently writing a book about mermaids and sheela-na-gigs in her idle moments.

Edwin S. Segal is a professor of anthropology at the University of Louisville, where he is one of the founders of the Women's Studies program. Professor Segal is also on the advisory councils of the university's Women's Center and the Multicultural Center. His research focuses on the countries of Eastern and Southern Africa, and he has done field research in Tanzania, Malawi, Kenya, and South Africa. Most of his writing has been about ethnicity and gender. His most recent publications are "Male Genders: Cross-Cultural Perspectives," in *Advances in Gender Research 2* (1997), edited by Vasilike Demos and Marcia Texler Segal, and "Confrontation in Academe: The Nairobi Faculty Strike," in *Humanity and Society 23*(1) (1999).

Laura Shanner is an associate professor in the John Dossetor Health Ethics Centre and the Department of Public Health Sciences at the University of Alberta (Canada) and is a coordinator of the International Network for Feminist Approaches to Bioethics. She previously taught philosophy at the University of Toronto and Georgetown University and has served on a federal advisory board on embryo research in Canada. Her publications on reproduction, genetics, women's health, and health policy have appeared in several journals and books in the areas of law, medicine, philosophy, and rhetorical studies.

Susan Shifrin is an art historian specializing in the field of early modern portraiture. She has contributed articles to a number of reference and encyclopedic works and to several essay collections. She is currently preparing an edition of collected essays titled *Women as Sites of Culture/Sights of Women as Culture* and is working on the manuscript for a book titled *"A Copy of My Countenance": Reading*

Biography, Iconography, and Likeness in the Portraits of Seventeenth-Century Women. Shifrin received her MA and PhD in art history from Bryn Mawr College. She is director of the visual resources collections at Swarthmore College and is an adjunct faculty member in the college's art department.

Mary Ann Stenger, PhD, is an associate professor of humanities at the University of Louisville. Her research and published articles focus on issues of feminism and religious pluralism and analysis of the thought of Paul Tillich. Her publications include "A Critical Analysis of the Influence of Paul Tillich on Mary Daly's Feminist Theology," first published in *Encounter* and reprinted in *Theonomy and Autonomy: Studies in Tillich's Engagement with Modern Culture;* "Feminism and Pluralism in Contemporary Theology" in *Laval theologigue et philosophigue*; and "Paul Tillich and the Feminist Critique of Roman Catholic Theology" in *Paul Tillich: A New Catholic Assessment*.

Ashwini Tambe is a visiting assistant professor of political science and intellectual heritage at Temple University. She has written on globalization, poverty and gender, and media representations of the sex trade. Her current work focuses on the history of prostitution. She has taught undergraduate courses in telecommunications, public speaking, and gender and globalization.

Nancy M. Theriot is the chairperson of women's studies and professor of history at the University of Louisville. She teaches courses on the history of childhood, history of medicine, and history of sexualities. She is the author of a book, *Mothers and Daughters in Nineteenth-Century America*, and several articles. Nancy's current research project is a book-length study tentatively titled, *Deciphering Illness: Nineteenth-Century Women and Their Physicians*. On a more whimsical note, she shares a house with four very contented cats.

Pamela Tracy is a doctoral candidate at Ohio State University. Her areas of specialization include media studies, pedagogy, and women's studies. She has written about adolescent girls, media impact, and identity issues. She has taught undergraduate courses in gender and media, argumentation and debate, and public speaking.

Sharon Varallo is an assistant professor of speech communication at Augustana College in Rock Island, Illinois. Her academic interests include the study of communication in close relationships, family communication, intercultural communication, and gender. Her dissertation, "Communication, Loneliness, and Intimacy," reflected on the experience and expression of loneliness in healthy relationships. She also researches social action issues, as illustrated by a recent article, "Speaking of Incest: The Research Interview as Social Justice." She has also taught communication in Beijing, China.

Jessica Weinberg is a doctoral student in the departments of linguistics and anthropology at the University of Arizona. Her research interests include the linguistic construction of identities and the ideologies of multilingualism and multiculturalism in the United States and Israel. Her current projects explore discourses among fans of *Xena: Warrior Princess* as responses to media representations of lesbianism and bisexuality, the negotiation of meaning in personal narratives in a women's studies class, and normative constructions of masculinity in mainstream movies.

Barbara L. Whitten is a professor of physics and women's studies at Colorado College. She received a BA in physics from Carleton College and a PhD in physics from the University of Rochester. Her physics research is in computational atomic physics; she has worked on problems in laser physics, plasma physics, and Rydberg atom collisions. A lifelong feminist, she discovered the feminist critique of science about a decade ago and has begun to teach and publish in that area. She is the mother of two children: Penelope is in ninth grade, a writer, artist, and swimmer; Jacob is in seventh grade, and is a computer expert and swimmer.

Foreword

In assembling the twenty-six essays that make up this new collection, the four editors of *Transforming the Disciplines* have accomplished something remarkable. They have put together a text ideally suited to function as a virtual primer in the burgeoning field of women's studies—a primary resource for undergraduate students, teachers, scholars, and interested laypersons eager to explore new feminist perspectives that have come to inform every academic discipline in the last three decades of the twentieth century. Invoking the modest rubric of transformation, the contributors successfully illustrate the profound impact of feminist thought on diverse fields of learning—from the arts and humanities, including rhetoric, philosophy, religious studies, music, art history, film, and literature; through social sciences such as history, archeology, anthropology, sociology, psychology, economics, and communications; to physical sciences such as biology, physics, mathematics, and technology; and to specialized professional areas such as education, law, architecture, library science, and sport. Each author surveys pivotal transformations brought about by the inclusion of women and the incorporation of female experience into a particular discipline, and most conclude with a superb bibliography for further reading.

Most women's studies instructors are familiar with a refrain frequently echoed in the halls of academe: "I'm not a feminist but . . . ." It is surely within the ambiguity of this ellipsis that pervasive misprisions of feminist thought in general, and of women's studies curricula in particular, haunt contemporary education. Even the most liberal of undergraduates may feel compelled to eschew invidious charges hurled by media pundits against caricatured "feminazis." But, paradoxically, the same student who adamantly rejects a feminist label often champions principles of gender equity: equal pay for equal work, fair treatment in school and in the workplace, women's right to reproductive control, and gender-blind standards in a professional meritocracy. Most college students at the dawn of this new millennium assume that they are training for careers that will absorb at least 90 percent of their adult working lives. They tacitly subscribe to the tenets of feminism, but nonetheless feel reluctant to associate their own progressive ideas with a women's liberation movement so frequently misunderstood by the American public.

This is where *Transforming the Disciplines* comes in, and its potential as a tool for education and understanding is truly transformative in the best sense of the word. All the contributors to this volume scrupulously avoid technical jargon and the kind of erudite language that might alienate a lay reader. The authors address an audience of common readers eager to learn more about the theory and practice of feminism. They show how women's ways of knowing have begun to reconfigure the terrain of our cognitive maps in startling and unprecedented ways. What *Transforming the Disciplines* does, like no other text in the field of feminist scholarship, is to provide a virtual guidebook for mapping the changing intellectual landscape of university education and responsible social practice. The authors tackle provocative but inarticulate issues: "What you always wanted to know about feminism, but were sometimes afraid to ask." Why, for instance, is the use of gender-inclusive language more than just a matter of semantics? And why have archaic categories such as "man the hunter" and the "ethics of man" been justifiably deleted from academic catalogues?

Historically, feminists have come to identify the second wave of the women's movement, inaugurated in the 1970s, as a pioneer period of struggle that gave birth to subtle but irreversible developments in Western thought. Germinal transformations in cultural consciousness and public policy take root so gradually that their pervasive influence, still evolving, continues to offer utopian visions of a gender-blind society in which social, sexual, and racial awareness might be amalgamated into a holistic philosophy of global equity and universal justice. Those theorists who have long insisted that the personal is the political, and that feminism is a humanism embracing all women, men, and children on the planet, might look to the essays in this anthology for further evidence of feminism's extraordinary promise for the twenty-first century.

Transforming the Disciplines will provide an excellent resource for a wide variety of classes in women's studies and feminist theory. It might serve as the primary textbook for undergraduate students in an introductory course in the field. Or, alternatively, it could be used as a supplementary text in more specialized courses where upper-level or graduate students attempt to situate their own feminist perspectives in the broader context of interdisciplinary research. By exploring the enormous impact of feminism on contemporary education, the authors have successfully collaborated on a primer elucidating the subtle power of women's ways of knowing to alter an astonishing array of scholarly disciplines.

I would urge any serious student or teacher of women's studies to read this book from cover to cover, to relish its breadth of knowledge and insight, to cherish its predictions for future feminist research, and to apply its premises to both scholarly and pedagogical practice. Any student uttering the familiar disclaimer "I'm not a feminist, but . . ." should be encouraged to fill in the ellipsis by reading this collection of thoughtful, informative essays. *Transforming the Disciplines: A Women's Studies Primer* will surely prove to be a transformative, indeed revolutionary, text. It will serve as an extraordinary and valuable contribution to the ongoing conversation about the way in which women's studies has redefined and utterly transformed our approach to every field of knowledge at the end of the twentieth century.

Suzette Henke
Thurston B. Morton Senior Professor of Literary Studies
University of Louisville

Introduction

The question "What is women's studies?" arises from time to time when we talk to people inside and outside the university. Perhaps you, too, have wondered about this new academic discipline. It is often difficult to give a reply in twenty-five words or less, especially after the subject of feminism enters the conversation. Once in awhile, questions such as "Why don't universities also have a men's studies program?" are voiced. This book is an attempt to answer these questions about feminism, gender, and women's studies. We would like to explain, simply and without highly technical language, how the perspective of feminism can affect our ways of knowing the world.

Virtually all of us have heard of feminism, and many may even recognize the academic category "women's studies." Yet many of us may be confused about the relationship between women's studies and feminism, and the ways in which feminist scholarship underlies much nonfeminist thinking about the various fields. It is no wonder confusion exists. At your university or college, you may encounter feminists who argue publicly over feminism's exact definition, while others, smarting under negative feminist stereotypes, wonder whether they ought to find something completely different to call themselves. Within feminist circles, you may hear accusations of people being "not feminist enough," while nonfeminists have been known to criticize others as being "too feminist." Besides the fact that no one can give a brief, simple definition of feminism that everyone agrees upon, most of the people who write about feminism are scholars who use highly specialized language to talk about what they know. You may be unable to casually pick up a university-level feminist book and read it without first engaging in a lengthy and sometimes tedious process of learning to decode feminist vocabulary.

Even if these problems are not enough to deter you, a number of notoriously popular but false depictions of feminists may discourage you from learning about feminism and women's studies. Since Sigmund Freud introduced the term "penis envy" into common parlance almost one hundred years ago, feminists have been accused of wanting to be men and/or wanting to castrate them. Today, radio talk show and television program hosts have been known to label feminists as "feminazis." Moreover, some broadcasters have asserted, among other absurd accusations, that feminists are nothing but a bunch of pro-abortion practitioners, whose primary aim in life is to prevent other women from becoming homemakers, mothers, or wives. Perhaps the most damaging calumny now being leveled against feminists is the popular claim that they urge women to falsely pose as "victims" of male aggression, especially in cases of sexual harassment. Such negative depictions of feminists make most students wary of the "F" word. No one wants to be a "man hater" or an "intentional victim," and confusion and fear of being labeled as such have prevented many students from seeking to learn more about feminism. Antifeminist backlash has even led to the concept of "postfeminism," which proclaims that all gender-related battles have already been won and that feminism is now passé.

Yet, as the saying goes, reports of feminism's death have been greatly exaggerated. Fortunately, feminists both inside and outside the university community continue to study and practice passionately their own particular types of feminism, of which there are a startling number and variety. All, however, are rooted in a shared belief in the equality of women and men. Whether we acknowledge it or not, feminist ideas have changed how we look at the world and ourselves.

You are likely to encounter these changes in your work life. The U.S. Department of Labor reports that 59.8 percent of women in the United States work for wages, and nearly half the labor force is female. Once ridiculed for seeking positions in fields such as plumbing and carpentry, women in the United States today are accepted in virtually every occupational field. They are also venturing into professional and academic fields once considered the domain of men. As Amy Bix's essay in this anthology shows, women are now much more accepted in scientific fields and are more likely to be recognized for their work. Changes can also be seen in our universities and colleges. The American Association of University Professors (AAUP) Web page shows increasing numbers of women teaching at all types of institutions (e.g., research universities with doctoral and/or master's programs, undergraduate-only schools, and community colleges). Within our colleges and universities, there are now 11.3 percent more women teaching than in 1974-1975, including 17 to 18 percent more women who hold entry-level, tenure-track faculty positions (Benjamin, 2000).

If you take a closer look at employment statistics, however, you will see that the need for feminism and women's studies continues. The 61 million working women in the United States in 1998 earned only 76 percent of what men earned, with more women (one out of five) working as teachers, secretaries, and cashiers than any other line of work (U.S. Department of Labor, 1999). When women do gain entry into some jobs, as Kathleen Kirby points out in another essay, the pay and prestige attached to those jobs are likely to decline. Even in colleges and universities, women faculty do not seem to be faring much better in receiving pay equity, although statistics reported by the AAUP suggest the pay gap is narrowing with new hires and part-time instructors. Whereas female professors averaged $8,186 less in 1996-1997 than male professors, women holding the rank of associate professor averaged $4,061 less; assistant professor, $3,626 less; and instructor, $1,247 less, according to AAUP data reported by the *Chronicle of Higher Education* (Freyd and Johnson, 1999).

In addition to employment issues, feminists are concerned with social issues and problems that women face, such as domestic violence. The number of women in the United States who are victims of domestic violence is shocking (Schwartz, 1997). Most experts argue that woman battering is probably one of the most underreported crimes in this country. Experts commonly report that the lives of 51 percent of women in the United States and their children are endangered on a daily basis due to brutal acts of violence committed by an intimate partner. In other words, approximately every fifteen seconds a woman is battered in the United States; while you are reading this paragraph, four women will be severely beaten. Half of the murdered women in the United States, or approximately four women a day, are killed by a current or former partner. Feminist activists and scholars, believing these statistics and issues just cannot be ignored, have played central roles in raising public awareness.

Although feminism has made strides in the public arena and continues to fight social injustices such as pay inequities and domestic violence, many people, including university faculty and administrators, still look askance at feminism and women's studies as a field of study. If asked, these people would probably be shocked to hear that the so-called "value neutral" and/or "objective" fields of knowledge, such as math or architecture, can be affected by feminism and, therefore, may be studied in women's studies courses. They do not usually understand that a feminist way of knowing—sometimes overtly, sometimes covertly—has found its way into virtually every academic discipline and has changed the way we study at the university. The changes may not be as dramatic or obvious as they are in the public realm, but they are quite real and, in some cases, these changes are immense.

This textbook is an attempt to demonstrate the directions in which feminism is moving the English-speaking academic world. The idea of the book was conceived by one of our editors, a comparative literature specialist whose field is feminist theory, as a result of her difficulty in finding a suitable women's studies textbook that actually explains feminism's influence on fields with which she is unfamiliar. When teaching introductory women's studies classes in the past, she tried to showcase not only the "interdisciplinarity" of feminism but also its "multidisciplinarity." However, because her areas of concentration are literature, philosophy, and psychology, she tended to emphasize these areas. She felt she could not do justice to fields such as math or architecture, and she preferred to teach what she knew best. Ideally, however, students being introduced to women's studies should be taught about fields other than the instructor's own. Women's studies courses may have students who like religious studies, film, and history as well as those who hunger for scientific subjects such as chemistry, physics, or math.

When searching for a textbook that could provide students with a simple explanation of feminism's influence on all fields, our editor discovered that women's studies textbooks tend to be historically oriented, fully detailed examinations of women's social, political, economic, spiritual, and domestic situations. Often these books attempt to encompass the entire nineteenth and twentieth centuries (sometimes more) in scope. While such books work very well in their own way, occasionally they can be "too much of a good thing." Literature and humanities professors would probably present novels, stories, poems, philosophy, and dramas as primary course texts. They need only a supplementary text that offers introductory ideas but does not go into extraordinary historical and political detail. For some students, too, the traditional women's studies textbook can be unsatisfactory. If, for example, students are not planning to major in history, political science, or other social sciences, they are often not willing to read lengthy discussions framed in the technical language of those fields. If dates and statistics do not fascinate them, these students may become bored or lost in the minutia of tomes like the traditional introductory texts. With these issues in mind, our editor began the process of compiling essays for her ideal course text, envisioning a book that would be geared toward first-year or lower-level undergraduate readers and designed to allow students to glimpse the "big picture" of women's studies.

Although this book does not cover every single discipline one might encounter in a university setting, *Transforming the Disciplines* closely approaches the ideal she envisioned. It contains almost thirty essays, covering a broad range of subjects from anthropology to chemistry to sport studies. In breaking down feminist scholarship field by field, this book seeks to describe exactly how feminism relates to various academic disciplines and, thereby, to explain what the field known as women's studies is. Without going into great detail or attempting to include fine nuances of scholarship, the essays spell out, in basic terms and concepts, exactly how the feminist approach has transformed (or how it could transform) each of the scholarly disciplines. Moreover, the essays have been written to avoid the often mystifying language of scholars, making the book accessible not only to undergraduate students but also to people in the general reading population who might have an interest in learning about different disciplines and how feminism affects academic pursuits.

The complexity of the essays varies greatly, so you can pick and choose readings suitable to your own interests and level of understanding. Some essays describe disciplines that have more or less acknowledged the changes made by feminism, while others discuss academic areas of interest in which feminist thought has only barely begun to provide scholars with new questions and perspectives. We have arranged the essays in sections according to the academic category where that subject is most likely to be found in a typical U.S. university setting. For example, art history, literature, and music are usually considered "Humanities" courses, while anthropology, communications, and history are labeled as "Social Sciences." Disciplines that use quantitative reasoning such as math and physics, on the other hand, are often spoken of as "Natural Sciences" or just plain "Sciences" because those disciplines try to explain "facts." Most fields taught beyond the bachelor's degree level, such as architecture or law, are called the "Professions."As you read through several essays, you will discover the manifold ways that feminism and women's studies have transformed the scholarship, teaching, and practices of these academic disciplines and professions. According to these essays, feminist scholars and teachers have challenged their fields to rethink what should be studied and valued. In the humanities, for example, scholars have questioned their fields' "canons," that is, the standard selection of what has been considered the best and most authoritative texts and individuals "practicing" in their fields. For example, Hildy Miller, writing about the field of rhetoric, points out that for two thousand years her field has been virtually dominated by men. A central and early task of feminist rhetoricians entailed rewriting their fields' histories to include the forgotten or neglected women who have made important contributions. Other contributors have also described a similar focus of early feminist scholarship. Ursula Rempel, for example, names early female musicians and composers who were accomplished and even popular performers in their time but later ignored by music historians. Georgia Rhoades tells a similar story about women writers as she investigates feminist efforts to transform the literary canon, as do Susan Shifrin and Robert Bambic in describing the history of women in art, as subjects of artists and as artists.

Besides rewriting a discipline's history and critiquing its canon, these essays reveal that feminist scholars question the basic assumptions, beliefs, and objectives of their fields. Jeanne Halgren Kilde, for example, describes how feminist scholarship has promulgated and questioned gendered conceptions of architectural spaces, so that certain places like the old saloons of the past or military schools of the present were built for men, while kitchens and sewing rooms were made for women. Kathleen Kirby describes how feminists in the field of educational psychology have challenged traditional categorizations of normal and deviant behavior for men and women, which were based on stereotypical notions of the feminine and masculine. Likewise, Haithe Anderson examines basic school practices, questioning curricula that create and maintain gender stereotypes. Similarly, Mary Childs explores the contributions of feminists in the field of law. For example, feminists have raised awareness about how some seemingly gender-neutral laws such as parental-leave laws can bring about inequality, and they have prompted the redefinition of issues such as domestic violence, which was once viewed as a private matter between spouses, not suitable for legal intervention.

All of our essayists describe ways that feminism has transformed their field's scholarship, changing the way a subject is studied and even written about in their disciplines. For example, Nancy Theriot explains that the first women historians told the same kinds of stories as their predecessors, usually white, upper- or middle-class men, except they reversed the genders. They might talk, for example, about great women and how they influenced politics and war. Today, they have broadened what historians may consider important subjects of study (i.e., how one's gender affects relationships in the private life of ordinary people).

Other scholars in the book report similar types of changes in their field's scholarship. In the field of linguistics, Jessica Weinberg describes how recent attention to women's language patterns has opened up a new awareness of language patterns for both men and women. In addition, communications scholars Sharon Varallo, Pamela Tracy, Debian Marty, and Ashwini Tambe describe a new kind of reflective mode of knowing that their field applies to its knowledge base. For example, instead of just describing new communications technologies, such as the answering machine, communication scholars now analyze a new technology to look for gendered assumptions that underlie it. A film specialist, Karen Chandler shows how feminist scholarship has changed film study. Comparing early feminist work in literature and film, she finds that both disciplines initially focused on documenting the ways women's subordinate status was recorded in literature and the movies. Today, feminist film scholarship is concerned with representations of women, men, and children in the context of their society, their viewers, and the film industry.

In addition to changing their discipline's research approaches and questions, some feminists have sought new ways to speak and write about their subjects. For example, Eileen John, writing about the field of philosophy, challenges two staples in philosophical discussion—argumentation and debate—as the best means of understanding an issue. She suggests that the field of philosophy should make room for alternative, nonargumentative forms of discussion that allow for subjective experience. Other contributors illustrate alternative academic writing approaches. Among them, Lyndie Brimstone examines in an autobiographical essay how our gender, class, race, and sexuality shape the way we read and interpret literature.

Feminism has been described in these essays as underlying significant changes in the way subjects are taught at the university. Barbara Burnell, an economist, and Edwin Segal, an anthropologist, describe changes in their classrooms that have occurred as a direct result of their feminist inquiries. For example, textbooks once considered canonical in anthropology can no longer be presented as giving an unbiased view of human culture. Mathematicians Julianne Lynch, Gilah Leder, and Helen Forgasz describe a North American program, SummerMath, which aims to create a learning community for young women studying mathematics. The program, delivered in a single-sex setting, offers an alternative to the traditionally competitive, hierarchical mathematics classroom. Similarly, physicists Barbara Whitten and Juan Burciaga describe how feminist educational theories and practices have prompted them to abandon the role of lecturer and redefine themselves as "facilitators" of learning in order to value their students' experience and accommodate their different learning styles. As a result, they describe restructured classes, now built around group work.

Feminist theories also have prompted many of our authors to reconsider how they understand the world and how they perceive the knowledge they create. In other words, feminism has transformed the *what* and the *how* of their fields of knowledge. In the fields of science, for example, Amy Bix and Laura Shanner show how the concept of factual knowledge has come under scrutiny, changing the way many scientists do research. Likewise, Gwyneth Hughes questions the scientific language of chemistry in order to show the relationship between culture and science. And in the fields of sociology and archaeology, Cynthia Negrey and Mara Greengrass show how our view of ourselves impacts the ways in which we view others, including those people who lived in the ancient past.

Finally, several of our essayists have described how feminist inquiry has prompted their fields to look to the future and beyond their disciplines and academia. Amy Begg DeGroff, for example, describes how the library profession could benefit from a return to its roots as a female profession and from the adoption of certain feminist principles. Another author, Mary Ann Stenger, describes in detail how feminist scholars in religious studies are working to transform the texts and practices of religious communities, develop leadership opportunities for women, and challenge theological positions on sexual issues such as abortion, heterosexuality, and homosexuality. Stenger, John, and Whitten and Burciaga have specifically linked feminist scholarship to social activism. No "town and gown" split exists in their visions of disciplinary work.

Social activism has always been at the heart of feminist thought, and many of our authors make it clear that the struggle of women for equality in academia is fully intertwined with that of people of color, and with the broader struggle of all disempowered groups. Most feminist academicians want justice, not only for women, and not only in academia, but for all people everywhere whose secondary place in the hierarchy is unfairly maintained.

If the preceding examples of feminist scholarship intrigue you, we invite you to read more about the feminist transformation now occurring in universities all over the English-speaking world. The book is organized so that you may read everything straight through or, if you prefer, you may skip around, reading only the chapters that interest you. Whichever essays you read, you should find them straightforward and free of highly technical jargon. Should you be interested in knowing more about one field or another, our authors have usually provided names of other writers or books that will give you a deeper understanding of that subject.

Because women's studies is an inter- and multidisciplinary approach, many of the fields discussed here overlap. As you will see, it is not uncommon for women's studies scholars to rely on studies produced by researchers in fields other than their own. Most feminists feel that sharing data between fields strengthens our understanding of the "big picture" for all women.

In the following pages, you will meet both national and international feminist scholars. As you read their essays about what feminism and women's studies has meant to their own fields, closely attend to their voices. Listen not only for what they say, but also how they say it. Notice that, in some cases, "scholarly" writing has been eschewed and/or a critique of feminism and women's studies might even have been made. As editors, we have chosen not to stifle or silence these writers. We see both forms of critique as healthy, for they help us grow. Whenever our authors' opinions and writing styles vary greatly from our own, we have made a conscious effort to allow those different voices to be heard. Discover for yourself that feminist scholars speak in different voices and from different perspectives and experience.

BIBLIOGRAPHY

American Association of University Professors. October 12, 2000. October 15, 2000. <http://www.aaup.org/index.htm>.

Benjamin, Ernst. "Disparities in the Salaries and Appointments of Academic Women and Men: An Update of a 1988 Report of Wommittee W on the Status of Women in the Academic Profession." *AAUP Reports. Association of University Professors.* October 15, 2000. <http://www.aaup.org/Wrepup.htm>, pp. 7-8.

Freyd, Jennifer, and J.Q. Johnson. "References on Chilly Climate for Women Faculty in Academe." 9 pp. May 11, 1998. June 11, 1999. <http://chronicle.com/chedata/infobank.dir...http://dynamic.uoregon.edu/~jjf/chillyclimate.html>.

Schwartz, Mary Ann, and Barbara Marliene Scott (Eds.). *Marriages and Families: Diversity and Change,* Second Edition. Upper Saddle River, NJ: Prentice-Hall, 1997.

U.S. Department of Labor Women's Bureau. April 1999. July 16, 1999. <http://www.dol.gov/dol/wb/public/wb_pubs/fact98.html>.

SECTION I: HUMANITIES

"Tools of Articulation" by Janet L. Gream

One of the three traditional divisions of academic study, the humanities has long been associated with the study of high culture (usually the study of Latin, Greek, or the masterworks of the great thinkers, writers, composers, and artists of Western civilization). The humanities, however, should be more broadly defined as a field of study that focuses on human culture and human values (contemporary and past, popular, and high). It encompasses many disciplines, including literature, language studies, the arts (e.g., painting, music, dance, theater, and film), philosophy, and religion.

As in the natural sciences and social sciences, scholars in the humanities ask certain kinds of questions, and they talk and write about their subjects in ways that reveal their particular methods of experiencing, thinking about, and investigating a subject. Whereas scholars in the natural sciences may be described (perhaps simplistically) as focused on studying natural phenomena and those in the social sciences as concerned with the behavior of groups of people, humanists—at least as we are defining them for this textbook—examine particular human productions. These include not only tangible artifacts such as a sonnet, a rap song, a watercolor, or a play but also intangible creations such as the philosophical belief "I think therefore I am" or the idea of the American dream. Typically, humanists analyze, interpret, and evaluate the meaning and significance of a human artifact, value, or activity so that we better understand and appreciate it.

Nine scholars representing seven disciplines have contributed essays to this section. Our first essay, "The Impact of Women's Studies on Rhetoric and Composition" by Hildy Miller, examines the effect that a male-dominated history of rhetoric has on writing, particularly its influence on those writing in the masculinist tradition of academia. Next, Eileen John's "Feminism and Philosophy" identifies the social and intellectual activism of feminist philosophers, whose projects include inquiring into the meaning and function of gender concepts and recasting philosophical discussion to allow subjectivity and collaboration. Similarly, Mary Ann Stenger explores how feminists are identifying patriarchal assumptions functioning within religious traditions and working to redefine women's roles and spirituality in "The Impact of Women's Studies on the Study of Religion."

In our fourth essay, Susan Shifrin and Robert Bambic examine the contributions of two generations of feminist art scholars in "Transgressing to Transform: The Feminist Engagement with Art History." The essay, similar to others in this book, reveals a shift in feminist scholarship from an early focus on rewriting the field's history and canon to include women artists and the "female aesthetic" to a more recent concern with reevaluating the field's assumptions, theories, and methods. Another of these essays is Ursula Rempel's "Women in Music." She outlines problems women musicians (past and present) have faced in gaining acceptance and explores current topics pursued by feminist musicologists, including investigations into the musical canon, and gendered "voices" and composition.

As you read the final three essays in this unit, pay attention to the authors' writing approaches as well as their content. All written by English professors, the essays variously illustrate the use of personal voice and subjective experience, two writing strategies recommended by some feminists calling for alternatives to the traditional, agonistic forms of academic writing and argumentation as discussed in Miller's and John's essays. In "Listening to Women's Voices and Reading Women's Words," Georgia Rhoades, a creative writer and performer from the southern United States, assumes a conversational stance, inviting her readers to hear her voice and locate her personal investment in feminist scholarship as she examines efforts to redefine literature studies and the literary canon. Karen Chandler takes a more traditional academic writing approach in "Feminism and Film Studies." However, she not only discusses the issues, objectives, and critical (i.e., interpretive, analytic) methods in this relatively new field of academic study, but also she illustrates the work of feminist film critics by describing her own investigations of a 1925 movie and its remakes. Finally, the author's history and voice are central to the form and "argument" of "Refusing to Close the Curtains Before Putting on the Light: Literature and Women's Studies" by Lyndie Brimstone. Exploring how feminist and lesbian scholarship have prompted new ways of reading literature, this autobiographical essay concretely illustrates how the author's responses to books and literature were shaped in part by her childhood, growing up in the 1950s in a white, middle-class neighborhood in Coventry, England, and by her subsequent education in school and out.

While reading the different disciplines in the humanities, think about how the authors have characterized their field of study and the contributions made by feminism and women's studies. What subjects, questions, and issues have traditionally concerned scholars and practitioners in their fields? What beliefs and practices have been valued? What role(s) have women historically played in each field? What new subjects, questions, issues, and methods have feminists contributed to the field's study and practice?

Chapter 1

The Impact of Women's Studies on Rhetoric and Composition

Hildy Miller

The field of rhetoric and composition in Western culture is one that dates back to antiquity. Aristotle and Plato, whose works are still read today, were among the first rhetoricians to look systematically at all we do when we compose. Stop and think for a minute about how you write. No, not just dotting "i"s and crossing "t"s or turning a sentence inside out so that you do not end it with a preposition. Think instead of all you do when you write. Find a topic and start generating some thoughts about it, perhaps testing them out on paper or with a friend. Wonder if your audience is going to like or understand it. Figure out a structure that can contain your ideas and communicate them. Trot off to the library to search for sources and worry about how to incorporate them into your paper. Enter a draft into a computer if you are lucky enough to have one. Revise, rethink, review the paper. Try to identify something that seems wrong even though you cannot quite put your finger on it. Ask a friend to read it and give you feedback. Enter it again into the computer and look it over one last time to try to catch all those words you seem to misspell in English ever since you took French. Turn it in and hope for the best.

Without question, composing is a complex and demanding activity, and it was these same elements we practice today when we write that Aristotle and Plato set out years ago. Of course, in ancient Greece, rhetoricians applied these principles to public speaking rather than writing, since writing was not widely practiced until printing presses were invented. But today in modern rhetoric and composition, our concerns are much the same. Composing is what can be called a "sociocognitive" process, meaning that it is a mix of internal decisions and attention to the needs of an actual writing situation.

Over the last twenty years, compositionists have focused on several important issues. First of all, empirical studies have tried to show step by step all that occurs when a writer writes. Writing, long thought to be a mysterious process, has steps that vary little from one writer to another. We all choose topics, and consider structure, audience, and purpose in writing. And yet we all have differences too. Some writers plan precisely what they will write before they write, whereas others refine their ideas through draft after draft. Some like to play with language—pausing to choose just the right golden word—while others scribble hurriedly whatever thoughts come into their minds. The field has taken much of what it has learned about writing processes in order to figure out ways to help people write better. Some writers can write circles around others. There are some people who enjoy writing and who seem to solve all sorts of rhetorical problems that vex others. They see immediately what structure will work or what an audience needs to know. They produce five pages in the amount of time that it takes another writer to produce one. By sharing what works for good writers with weak writers, we have tried to make composing something that everyone—not just the gifted—can do.

The field has focused too on learning about what goes on in the minds of writers and how they respond to different rhetorical situations. Cognitively, writers have been compared to switchboard operators who must coordinate a score of ideas. If we could see into the mind of a writer, we would be surprised at the flow of ideas: "How can I explain my idea—perhaps by referring to that book I read last year—no, it was that other one; what was its name?" When writing on the job, a writer probably wants to consider his or her position in the company, its writing conventions, and a host of other issues that make that writing situation unique. From these sociocognitive concerns, compositionists have also focused on the kinds of written texts we commonly produce in response to a cognitive aim or a social situation. An academic essay, a Sunday paper editorial, an informal letter, an autobiography, a poem, a feasibility study, a country and western song—these products, or genres as they are called, can be quite varied. Each can be studied, described, and taught to others. Some genres come into fashion in certain eras of rhetoric's history and become valued above others. Today, for instance, much of the writing that scholars do in professional journals, as well as the essays expected of undergraduates, is based on the method of argumentation laid out by Aristotle.

How we compose, how to improve writing, what the sociocognitive dimensions of writing are, and what categories our written products can be classified into: these are the areas on which most composition research has focused. But since the mid-1980s, we have begun to look more closely at different worlds of writing, or "discourse communities." The community of business writing, for example, has a whole different set of expectations and requirements from that of academic writing. What is more, each writer may be oriented to think and write in different ways, in part, because of the "worlds" to which he or she belongs. An upper-class male student at Harvard will no doubt bring a different set of experiences and expectations to writing than does a middle-class woman at a local community college. How could he not, when you imagine the differences in the language the two of them grew up hearing and in the ways they were likely encouraged or discouraged in their writing.

Out of these cultural concerns, gender emerged as an especially important marker of social difference among writers as we began to ask what it meant to "compose as a woman." We wondered, did women write in significantly different ways? Were writing conventions and writing instruction really geared to women's needs and expectations? Or had we done what most academic disciplines have done in making a male "world" the universal standard, discounting the experience and input of women? Such questions arising from interdisciplinary applications of women's studies have led to nothing less than a total revision of much of the research in rhetoric and composition over the last two decades.

Several issues stand in this revision. One issue is that of recovering and revising women's place in the Western history of rhetoric. The canon, or standard selection of rhetoricians, has traditionally consisted only of males, even though it stretches back a full two thousand years. When you consider that education has been accessible to all classes of Western women only in this century, it is not hard to see why. Few women until recently could read or write. Those who did were from wealthy families and had access to their fathers' libraries. And even those women were discouraged from speaking or writing publicly. As a result, much of the recovery work that has gone on is turning up missing women rhetors wherever and whenever possible. Sometimes their work is found in private diaries or in religious orders, those places in which literate women might have recorded their thoughts. Sappho from ancient Greece, Christine de Pisan from Renaissance Italy, Sojourner Truth and the Grimke sisters from nineteenth-century America—little by little significant feminine figures such as these are being rediscovered and added to histories of rhetoric.

A second project has been to identify and describe ways that our male-dominated history of rhetoric produced approaches to thought and language that only reflected the perspectives of the educated men who shaped rhetoric. In rhetorical situations we think as we write and we write as we think, so, you might say, writing really *is* thinking. The ancient Greek rhetoricians referred to this aspect of rhetoric as "dialectic" and set out rules of systematic reasoning that still dominate Western academic thought today. When we reason by cause and effect, search for proof, or draw inferences from evidence, we practice the dialectic they articulated for us. This tradition is called rationalism. We find it not only in the thinking and writing practiced throughout the academy but also in the way we conduct scholarly research. Descartes, a seventeenth-century philosopher, adapted the principles of dialectic to develop what we know today as the scientific method. Surely, he thought, if we reason systematically, we can arrive at reliable truths. Yet today, we recognize that rationalism is only one of many ways to think, and one that has been associated with the educated males who developed rhetoric.

What are some of the alternatives to this perspective? One that women have been pointing to is the importance of personal experience. Much of what we know, we learn as we go through life. Chances are that when you first encounter a new concept in a class—say, that women in this country got the vote in 1921—you probably first associate it with something from your own experience. Let us say that you feel guilty for not voting in the last election, given that you see how hard women worked for the right to vote. By connecting that personal experience to the new piece of historical information, you may realize the importance of voting in a way that no pure systematic reasoning can match. Because of the field's willingness now to consider such alternatives, we are seeing changes in the way scholarly research is written. For example, writers now often explain their own experiences autobiographically before presenting results of their research, thus identifying their shaping perspectives. We have come to think that scientific objectivity is not always a strength—and some would say, not even possible. Such changes are leading us to perspectives on rhetoric that are more inclusive of diversity, not only in gender but in race, class, and sexuality.

A third concern has been to critique ways in which women may be excluded in contemporary research on composing. Many studies of composing processes were biased from the start because they included only male writers and then generalized from them to *all* writers. Or they included a mix of male and female writers without accounting for ways these men and women may have done things differently. Sometimes the research designs themselves were so biased that women were almost sure to have performed poorly. Or researchers fell into sexist stereotypes in interpreting their findings. Suppose a research project asked teachers to comment on the quality of the work of students in their classes. Did you ever stop to think that the gender of these teachers might affect the way they respond to student writing? Some studies have found that many male teachers tend to be more judgmental about student writing, more likely to demand that a paper fit their preconceptions of how it should be. Many female teachers, in contrast, are more likely to open up a dialogue with the writer, trying to determine what his or her conception of a text is. Though not *all* men or women can be said *always* to do anything, these are interesting observations and trends. Now that we are more aware of the need to account for diversity in gender, race, class, and sexuality, compositionists try to keep these issues in mind as we work.

We also focus more today on the particular writing needs and experiences of women. Some have gender-related problems. Women often have a special kind of "writer's block," or fear of writing, that stems from a long history of being silenced. With less encouragement to excel at rationalist kinds of thinking and often less attention and interest in what they say and write, many women feel considerably less confident than men at writing. In other ways, many women have special strengths. With less investment in rationalist thinking, women writers are often more willing to experiment with personal experience, autobiography, and alternatives to the standard academic essay. With their long experience of working cooperatively with others, many women can collaborate especially well in research and writing.

Finally, compositionists have begun to depart from conventional genres, rooted in masculinist constructions of rhetoric, and to envision new forms of discourse. In the academy, much of the writing we do is based on argumentation, a form that many women find problematic. They say that if we are to change a society that oppresses women, we should change the forms of discourse that underlie it. Did you ever think of how warlike much of the writing is in the academy? We attack a position, defend a point, set out strategies for demolishing opponents, and try to dominate our readers. Some women say that we should make academic writing more humane. Only writing that is more cooperative and respectful of one another, they say, can help to change the imbalance of power in our society. Others say that women need to learn exactly these battle tactics in writing if they are to compete in our tough society. If it were not for the impact of women's studies on composition, we would probably not be asking why we write the way we do and whether we should change it.

As we enter a second decade of interdisciplinary studies of women and writing, we still have many rhetorical questions to answer. What new descriptions of writing processes and products will appear? Will traditional forms of discourse, such as argumentation, really change? How can we consider not only gender but also other variables such as race, class, and sexuality? How can we keep from overgeneralizing what women do, thereby "essentializing" women by treating women writers as if they were all the same? How can we develop research methodologies not always based in rationalist rhetorics? How can we develop new theories of rhetoric that include women or are about women? How can we expand our notion of who should be included in histories of rhetoric in order to take women's contributions into account? These exciting issues promise a future in which women's studies will continue to exert its strong impact on our field.

Chapter 2

Feminism and Philosophy

Eileen John

Feminism is expanding and changing the content of philosophical work, it is producing new readings of the history of philosophy, and it is challenging philosophy's traditional methods and goals. I discuss here feminism and philosophy in the culture I live in—roughly, Western culture. Non-Western cultures have different philosophical traditions and, in many cases, different feminist movements, so this discussion is not likely to apply directly to feminism and philosophy in other cultures.

Let me begin by saying a few things about philosophy. It is devoted to studying some of the "basics" about the world and our place in it. Philosophers try to answer questions that we usually do not worry about in getting through the day, in catching the bus, eating lunch, and so on. Often we take it for granted that we know how to answer these questions, but in fact we may find them much harder to answer than we suspect.

Here is a sampler of questions philosophers have raised. First, on how we ought to live: Why should people not be egoists, only out for themselves? What makes actions morally wrong or right? Is the right action in a given situation the one that will cause the most pleasure? Second, concerning the nature of the universe and the things in it: Can we know for sure either that there is a God or that there is not one? Is there really a physical world outside of people's thoughts? And what is a person—meaning what is essential to being a person? Third, concerning our beliefs and knowledge about the world: Is there any route to knowledge besides the evidence of our five senses? Is my belief that 2 + 2 = 4 a different, stronger kind of knowledge than my belief that the sun will rise tomorrow? Can we *know* anything at all anyway (assuming knowledge involves being *certain* about something)?

In general, philosophical work involves studying the basic concepts and beliefs we use in understanding the world. Philosophers test whether those beliefs and concepts reflect our experience of the world in the best possible way. If they do not, the philosopher tries to figure out what beliefs and concepts would do a better job. Imagine, for instance, that a philosopher was investigating the above question "What is a person?" and found that the meaning we attached to personhood was a "two-legged creature that can talk." The philosopher would probably suggest that this concept was not capturing what we really need to capture with our person-concept: there are beings who cannot talk and some without two legs who still count as people, and there may even be two-legged, talking creatures that are not people (parrots, perhaps). Philosophers are in this way often critical of the concepts and beliefs we rely on, although usually with less obvious targets than the "bad concept" I just made up.

Because both philosophy and feminism are critical of current concepts and beliefs, they start out with something very important in common. One of the central projects of recent feminism has been to examine such concepts as *woman, man, femininity,* and *masculinity* to see what they mean and how they function for us. Feminist thinkers have made it clear that the concepts involved in our understanding of gender are indeed problematic and deserving of critical attention. With regard to the concept of *woman,* for instance, it seems at first as though it just sets up a biological category: is being a woman just a matter of having certain chromosomes? But feminists have argued that the biological meaning does not capture the whole meaning of *woman.* Much of the nonbiological "baggage" attached to the concept builds the historically dominated, lesser status of women into the very meaning of womanhood: womanhood has been associated with weakness, passivity, and attachment to the body rather than to the mind. Manhood, in contrast, has been associated with strength and action, rationality and mental life.

When the concept of *woman* has a biased definition of this sort, it does not accurately describe all of the people to whom it is applied and, furthermore, it does not capture what is essential to the female human beings who may seem to satisfy the definition. It thus can be rejected as a "bad concept." But the concept is nonetheless powerful and damaging. The concept affects our expectations and treatment of the people we call women. Feminists are thus working on developing concepts that leave behind the harmful "baggage" attached to our current ways of thinking about gender and persons. Can we, perhaps, understand the person as a creature who does not stand alone, who is not the aggressive individualist, but whose identity depends in large part on relations to a community of other people? More broadly, feminists are trying to find ways to avoid categorizing people in terms of so many strict oppositions, such as weak versus strong, active versus passive, rational versus emotional, masculine versus feminine. These alternatives are too crude to capture the complex characteristics of actual people. In general, then, feminists have had an impact on philosophy in part by expanding the set of concepts studied by philosophers, to include concepts of *gender* that are basic to the shaping and understanding of women's existence.

Along with the new focus on gender concepts, feminist thinkers have also helped bring issues of special concern to women into the mainstream of philosophical discussion. The issues of abortion, affirmative action, and pornography, to name the most prominent, have become lively centers of debate in ethical and political philosophy. Getting these and other issues into the limelight is of course only part of the feminist achievement. Feminists have made sure that feminist positions on these issues have been well represented. With regard to abortion, for instance, in which discussion has often focused only on the fetus, feminists have worked to include the pregnant woman's rights and well-being in the debate. Usually there is not just one feminist position—controversy occurs among feminists about how to deal with these problems. In general, feminists have helped to make it normal for philosophers to study questions that concern, in special ways, the treatment, rights, and flourishing of women, and feminists have argued, with some success, for specifically feminist positions on these issues.

So far, I have talked about kinds of feminist impact that are easily identified as feminist. There is also a body of philosophical work that is feminist in more complicated and controversial ways. This work is not just concerned with finding evidence of blatant sexism in philosophy (the history of philosophy gives plenty of evidence of that); it tries to see whether philosophy shows a bias against women and the feminine even when women and women's concerns are not being discussed. This work is controversial because it often involves making claims about what is and is not appropriately associated with women, and there is much disagreement about that. Feminists want to avoid stereotyping women as well as being critical of trends in philosophy that have harmed women. However, that kind of criticism sometimes depends on claims about women's needs, capacities, and experiences, and that brings a danger of stereotyping women into the critical work itself.

Here are a few roughly sketched examples of this kind of feminist work. Western philosophy has a long tradition of treating reason, roughly meaning our ability to form beliefs on the basis of evidence, as the defining and highest activity of people. Our capacity to reason has frequently been said to be superior, in particular, to our capacity to feel emotion. Many philosophers have considered the emotions to be primarily dangerous and destructive—they have been thought to make us "irrational," steering us away from constructive, appropriate behavior. Now, although it seems quite true that we can do silly things when feeling strong anger, hate, jealousy, love, and so on, such a general bias against the emotions seems quite unwarranted. Our emotional experience seems like a crucial and valuable part of human life, helping to make us who we are. And furthermore, it seems wrong to separate and oppose our reasoning and feeling activities so radically. Our emotional response is often not an "irrational" one at all, but rather it contributes to an appropriate awareness of our circumstances. Feminists not only argue that privileging reason over emotion is a mistake, but they also argue that the philosophers' tradition of favoring the one over the other is evidence of male bias. Women, long associated with emotion, have been thought to be controlled by passions rather than "cool reason." Feminists have thus charged that not only is the special pairing of women and emotion unjustified but philosophical theories that elevate reason over emotion also implicitly denigrate women.

Similar arguments have been made for philosophers' elevation of the mind over the body, and for the treatment of abstract, general knowledge as an ideal, while devaluing forms of knowledge about individual people and things, such as insight into specific human relationships. On all of these issues, I think it would be difficult to resist the feminist conclusion that the philosophical tradition has had a habit of subordinating a stereotypically female element to a stereotypically male element. It is much harder to move on constructively from that conclusion. As many feminists have warned, it is not enough to respond to these rereadings of philosophy's history by embracing emotion, bodies, and context-specific knowledge in our philosophical views—though that must be done. For feminists simply to celebrate these stereotypically female elements would help cement a stereotype of woman that is not adequate to the varieties of women's experience. It could also backfire, if the revaluation of such things as the body were not adopted by the wider community and if women were even more firmly associated with the traditionally "lesser" elements. However, feminists have made progress by making the philosophical world recognize the pattern of subordination, as well as by showing that the pattern does not do a good job of reflecting the complex capacities of real people.

Feminists have encouraged change in philosophy at two other very basic levels. First, feminists have reflected on traditional methods of philosophical work. Since at least the time of the ancient Greek philosopher Plato and his teacher Socrates, there has been an ideal of philosophical activity as a matter of *debate,* of presentation of opposing arguments, leading to the triumph of the strongest argument. Notice that I have used some of this vocabulary of debates and strong arguments in this essay. For example, I spoke earlier of it being "hard to resist" a certain feminist conclusion and of feminists arguing "with some success" for feminist positions on abortion and other issues. Even this rather mild language indicates the goals of putting pressure on an opponent and of using argument to defend a position and to win. Second, it has been commonly thought that philosophical work uses pure, impartial reason. This means that the philosopher's activity is not supposed to be tainted by the personal interests and viewpoint of the philosopher. Sometimes philosophers are said to aim at objectivity: objective philosophical thinking should be guided only by what is relevant to the object of thought and it should therefore be found reasonable by any properly reasoning person. Philosophy is not supposed to be an activity guided by the philosopher's particular, subjective position (the position she or he has as the subject of her or his thoughts and experiences).

Feminists have challenged these notions in one way by rejecting the "triumphant combat" view of philosophical work. It is, in part, simply not an accurate description of what philosophers do. It ignores all the exploratory, imaginative, and collaborative thinking that contributes to a philosopher's work, and it gives priority to strong arguments as the goal of philosophy when sometimes the philosopher's achievement lies in asking an important question or in leading discussion in a new direction. However, there is some accuracy to the combat view, not only because strong arguments are indeed important to philosophy, but also because philosophers frequently present their work using the combat model. Published papers and books often emphasize the combat of arguments, and public and private philosophical discussions often pursue the goal of demolishing a position. Feminists have thus emphasized the need to acknowledge and encourage philosophy's cooperative, exploratory, less victory-oriented work. Feminists are thereby urging a view of philosophical activity that is, of course, less stereotypically masculine. Given that women in our culture are not encouraged to disagree, or to be forcefully argumentative, one practical effect of this revised view of philosophical practice may be to make it a more welcoming field for women.

With respect to the notion that philosophy is guided by pure, impartial reason, feminists point out that, as with any other human activity, philosophy is done in particular social contexts, under the influence of whatever values, needs, and experiences the philosophers have. No purity is to be had from these things. So what philosophers do is shaped not just by principles of reason alone (if there are such principles) but also by many factors that vary over time, between cultures, and even between individual people. If there are substantial differences in the values, needs, and experiences of people (say, differences between the experiences of men and women) that do not get represented in philosophical work, the philosopher's claim to objective knowledge may well be wrong. The philosopher's work may only show how things seem from certain philosophers' subjective positions. For example, if philosophers have ignored the body in understanding what it is to be a person, and if the body has been more central to women's self-understanding than to men's, then philosophers' claims about persons might in fact only make sense when considering men's (or some men's) experience.

Feminists have thus argued that, at the very least, philosophy needs to revise its goals of reasoning purely and achieving objective knowledge. Some feminists urge that our project must be to discover the range of different views and experiences of the world, and to grant them all a legitimate place in our discussions. According to this view, we should have the goals of complete inclusiveness and appreciation of the differences we find rather than an aim to capture unifying basic truths about the world. Other feminists, while agreeing that the old philosophical goals are misguided, worry that complete inclusiveness and appreciation of difference will prevent feminists from doing necessary critical work. That is, if we want to say that it is really true that some traditional concepts and beliefs misrepresent women and persons in general, and hence need to be changed, then it can be dangerous to take a relativistic position and say things such as, "Everyone has different experiences, so everyone has a different 'truth.'" (The notion that there can be a different truth for everyone is usually called "relativism.") Presumably sexists, for instance, have a way of experiencing the world that makes it seem true that women are worthy of less respect. How can we say that there is something wrong with the sexist experience? The upshot is that we need a way of being inclusive, and appreciative of difference, that allows us to be critical.

Finally, as I hope this discussion has illustrated, feminist philosophers have the very broad goal of integrating their intellectual activity with their activism. The content, methods, and goals of philosophy can make a positive difference in the world, so feminists try to approach philosophical work with an awareness that it is not an isolated pursuit of knowledge but is an opportunity for pursuing positive social change. Feminism has thus led itself, and philosophy, to a very interesting point. It has set up the following challenge: investigate basic concepts and beliefs in ways that allow for the important differences in human experience but also make it possible for oppressive, destructive concepts and beliefs to be criticized and changed.

BIBLIOGRAPHY

Cole, Eve Browning. *Philosophy and Feminist Criticism: An Introduction.* New York: Paragon House, 1993.

Frye, Marilyn. *The Politics of Reality.* Freedom, CA: Crossing Press, 1983.

Garry, Ann and Marilyn Pearsall (Eds.). *Women, Knowledge, and Reality.* New York: Routledge, 1996.

Grimshaw, Jean. *Philosophy and Feminist Thinking.* Minneapolis: University of Minnesota Press, 1986.

Pearsall, Marilyn. *Women and Values.* Belmont, CA: Wadsworth, 1993.

Chapter 3

The Impact of Women's Studies on the Study of Religion

Mary Ann Stenger

Because the modern study of religion is multidisciplinary, looking at religion from a variety of academic perspectives and with diverse methods, feminist approaches to religion draw from the insights of feminist scholarship across the academic world. History, philosophy, textual-literary analysis, cultural studies, sociology, psychology, political science, and anthropology include some study of religion as it affects their specific disciplines. Accordingly, feminist analysis within these academic disciplines has included study of the influence of religion on women.

Until recently, the study of sacred scriptures and the development of theology had been seen as part of the religious domain, in other words, occurring primarily in religiously based settings (seminaries, divinity schools, and religiously identified colleges and universities). Such studies continue in these contexts but can also be found in independent or state-supported universities. The modern study of religion emphasizes the plurality of religious traditions rather than privileging one religious tradition as the only true one. As a result, there has been increased influence of secular scholarship on scriptural study, theology, and the history of religions. Feminist scholarship, developing simultaneously with the modern study of religion, has been a significant part of this influence.

Feminist scholarship in the study of religion and women can be divided into three areas, listed in the order of their chronological development within the field: (1) critical review of religious traditions, (2) reconstruction of religious traditions, and (3) development of new religious options. Overlap among these three activities is inevitable, but this division helps to clarify the approaches used in the feminist study of religion. Within each of these areas, the experience of women in their religious traditions and the understanding of the spiritual dimension or ultimate reality are included.

In the critical review of religious traditions, scholars have uncovered the deep patriarchal assumptions that dominate most religious ideas and practices. Even when much of the spiritual teaching of a religious leader was open to women, patriarchal attitudes, seeing women as inferior to men, became part of the early tradition. For example, the historical Buddha, Siddhartha Gautama, after being persuaded by a female relative, agreed to allow women to form monastic orders similar to the male monastic communities. But the tradition also includes his comments that the tradition would not last as long with women included and details monastic rules subordinating females to males. The stories of Jesus suggest equal treatment of men and women, and in 1 Corinthians Paul suggests mutual relationships in marriage and an absence of social distinctions in relationship to Christ. But by the early second century of the Christian tradition, the hierarchical Roman social codes subordinating wives to husbands (and slaves to masters) were put forward in the Christian communities and became part of the New Testament. Earliest Hindu practices included priests and priestesses, but as the tradition became more complex, women's religious roles were relegated to individual religiosity rather than official public roles. In the Qur'an (Islamic holy scripture produced around the seventh century), women and men are created equal and are given more economic and social rights than usual for women almost anywhere before the nineteenth and twentieth centuries. But later Islamic traditions emphasized inferiority and subordination of women to men. Most disturbing to contemporary feminists are statements of spiritual inequality along with social inequality. These statements are found mostly in individual theologies developed after the Scriptures, but many of these theologies became strong influences in the traditions, making the anti-female views strong parts of the tradition as well.

When religion claims that women are inferior and should be subordinated to men, many people accept it as God's will or absolute truth. Thus, religiously legitimated roles and rules are the most difficult to criticize or to change. Sociological studies often show the high participation of women in religious and spiritual activities while the positions of public power belong mostly to men. With a few exceptions, women through the centuries have accepted these social positions as normal and right.

In some traditions, religious roles offered women more options and opportunities than traditional social roles of wife and mother. To become a Buddhist nun or a Christian nun could mean freedom from family and household responsibilities and freedom to study, meditate, and pray. But the religious choice might also mean harder physical work and ascetic practices, all seen as part of one's progress toward a higher spiritual goal. This religious option further decreased the status of the traditional, married woman, and many movements started by and for women were forced to be under male rule or were destroyed for their independence.

Sometimes women with highly respected spiritual gifts were quite influential in the politics of religious or state institutions. Or some women were elevated to high spiritual positions as saints who could give spiritual guidance to ordinary people. But such spiritual elevation of a few females did not lead to higher social status for women or better treatment of ordinary women. It often had the opposite effect of serving to highlight the differences between these ideal female saints and ordinary women.

Images of God have been strongly patriarchal in Western religious traditions, even though sophisticated religious thinkers would argue that God is beyond both male and female. The image of God as Father has dominated Christian tradition and can be found in Jewish tradition, but both traditions also have scriptural images of God in female symbols, such as mother or breadmaker.

One can also discover the important role of goddesses in some religious traditions. But as with female saints, these positive female images did not lead to higher spiritual or social roles for women. Although the female qualities of such spiritual figures are a central part of their attraction for both men and women, those same female qualities often are seen negatively within the ordinary social communities. The image of mother goddess can be found in numerous cultures, but mothers within those cultures are often treated as necessary means for producing males rather than valued for mothering, nurturing qualities or as full female persons.

Feminist critical studies of religion have forced scholars to recognize the patriarchal assumptions that penetrated past historical and social studies of religions. Not only have questions about the roles and images of women or about gendered imagery for God(s) become a standard part of scholarship, but also these studies have worked together with critiques, focusing on other issues, such as economic or social privileges and the relationship of diverse religious traditions. Although the negative images and roles stand out in these studies, more positive female images and roles for both humans and deities also have been highlighted, making them part of standard histories and social analyses. Because religion is not only studied but also practiced, the impact of these studies on ordinary religious persons has been strong. Some become bitter and angry, choosing to leave a particular tradition. Others reject the negative images, seeing them as part of past tradition, and work to build on the positive images to create a more equal status for women within particular religious traditions.

The feminist process of reconstructing the roles of women within religious traditions often involves "reading between the lines" of Scriptures and other traditional texts and inferring social roles or likely psychological profiles of women from the sparse information available. For example, laws prohibiting women's participation in public positions of religious leadership or relegating women to set subordinate social roles may reflect an effort to remove women from public leadership and to establish more firmly a patriarchal structure.

Reconstruction can also mean highlighting those women whose qualities or roles are mentioned in the Scriptures and traditions but who have been ignored in most "official" histories or social studies of the traditions. It also involves recognizing oppressed groups whose history, psychology, and social position were often ignored in the past. Feminist concern for liberation from oppression has increased awareness of these "forgotten" groups. Ironically, these very groups were often at the center of early religious development in traditions. The politically powerless, the economically deprived, and the lower social classes were frequently key groups in building the social support and early communities of new religious movements. Desire for liberation from current oppression and hope for a better spiritual (and sometimes social) future were motives for joining the new religious movement. The story of the Exodus from Egypt, the social picture of the first Christians, and the rejection of social caste within Buddhism are examples of new religions building on liberation from more oppressive social structures. Emphasizing these liberating dimensions in reconstructing religious traditions can act as a counterpoint to later development of hierarchical, oppressive structures within those same traditions.

Reading traditional stories and Scriptures with new insights is another dimension of feminist reconstruction. For example, one can look at Eve as the culmination of creation rather than the inferior offshoot of Adam. One can think of how Sarah must have felt when Abraham took away Isaac to offer him as sacrifice. Other examples include imagining the situation of women present at Sinai, considering the implications of deaconesses or female heads of early house churches, exploring rituals designed for Hindu women, and pulling out the stories of Sufi women (Islamic mystics).

Renewed images for God(s) have been part of this reconstructive effort. For example, Sophia (Wisdom) is a female image of God found within biblical traditions as well as outside them. Scholarly studies of the development of this traditional but often suppressed image of God have shown the importance of the female image through Christian history, rather than assuming it was a leftover of Greek tradition.

Although feminist reconstruction involves some application of imagination, the results of these efforts have broadened our understanding of religious interpretation, history of religions, and social analyses of religions. Such scholarship works at filling in the gaps of traditional studies, offering a strong critique of traditional approaches even while it enhances the positive dimensions of the traditions.

Within religious traditions, feminist scholars have used the above historical and social studies to suggest the possibility of new approaches within religious communities. Examples include developing new translations of scriptures in inclusive language, publishing feminist commentaries on scriptures, proposing new positions of leadership for women within religious communities, and creating new theological images for God(s). Such studies have affected not only the academic understanding of religion but also the religious communities themselves. These studies have helped some communities use inclusive language on a regular basis in their rituals and liturgies. Some traditions have elevated women to new positions of leadership (such as priests and rabbis) as a result of feminist critical studies. New metaphors for God(s) include imaging the divine with female qualities such as those of friends, erotic lovers, and mothers.

Similarly, feminist scholarship looking at past theological positions on sexual issues, such as abortion, heterosexuality, and homosexuality has brought about some proposals for new approaches. Scholars often find that the past traditions were not as settled or absolute as many have thought. Changes in the future, then, can be seen as fitting with past traditions (or at least parts of those traditions). Feminist efforts argue for justice as a primary criterion, rooted in many religious traditions although not always established in religious practices. Concern for communities among women, solidarity with all oppressed, and political and social empowerment of the oppressed are emphasized more than the rights or upward mobility of a few individuals. Many feminists see their scholarly studies and proposals as playing an active role in the liberation of oppressed people.

Moved perhaps by anger or a sense of disconnection to patriarchal religions, many women today have turned to new (or returned to old) options outside traditional religions. Interest in bodies, nature, and ecology has brought a renewed interest in goddess traditions. Some feminist studies connect the characteristics of goddesses with psychological dimensions of contemporary women. Others emphasize the connection of goddesses to natural phenomena, ranging from trees and the moon to the bodily cycles of females. In addition, scholarly studies have correlated with renewed interest in pagan traditions, which often allow more leadership for women and celebrate women's lives more than traditional religions. These options can be controversial, however. Images of the mother goddess are presented as empowering by some analysts and criticized as relegating women to stereotypical roles by others.

This overview cannot do justice to the extensive feminist scholarship in the study of religion and its impact on the subdisciplines within the academic field. The transformation of the study of religion is in progress, with all three areas of scholarship still continuing. Yet, there are still numerous scholars in religious studies who take no account of the above studies or who miss the relevance of these studies to their own subdisciplines. To a great extent, the study of women and religions and the feminist critique and reconstruction of religions have developed as subdisciplines rather than pervading the whole discipline. But publishers and organizers of academic conferences on religion have begun to demand inclusion of women's issues as well as inclusive language. Perhaps most important, feminist issues share common concerns with other movements of liberation (African-American, Asian-American, and Hispanic) and with renewed interest in cultural and religious diversity. Womanist (African-American feminist) studies and feminist issues in interreligious dialogue are examples of combined efforts for liberation. When taken as a total effort to critique past assumptions of religious scholarship as well as past theologies and social structures, the movements for liberation are transforming the scholarly study of religions *and* the practices of religions and developing new options.

BIBLIOGRAPHY

Carmody, Denise. *Women and World Religions.* Nashville, TN: Abingdon Press, 1979.

Carr, Anne. *Transforming Grace: Christian Tradition and Women's Experience.* New York: Harper & Row, 1988.

Christ, Carol P. and Judith Plaskow (Eds.). *Womanspirit Rising: A Feminist Reader in Religion.* New York: Harper & Row, 1979.

Clark, Elizabeth A. and Herbert Richardson (Eds.). *Women and Religion: A Feminist Sourcebook of Christian Thought.* New York: Harper & Row, 1977.

Daly, Mary. *Beyond God the Father: Toward a Philosophy of Women's Liberation.* Boston: Beacon, 1973.

Falk, Nancy Auer and Rita M. Gross (Eds.). *Unspoken Worlds: Women's Religious Lives.* Belmont, CA: Wadsworth, 1989.

Fiorenza, Elisabeth Schussler. *In Memory of Her: A Feminist Theological Reconstruction of Christian Origins.* New York: Crossroad, 1983.

Lerner, Gerda. *The Creation of Patriarchy.* New York: Oxford University Press, 1986.

Loades, Ann (Ed.). *Feminist Theology: A Reader.* Louisville, KY: Westminster, 1991.

Olson, Carl (Ed.). *The Book of the Goddess: Past and Present.* 1983. New York: Crossroad, 1986.

Plaskow, Judith and Carol P. Christ (Eds.). *Weaving the Visions: New Patterns in Feminist Spirituality.* New York: Harper & Row, 1989.

Ruether, Rosemary Radford. *Sexism and God-Talk: Toward a Feminist Theology.* Boston: Beacon, 1983.

Sharma, Arvind (Ed.). *Women in World Religions.* New York: State University of New York Press, 1987.

Chapter 4

Transgressing to Transform: The Feminist Engagement with Art History

Susan Shifrin
Robert Bambic

> Feminist art history is there to make trouble. . . . At its strongest, a feminist art history is a transgressive and anti-establishment practice, meant to call many of the major precepts of the discipline into question. (Nochlin, 1988)

Although the history of art, incorporating theory, criticism, philosophy, and aesthetics, has existed in writings since antiquity, the disciplinary practice of art history is largely a product of nineteenth-century scholarship. Earlier writers concentrated on the biographies of acknowledged masters and their contribution to the progress of art. Nineteenth- and twentieth-century scholars codified the principles and methodologies for formulating notions of stylistic or formal development in art: how the artist deploys the forms of art such as line, surface, volume, plane, depth, and color. In addition, art historians had become interested in investigating the meaning of artistic works and assessing their value.

In tandem with a focus on form and style, art history has also traditionally concerned itself with examining the meaning of the subject of art. In the twentieth century, Erwin Panofsky codified this disciplinary interest in his 1939 text, *Studies in Iconology.* We might think, for example, the subject of a painting depicting a woman holding a sword in her right hand and a platter with a decapitated head on it in her left to be self-evident, but Panofsky demonstrated that this merely identifies the first level of subject matter or meaning. Although the first level of interpretation moves beyond purely formal analysis, it does not account for precisely who is represented in the painting. To ascertain this, we must turn to narrative or literary sources. For example, the Bible recounts that the head of St. John the Baptist was brought to Salome on a charger, but it does not mention Salome's use of a sword. The Bible also tells the story of Judith, another woman associated with a decapitation. We are told that Judith decapitated Holofernes with a sword, but there is no mention of a platter; indeed, the text explicitly states that the head of Holofernes was placed in a sack. Whether we interpret the woman pictured in the painting as Salome or as Judith, in neither case can we satisfactorily account for the extra element, the sword in one instance or the platter in the other. Panofsky resolves the conundrum by observing that we must modify our knowledge of literary sources by examining how, under a variety of historical conditions, themes might have been expressed differently. It turns out that there is a pictorial tradition in which Judith is represented with a platter, but there exists no traditional type of Salome with a sword. According to Panofsky, because the sword traditionally served as an established and honorific attribute of Judith, as well as of many martyrs and personifications of abstract virtues such as Justice, it therefore could not have been properly associated with the figure of the lascivious and capricious dancing girl Salome. He therefore concludes that the painting represents the legendary heroine Judith.

Connoisseurship comprises a third area of traditional art historical investigation, encompassing both the study of style and that of subject. Drawing on a broad familiarity with the makers and styles of art, developed through extensive firsthand contact with the works themselves, the connoisseur attributes and dates art objects. Based substantially on the assessment of relative quality among works of art and artists, the practice of connoisseurship inevitably leads to the formation of a canon, or a widely acknowledged selection of so-called masterpieces. These works are judged to represent the greatest and most innovative achievements of a culture's "masters."

In 1971, therefore, when art historian Linda Nochlin's essay "Why Are There No Great Women Artists?" was first published, the discipline of art history largely focused on the analysis of style and formal composition, and on the determination of subject and meaning. Art historians predominantly studied the established canon, documenting and celebrating the life and work of great male artists. The title of Nochlin's essay ironically questioned the seeming omission of female artists from this canon. With its origins in the works of the sixteenth-century artist-biographer Giorgio Vasari, the canon traditionally defined great art as the expression of individual, inevitably male genius. Texts by Vasari and later writers explicitly situated the work of the artist-genius as transcending the social, economic, and political contexts of his time. As several scholars have pointed out, our most popular art history textbooks today still exhibit origins in Vasari's canon.

Since the early 1970s, feminist art historians have sought in a variety of ways to reform the discipline's standard expectations and methodologies. Nochlin's 1971 article disputed the validity of standards of artistic quality based on patriarchal notions of artistic genius and mastery. She argued that the myth of the artist-genius presumed male preeminence, disregarded the cultural and socioeconomic conditions that (she asserted) had historically excluded women from the likely achievement of "mastery," and sanctioned the biologically determinist assumption that women were incapable of such cultural achievement. Nochlin also disputed the prevailing assumption that women historically had worked as artists in virtually negligible numbers, reminding her readers of a range of women artists such as Mary Cassatt, Angelica Kauffmann, and Artemisia Gentileschi (among others) who had achieved lasting recognition.

To redress the exclusion of women from the canon, the first generation of feminist art historians produced a number of monographs on women artists, working to "complete art history by restoring its female half" as Broude and Garrard described it in 1982 (Tickner, 1988, p. 119). Others proposed to recover not only suppressed women artists but, in addition, a previously unidentified "women's imagery" based on women artists' experiences of their bodies and of their otherness in a patriarchal society. For example, feminist art historians explored the so-called vaginal imagery in the works of Judy Chicago and Georgia O'Keeffe and the scenes of domesticity in the paintings of Berthe Morisot and Cassatt. Others examined Gentileschi's picturing of male disempowerment effected by legendary female protagonists such as Judith, who, in decapitating Holofernes, figuratively castrated him. The idea of a uniquely female imagery was ultimately abandoned by most feminist scholars as reinforcing the biological determinism that feminism was striving to invalidate. As feminist art historians have pointed out, however, it increased sensitivity to the ways in which women artists could be understood to have critiqued in their own works male artistic formulas and conventions. In 1976, Nochlin and Ann Sutherland Harris produced one of the earliest manifestoes of these themes, *Women Artists: 1550-1950,* to accompany the landmark exhibition of the same title. They curated this potentially ghettoizing exhibition in the hope that it would be the last of its kind to focus exclusively on the works of women artists, that it would prompt instead their integration into the canon.

Indeed, the project of filling in gaps and striving for a more equal representation for women artists within the field of art history has, over time, represented for the majority of feminist scholars an insufficient enterprise. They have called for not only a recuperation of "the female half" of art history but also the construction of a theoretical feminist framework in which to review, critique, and revise an art history consisting of the works of Old Masters and of historical practices that privileged the patriarchal viewpoint of the male viewers who were presumed to have constituted those works' audience. Most feminist scholars agreed that many of the discipline's conventional assumptions were contrary to feminist ideology, which insists on the social character of all practices—including artistic practices—and argues that the production and reception of art should be understood in terms of a social order based on gender divisions. As early feminist art historians amply demonstrated, even the most basic assumption that gender and sexual difference might play a role in defining issues of significant inquiry had been consciously dismissed or negligently overlooked in the nineteenth century when women artists were omitted from the annals of art history.

The exploration of gender divisions presupposed the methodological tools for evaluating the effects of men's and women's differing experiences of the socioeconomic and cultural conditions prevailing in any historic period. Investigating the role of gender in art also demanded deconstruction of sexual difference itself to allow for understanding femininity and masculinity as culturally rather than biologically determined, as sexual metaphors rather than as designations of fixed, anatomically based characteristics. It presupposed a social history of art that integrates the practices of related disciplines and revisionist methodologies into the study of art.

The second generation of feminist art historians was spurred to action by a widespread call to refashion the discipline of art history rather than to complete it, to review and revise its assumptions regarding the nature of the work of art, its social functions, and how it conveys meaning. It was at this point, early in the 1980s, that what Lisa Tickner refers to as a "tension between feminisms" (1988, p. 99) emerged in the feminist critique of art history. Responding to Nochlin's and other American feminists' accounts of the social, institutional, and psychological repression of women as historical by-products of prevailing socioeconomic conditions, the English feminist art historian Griselda Pollock suggested a different scenario to account for the comparably small number of accomplished women artists recorded by art history. She viewed the discipline's marginalization of women artists as instances of a patriarchal society's systematic, ideological suppression of women. Pollock called upon "feminist art historians . . . to critique art history itself, not just as a way of writing about the art of the past, but as an institutionalized ideological practice that contributes to the reproduction of the social system by its offered images and interpretations of the world . . ." (1987, p. 3). She dismissed as counterproductive conventional art history's reliance on what she called "evaluative criticism," the practice of judging positively or negatively the relative quality of artists and their work. Her stand on this issue divided her from a number of other feminist scholars within the field, such as Norma Broude and Mary Garrard. Like her, they conceived of the production of art as a social practice. They construed the work of art as a text with multiple meanings for multiple readers, integral in forming as well as reflecting ideologies. Nonetheless, they rejected her claim that the discipline's continued, fundamental reliance on judgments of quality rather than on the analysis of the social positions and functions of artist and art object, for instance, would prove destructive to the concerns of the new art history. They critiqued as well the potential incompatibility with the feminist art historical enterprise of such "new methodologies" as semiotics. They suggested that the deployment of such methodologies focused more on theorizing than on "understanding works of art" and could be viewed as a throwback to the "formalist disregard for content," that is, to an emphasis on the analysis of structure and form rather than on contextualization and interpretation of meaning (Broude and Garrard, 1987, pp. 13-14). They argued that such methodologies implicitly opposed "a feminist scholarship and sensibility that stress content and interpretation" (p. 14). Pollock, Tickner, and others contended that, to the contrary, a crucial task of the new art history—to provide explanations of women's artistic production through history—required the consideration of both works of art and of women themselves as cultural representations endowed with a variety of societal meanings, to be read, interpreted, and understood based on their circulation and interchange with other such cultural representations. Despite methodological divisions among feminist art historians—or perhaps, in part, because of them—the influence of feminism and women's studies has broadly expanded the range of practices now viewed as within the domain of art history. The inaugural challenge of the feminist engagement with art history—"Why are there no great women artists?"—addressed crucial and specific concerns of feminist scholars in the language of the discipline as it then existed. Nochlin posed the question ironically, calling the bluff of those who assumed that there *were* no "great" women artists capable of producing art valued as innovative or influential. Tickner's revision of the question, almost two decades later, as "How [and to what effect] are the processes of sexual differentiation played out across the representations of art and art history?" (1988, p. 99), suggests through its altered emphasis and different vocabulary the degree to which the field had already changed. The "woman question" had asked why women had not had a visible role in the annals of art history and how social, economic, and other cultural conditions had historically shaped women's production of and responses to art. The more complex question of "sexual differentiation" asked, in addition, how the production and reception of art is shaped by women's and men's differing, gendered experiences of the world.

The feminist critique of art history prompted a reevaluation of the ideologies underpinning the discipline. It also urged (re)consideration of the implicit prescriptions and prohibitions of traditional approaches as well as of their impact upon the scholarship of art history and upon the viewing of art itself. For example, the positioning and outlook of the viewer, virtually invisible in the old art history (or visible at best as an implicitly univocal white, male, heterosexual spectator), now figures focally in many art historical studies. The notion that a gendered "gaze" is presupposed by the language of conventional criticism as well as by much art—that the viewer is assumed to be male and to derive pleasure from a voyeuristic relationship with the female body as portrayed in works of art—has been borrowed from other disciplines' scholarship such as Laura Mulvey's film criticism and is now implicit in much of what is written within the field.

We have focused in this brief synopsis of change and transformation on just a few of the many feminist scholars who have shaped changes to art history, and on just the most basic elements of the methods and approaches they have espoused. The need to be concise has necessarily meant that complex and detailed issues have been condensed and oversimplified. Fortunately, feminist art history is an intensely self-conscious, self-reflective enterprise. Much of the material in our text has been drawn from the numerous works written since 1971 to document, critique, and revise the progress of the feminist project within art history. We encourage our readers to return to these primary sources, the founding documents of feminist art history.

BIBLIOGRAPHY

Broude, Norma and Mary D. Garrard (Eds.). *The Expanding Discourse: Feminism and Art History*. New York: HarperCollins, 1992.

________ (Eds.). *Feminism and Art History: Questioning the Litany*. New York: HarperCollins, 1982.

________. "Feminist Art History and the Academy: Where Are We Now?" *Women's Studies Quarterly* 15(1-2) (1987): 10-16.

________ (Eds.). *The Power of Feminist Art: The American Movement of the 1970s, History and Impact*. New York: Abrams, 1994.

Broude, Norma, Mary D. Garrard, Thalia Gouma-Peterson, and Patricia Mathews. "Discussion: An Exchange on the Feminist Critique of Art History." *Art Bulletin* 71(1) (1989): 124-127.

Gouma-Peterson, Thalia and Patricia Mathews. "The Feminist Critique of Art History." *Art Bulletin* 69(3) (1987): 326-357.

Harris, Ann Sutherland and Linda Nochlin. *Women Artists 1550-1950.* Los Angeles: Los Angeles County Museum of Art, 1976.

Mulvey, Laura. "Visual Pleasure and Narrative Cinema." *Screen* 16(3) (1975): 6-18.

Nochlin, Linda. *Representing Women.* New York: Thames and Hudson, 1999.

________. "Why Are There No Great Women Artists?" In Vivian Gornick and Barbara Moran (Eds.), *Woman in Sexist Society: Studies in Power and Powerlessness* (pp. 480-510). New York: Basic Books, 1971.

________. *Women, Art and Power and Other Essays.* New York: Harper & Row, 1988.

Panofsky, Erwin. *Studies in Iconology: Humanistic Themes in the Art of the Renaissance.* 1939. New York: Icon-Harper & Row, 1972.

Parker, Rozsik and Griselda Pollock. *Old Mistresses: Women, Art and Ideology.* New York: Pantheon, 1981.

Pollock, Griselda. *Vision and Difference: Femininity, Feminism, and the Histories of Art.* London: Routledge, 1991.

________. "Women, Art, and Ideology: Questions for Feminist Art Historians." *Women's Studies Quarterly* 15(1-2) (1987): 2-9.

Salomon, Nanette. "The Art Historical Canon: Sins of Omission." In Joan E. Hartman and Ellen Messer-Davidow (Eds.), *(En)Gendering Knowledge: Feminists in Academe* (pp. 222-236). Knoxville: University of Tennessee Press, 1991.

Tickner, Lisa. "Feminism, Art History, and Sexual Difference." *Genders* 3 (Fall, 1988): 92-128.

Chapter 5

Women in Music

Ursula M. Rempel

When we think of the study of music, we automatically associate it with the study of a specific musical instrument because this is, of course, where students begin. We sing, or we play. Although we may not realize it at the time, music students are also learning about theory (rhythm, melody, and harmony); about history (the lives and times of the composers of the music we play); about the structures and styles of music (its organization and language); and about how to listen. Because the theoretical and historical aspects of music training are usually peripheral to the practical skills taught to beginning students, many of us, unless we pursue advanced musical training, may not be aware that music does not exist without contexts (e.g., cultural, social, political, and artistic). Feminist scholars investigating the roles of women musicians, however, are showing that these contexts are not incidental to the creation, performance, interpretation, and preservation of music.

My field is music history, a discipline that goes far beyond biographical studies of composers to a deeper exploration of the musical styles, structures, and contexts of both the composers and their works. Although I teach general music history courses, I have specialized in the history of women in music, which until recently was a very neglected field of study. The question I hear most frequently from my students is, "Why aren't there any women composers?" My response is always, "I'm amazed that there are so many!"

Alas, their absence from general music history books is still all too apparent. The token appearances of a few women composers, teachers, performers, and conductors within these texts are literally framed within boxes with headings like "Where Were the Women?" The problem is one of ignorance, compounded by the refusal of "old guard" musicologists to acknowledge women's contributions to music or to include their achievements in traditional undergraduate music history that emphasizes dead white European males (dwems). It is still generally men who write the standard music history texts, so the marginalization of women continues, thus necessitating independent courses on women in music. It is only in the specialized texts *on* women in music (mostly written *by* women) that we see the great wealth of information available on women musicians both past and present.

The women's movement(s) of the 1960s and 1970s hastened the awareness of gender studies and promoted the establishment of women's studies programs. The transference of methodologies to the discipline of music was slower, and it has only been in the last twenty-five years that we have seen systematic studies of the various roles women have played in musical history. The first work on women in music in the 1970s involved discovering who they were, what they wrote, where their works were available, and how they could be recorded; consequently, biographical information, editions of the music, and performances were the priorities. Although this is ongoing work as we continue to discover "new" composers from the past, we now have rich sources of information about women throughout the ages, from the medieval visionary Abbess Hildegard von Bingen to the late-twentieth-century, Pulitzer prize winner Ellen Taaffe Zwilich.

Feminist musicologists have made us aware of Hildegard, the twelfth-century composer whose stirring Gregorian melodies have been revived and recorded—even popularized; of the Renaissance composer of complex madrigals, Maddalena Casulana; of Francesca Caccini, whose early Baroque opera was the first to have been performed outside Italy, her native country; of Barbara Strozzi, a mid-seventeenth-century composer of passionate cantatas; of the late-seventeenth-century nun-composer, Isabella Leonarda; and of the harpsichord virtuosa, composer, and favorite of the Sun King, Louis

XIV of France, Elisabeth-Claude Jacquet de la Guerre, whose performances and compositions were such that at her death, a medal was struck in her honor. These were women admired and recognized in their own lifetimes but filtered from or neglected by later historical sources.

Women's roles in music have historically been defined by their education— or rather their *lack* of education; we confront the same problems when we consider women in art or women in literature. For centuries, women were excluded from the privileged education afforded to men—and defined by men; women's education was limited to housewifery and to childrearing, and their participation in the arts was, at best, decorative. Although the medieval, Renaissance, and baroque eras allow us glimpses of women musicians who transcend the norm, these are either women born to musical families, encouraged and taught by musician-fathers who realized the potential of their daughters, or women who were educated in convents and later became nuns. The music they performed and created was for private consumption: thus, nun composers wrote sacred works for use in their convents while women in the secular world wrote small-scale works for domestic entertainment. For the most part, the musical forms women composed were designed to be performed in the home—for a single instrument, for a small group of instruments, or for an instrument with voice. Song forms like madrigals, harpsichord suites, and later, dance forms, sonatas for piano, *Lieder,* and themes and variations were musical structures accessible both to domestic performance and compositional capabilities. Large-scale forms such as operas and symphonies were complex: few women had the theoretical/musical knowledge necessary to attempt these and, as well, large-scale public forms were male domains, which required both money and power.

The two major women composers of the nineteenth century (Fanny Mendelssohn Hensel and Clara Wieck Schumann) fell victims to the prevailing view of women as only "re-creative beings," an assumption that continues well into our own century. (In the 1970s, for example, there was a thriving debate about the creative/re-creative abilities of women in music. Psychologists proclaimed the re-creative capabilities of women [musical performance], but completely dismissed any potential for creativity [musical composition]:

only men had the creative impulse; only men could compose great music. Although less vociferous today, the debate continues.) Fanny Mendelssohn Hensel (1805-1847) wrote more than 400 compositions but was, on several occasions, reminded by her father that her role in life was that of wife and mother: that for *her,* music could *only* be an ornament, an art to be enjoyed in the domestic sphere among friends and family but *never* in the public arena. When she had a few early works published, they were published under the name of Felix, her brother, because, as he explained to her, as a woman she should not be subject to public scrutiny and criticism.

Clara Wieck Schumann (1819-1896) was a near contemporary of Fanny, but Clara's middle-class upbringing allowed her both performance and compositional opportunities that the "elite" Fanny was denied. Clara's performance career far exceeded the financial expectations of her husband: she made more money in three weeks of performing than he made in two years of composing, and although she showed promise as a composer, she basically relinquished composition after her marriage to Robert. He needed his space and quiet time for composing. She was organizing the household, performances, concert tours, finding practice time, and changing diapers. It is hard to be creative when you have no solid blocks of time: the Schumanns had eight children.

Like Hildegard 700 years before her, Clara questioned her abilities as a composer on the grounds that there had been no great women composers: that is, she did not know of any because none had been "discovered" in her time. And she, like the twelfth-century Hildegard, lamented her poor woman's brain, which she assumed to be inferior, and wondered at her presumption in composing music, which she viewed as a masculine enterprise.

Clara, Fanny, and untold other women from the Middle Ages to the present have been involved in the making, performing, and teaching of music. Their supporting functions as wives, mothers, sisters, daughters, and muses were the focus of earlier studies about women's roles in music; slim volumes from the late nineteenth and early twentieth centuries reaffirmed earlier beliefs and advocated for these supportive roles as part of women's work in music.

The late nineteenth century gave us such musical women as Louise Farrenc, Cécile Chaminade, Amy Beach, and Pauline Viardot-

Garcia, and in the early twentieth century, the indomitable Ethyl Smyth, a suffragist as well as a composer of large-scale works such as operas. The last sixty years have seen a greater acceptance of women as composers (Rebecca Clarke, Germaine Tailleferre, Lili Boulanger, Thea Musgrave, Ruth Crawford Seeger, Pauline Oliveros, Joan Tower, Ellen Taaffe Zwilich, Alexina Louie, Violet Archer, Barbara Kolb, Libby Larsen, as well as hundreds of others). Their works range from solo songs to symphonies to operas: from small-scale to large. Their success in large forms is due, in part, to their training in musical composition (formerly a masculine preserve) and to an awareness of women as performers of *all* musical instruments. The hurdle facing women in composition today is the acceptance of their technological capabilities: many women write electroacoustic music (music that combines acoustic instruments with taped sounds), but technology continues to be a male-dominated field.

For centuries, women were denied the theoretical musical education afforded to men. From a more practical (but parallel) perspective, women were also discouraged from playing musical instruments deemed to be masculine. Today, a female music undergraduate who wishes to study tuba or trombone may not be commonplace, but her desire to do so is generally accepted and she will be admitted to a music school as a tuba or trombone major. But until the 1960s, brass—and some wind—instruments were male prerogatives: these instruments distorted the face. Until the early twentieth century, even stringed instruments were considered to be "unfeminine": violins "scrunched" the chin; the cello was unseemly with its physical posture of splayed legs, which invited rude comments (some late-nineteenth-century teachers advocated a sidesaddle position for female cellists); brass and timpani were military instruments, associated with the battlefield in the eighteenth century and thus considered to be masculine instruments. The harp, harpsichord, and piano were the truly feminine instruments because they displayed the female figure to great advantage with a well-turned ankle, graceful arms, and elegant profile. In the last half of the nineteenth century, female and male students at the Paris Consérvatoire were assigned different repertoire: male students were given "masculine" works (Beethoven) to play; women students were assigned Chopin. Such thinking still persists.

Although during times of war women replaced men in major orchestras, they lost their positions when the men returned. The emergence of women's orchestras to counteract such discriminatory practices began well over a hundred years ago, and some continue to this day. Even now we are faced with gender discrimination: several major European orchestras do not willingly hire women musicians; the Vienna Philharmonic, for example, affirms its right to retain its 150-year-old tradition as an all-male "Austrian" orchestra, citing reasons completely unacceptable to my conception of gender and race equality.

If women composers and performers are gaining greater acceptance in our century, what is happening in that last male bastion—conducting? It was not until the late nineteenth century that the art of conducting was given any kind of elevated status: it carries the illusion of physical power over not only the performing (male) musicians but also over the music itself. How could women possibly ascend to this power? Conductors of symphony orchestras are symbolically akin to presidents of corporations: how many women are presidents of corporations? The twentieth century has seen some fine female orchestral conductors (e.g., Antonia Brico, Sarah Caldwell, Catherine Comet, JoAnn Falletta, and Marin Alsop), but women in the position of wielding a baton—as orchestral conductors do—are suspect. Women choral conductors, who use their hands as a medium of direction rather than the orchestral baton, are more widely accepted. The baton remains the phallic symbol of power, and women conductors who aspire to this power find that critics and audiences cannot separate the gender of the conductor from the conductor. For example, Marin Alsop's conducting style is seen as masculine because it is energetic and athletic; JoAnn Falletta's style is seen as more gentle and feminine. Women conductors of great symphony orchestras may be a vision of the future; they are not, at present, a reality.

Currently, feminist musicologists are exploring such issues as gender differences in the compositional process: do women composers write differently from men? Is there a difference between masculine/feminine musical language? How can we redefine the canon—the great body of accepted, usually male musical repertoire—to include music by women? These are complex issues with unresolved answers. Until women composers are accepted as composers without a gender affiliation, there will be no equality. Yet, many women composers, profoundly concerned with issues of gender and ethnicity, argue that they do compose from a feminine perspective and that their compositions reflect the issues important to them as women: nurturing, the environment, family, sexuality, and cross-cultural ethnic roots. In music with text, the differences are more readily apparent—as they have always been. What is more difficult for listeners to discern is what happens in nontexted music. Can we really tell the difference between an orchestral work of a male or female composer, or between a heterosexual or homosexual composer? Can we, as listeners, hear differing sexual orientations in the music itself? Without a text or program to guide us, the answer is probably no. These are current questions for which there are no easy answers.

Within the past ten years, the proliferation of information about women in music (published articles, journals, books, CDs, as well as Internet lists and Web sites) has been wonderfully overwhelming. What once seemed to be an isolated field of study for many of us for such a long time has become an all-encompassing expansion of shared knowledge and mutual interest. Internet lists such as IAWM (the International Alliance for Women in Music), GRIME (Gender Research in Music Education), and Gen-Mus (Gender-Music) explore and discuss immediate and relevant issues; scholars in the field of women in music now have the means to exchange views, to publish Web Sites and home pages, and to make public the work of women musicians—past and present.

Many colleges and universities in the United States and Canada in the 1970s, 1980s, and 1990s devised separate courses on the "history of women in music." I suspect that many of these courses were instituted—and continue now—for reasons of "political correctness." And, I think, most of us teaching these courses hope fervently for a time when they will not need to be taught as separate courses, a time when the contributions of women can be integrated fully within a general music history curriculum.

BIBLIOGRAPHY

Bowers, Jane and Judith Tick (Eds.). *Women Making Music: The Western Art Tradition 1150-1950.* Chicago: University of Illinois Press, 1986.

Briscoe, James R. (Ed.). *Contemporary Anthology of Music by Women.* Bloomington: Indiana University Press, 1997.

________. *Historical Anthology of Music by Women.* Bloomington: Indiana University Press, 1987.

Cook, Susan C. and Judy S. Tsou (Eds.). *Cecilia Reclaimed: Feminist Perspectives on Gender and Music.* Chicago: University of Illinois Press, 1994.

Furman, Martha Schleifer and Sylvia Glickman (Eds.). *Women Composers: Music through the Ages.* 5 vols. to date. New York: Schirmer (G. K. Hall), 1995- .

McClary, Susan. *Feminine Endings: Music, Gender, and Sexuality.* Minneapolis: University of Minnesota Press, 1991.

Neuls-Bates, Carol (Ed.). *Women in Music: An Anthology of Source Readings from the Middle Ages to the Present.* Revised Edition. Boston: Northeastern University Press, 1996.

Pendle, Karin (Ed.). *Women & Music: A History.* Bloomington: Indiana University Press, 1991.

Sadie, Julie Anne and Rhian Samuel (Eds.). *The New Grove Dictionary of Women Composers.* London: Macmillan, 1994.

Chapter 6

Listening to Women's Voices and Reading Women's Words: How Women's Studies Has Helped to Transform the Teaching of Literature

Georgia Rhoades

The tradition of scholarly writing in literature has always included the personal essay, in which the writer draws connections between observation and experience and the chosen topic. In the field of literary criticism, especially as it applies to the canon, a landmark essay is Adrienne Rich's "When We Dead Awaken: Writing As Re-Vision" (1971) in which she used her own development as a creative writer to explain how the traditional texts by white heterosexual males were unable to provide her with adequate models for finding her voice as a Jewish lesbian. This model offered an alternative to women writing in the profession and is now a common practice of many feminist writers such as Jane Tompkins, Carolyn Heilbrun, bell hooks, Gloria Anzaldua, and June Jordan. I am thankful to write about literature at a time when the observations and experience of the writer are valued and expected by feminist readers and, to some extent, by others in the profession. In contrast to a heavily academized writing style that attempts to impress the reader into agreement, feminist writing as it is now practiced tries to be clear, to draw upon examples that are accessible to most intended readers, to acknowledge its own perspective, and to be applicable to life knowledge as well as academic knowledge (in fact, we try to make these the same).

During my undergraduate years in Kentucky, I worked in the university, married, had a child, and got a divorce, but these dramas were not part of my academic (or my personal) response to the fictional marital problems of Isabel Archer or Molly Bloom. A disciple of T. S. Eliot's "Tradition and the Individual Talent," I wanted in those days to be objective, to be recognized and rewarded as the kind of rigorous thinker whose work was sexless and timeless. As an academic, like Rich, my academic models were either male or male-identified women (i.e., women considered exceptional because they had been successful by male standards). I thought being a literary scholar meant being sexless, but it really meant being patriarchal.

Today, at least in many universities, literature is presented differently than in 1969. Even teachers who are fairly traditional will often ask literature students to write journal entries that reflect personal connections to texts. We are likely to use groups in classes for collaborative learning, often asking the group to teach the class. We look for ways to shift authority from the teacher who "knows" what the work means to a variety of perspectives that lead students to different interpretations, all honored as valid readings. I have watched this transformation occur in the universities that I have been part of for the past twenty years. And I believe much of this change to be the work of feminists, some of us working overtly, some of us gradually bringing about consciousness-raising through a more feminist way of seeing the roles of teacher, student, and multicultural education. Certainly some change is inextricable from the attitudes of the 1960s, the Civil Rights movement, the antiwar movement, and the movements for Native American and gay/lesbian/bisexual rights, as each of these called for other voices to be heard. In calling for the recognition of many voices, these movements helped lead to the feminist ideas of listening to students, of imagining antihierarchical structures in the classroom, and of recognizing multiple viewpoints in choosing texts and interpreting them.

These changes have naturally moved to the literature classroom. In the past two decades, literature teachers also have been affected by a new interest in the response of the reader. In respecting many views, feminism respected student readers as well. Some critics began to write about how we could take into account individual reactions to a novel as students make sense of it using not only their own reading experience but also the experiences of their lives. Ideas about what it means to interpret a work began to soften; the clearly defined edges began to blur. Teachers began to be less likely to tell students what a work meant and less likely to expect that right answer on a test because the text could mean many things.

As we began to change *how* we taught, *what* we taught began to change as well. Teachers began to realize that we must honor other texts than those traditionally taught by white heterosexual males. As an undergraduate, I read Virginia Woolf and Emily Dickinson, some Langston Hughes but no texts by African-American women, Native Americans, or Latin Americans. Woolf and Dickinson, considered as good as men, were exceptions to the exclusion of women from the canon. To be considered good, a writer had to be "classic," which generally meant that he (or Woolf, Dickinson, Jane Austen) had stayed in print and remained on college reading lists. (As late as 1993, my university included only two women writers on the graduate reading list.)

Feminists began to question these criteria. Scholars such as Lucy Freibert, Barbara A. White, Sandra M. Gilbert, and Susan Gubar pointed out that writers often stayed in print through good networking, which often meant that the writer was well known and was taught in colleges. Thus, Ralph Waldo Emerson stayed in print, but Margaret Fuller, the first editor of *The Dial,* did not. Not finding many works in print that celebrated female experience, women and men teachers taught the texts they had been taught. Women teachers were themselves often unaware of women's literary history. Publishing remained a male province: as Woolf had argued, women artists were kept illiterate or discouraged from writing, so it was a miracle that any of their stories existed in any form. Alice Walker extended Woolf's research to point out that many African-American women were forced to express their artistry through gardening and quilting in a society that did not believe these women had artistic gifts.

Fortunately, in the 1960s many of the women's texts that had gone out of print were recovered through the networking of the women's movement. Women passing around battered photocopies of such classics as Charlotte Perkin Gilman's "The Yellow Wallpaper" and Kate Chopin's *The Awakening* created women's presses such as The

Feminist Press and Virago to make texts available again. Eventually, large presses began to include women's writing in their anthologies and to republish classic women's works.

For some teachers who have tried to enlarge the canon and for some writers of textbooks, this mission has seemed gargantuan because they have kept the same patriarchal values and merely added women to the traditional reading list. I first understood how feminism might change education while listening to an address given by Peggy McIntosh in Louisville, Kentucky, in 1987. McIntosh's metaphor for patriarchal thinking, which is the basis for the traditional canon, is a mountain summit. Few can stand on top, and their priority is to stay there and keep others off. Literature seen in this way is competitive and elitist. For traditional anthologists, this has meant that "classic" works, those at the pinnacle, have been those that are white, heterosexual, and male-identified. "Objectivity" has long been a standard of classic works, suggesting that a writer's own experience must be universal to be valuable. Yet James Joyce's *A Portrait of the Artist As a Young Man,* based on his life, has obviously been judged by far different standards than Kate Chopin's *The Awakening,* also based on real experience but considered too vulgar by the reading public because it was written by a woman.

The plateau, McIntosh's metaphor for feminist thinking, allows much more room at the top and encourages growth and nurturing for newcomers. Many voices, many writers, many readers decide what they choose. Therefore, a feminist perspective shifts the center away from the pinnacle to a more egalitarian place where many of us have the opportunity to define authenticity. Rather than creating a canon that expands by adding works to those already considered classic, some feminist scholars suggest that we find a new way to see classic works with perhaps a separate canon of literature that defines the Asian-American woman, another that helps to explain Jewish culture in the United States, and so forth. Under these standards, "objectivity" probably would not matter as a value or be an interesting point at all.

As women's literature has moved into the mainstream in the context of universities interested in exploring multiculturalism, literary criticism has been forced to make room for more political criticism, especially feminist critics. A sampling might include Julia Kristeva,

Hélène Cixous, Barbara Smith, Audre Lorde, Barbara Solomon, Nina Baym, and Carolyn Heilbrun. These writers help readers focus on the balance of power and gender within texts. Several collections of feminist critical essays and books about feminist criticism are available. An excellent example is Henry Louis Gates's *Reading Black, Reading Feminist* (1990). Most courses in literary criticism now include a discussion of feminist criticism.

I am not sure whether we will ever be able to mainstream the writing of women in traditional literature courses (such as English literature surveys) so that specialty courses will be unnecessary. Today most English departments offer a course or two in women's literature, African-American literature, and perhaps Native-American literature. In these courses, teachers are likely to avoid comparisons to mainstream or traditional literature, maintaining a perspective that is less competitive and hierarchical. When women are included in mainstream courses, often these writers are tokens, included so that the course will appear to fulfill the requirement of multiculturalism. In fact, for some teachers and the anthologies they choose, the women writers taught are the least threatening or less radical. For example, Woolf's "The Mark on the Wall"—early, experimental, and relatively nonpolitical—is a more likely choice for mainstream courses than her essay "22 Hyde Park Gate," an indictment of her stepbrother's sexual abuse of her and her sister. Until teachers are themselves exposed to a wide variety of women's texts, courses focusing on women's writing remain necessary.

Some women have had undeniable popularity and longevity, traditionally considered part of the teaching canon, such as Mary Shelley, Jane Austen, Gwendolyn Brooks, Charlotte Brontë, Emily Brontë, Lorraine Hansberry, Lillian Hellmann, Joyce Carol Oates, Flannery O'Connor, Carson McCullers, and Eudora Welty. Although some women writers, particularly Emily Dickinson, Elizabeth Barrett Browning, George Eliot, and Edith Wharton, are included, they are not often represented by their radical and clearly feminist works, and often their biographies have focused on their sexual lives. Many women writers now taught in mainstream courses are considered foremothers and have gained canonical standing because feminists have stressed their significance. These include Mary Wollstonecraft, Phillis Wheatley, Sojourner Truth, Elizabeth Cady Stanton, Susan B.

Anthony, Linda Brent, Kate Chopin, Charlotte Perkins Gilman, Virginia Woolf, Zora Neale Hurston, Alice Walker, Toni Morrison, Paula Gunn Allen, Grace Paley, Carolyn Heilbrun, and Adrienne Rich. These foremothers' works have been reprinted and remain in print. Unfortunately, sometimes only one work of these writers is included in mainstream courses, so a college graduate may have been asked to read "The Yellow Wallpaper" several times, receiving the impression that this one work sums up Gilman's contribution.

Feminists could, of course, expand the reading lists with many other writers, particularly in our attempts to offer a multicultural canon: such a list might include Margery Kempe, Aphra Behn, Maxine Hong Kingston, Amy Tan, Toni Cade Bambara, Audre Lorde, Maya Angelou, Rita Dove, Caryl Churchill, Gloria Anzaldua, Leslie Marmon Silko, and Linda Hogan. Other feminists might wish to add names from science fiction, particularly Ursula LeGuin, Joanna Russ, Octavia Butler, and Marge Piercy, and also in detective fiction, including Dorothy L. Sayers, Agatha Christie, Sara Paretsky, and Katherine Forrest. (Some readers, I imagine, are wondering why these women are not on my foremothers' list: I am reluctant to list names in any category at all, not wanting to box us into a canon. I offer these as a beginning, reflecting on what seems to me to be common practice at this late point of the century.)

In my own teaching experience, I have watched one book I felt to be a classic, which I had taught several times, disappear from print. *The Seven Ages,* by Eva Figes (1986), is an epic about a family of midwives, incorporating women's history and political commentary. It is not possible to teach unusual choices and be unaware of the politics of publishing: we have to teach books to keep them in print, but sometimes that act is not enough. In my own course recently, we read Octavia Butler, Dorothy Allison, Barbara Kingsolver, Rigoberta Menchu, and Katherine Forrest. The semester before I included Vita Sackville-West, Marise Conde, Caryl Churchill, and Audre Lorde. None of these is considered classic, perhaps, but I have come to see my job as introducing those writers that students may not hear of otherwise. In keeping women's books before the public and in publishing new ones, several publishing houses are significant: The Feminist Press, The Women's Press, Virago, Kitchen Table—Women of Color Press, Seal, Naiad, Aunt Lute, and others.

For those of us who teach women's studies, certain collections of women's writing have been invaluable. Gilbert and Gubar's *The Norton Anthology of Literature by Women* (1996) is a chronological collection of U. S. and British women writers: many of the women mentioned previously are included in their book. Mary Ferguson's *Images of Women in Literature* (1991) and Sandra Eagleton's *Women in Literature* (1988) are thematic anthologies. The *Bloomsbury Guide to Women's Literature* (1992) is a helpful commentary. Mary Helen Washington's *Black-Eyed Susans/Midnight Birds* (1990), Paula Gunn Allen's *Spiderwoman's Granddaughters* (1990), and Gloria Anzaldua and Cherrie Moraga's *This Bridge Called My Back* (1984) also created landmark collections of women's work.

The reading and teaching of women's texts, as the writing of them, is a political act. It is one powerful way to witness women's experience and to ensure that we always have a voice, in schools and out. It is also the medium through which second- and third-wave feminists may speak to each other, to allow us to know the spectrum of written women's experience, and to give us heart.

BIBLIOGRAPHY

Allen, Paula Gunn. *Spiderwoman's Granddaughters.* Boston: Beacon, 1990.

Anzaldua, Gloria and Cherrie Moraga. *This Bridge Called My Back.* New York: Kitchen Table, 1984.

Chopin, Kate. *The Awakening.* 1899. Margaret Culley (Ed.). New York: Norton, 1976.

Claire Buck (Ed.). *The Bloomsbury Guide to Women's Literature.* London: Bloomsbury, 1992.

Eagleton, Sandra. *Women in Literature.* Englewood Cliffs, NJ: Prentice-Hall, 1988.

Ferguson, Mary. *Images of Women in Literature.* Boston: Houghton-Mifflin, 1991.

Figes, Eva. *The Seven Ages.* New York: Ballantine, 1986.

Gates, Henry Louis. *Reading Black, Reading Feminist.* New York: Meridia, 1990.

Gilbert, Sandra M. and Susan Gubar (Eds.). *The Norton Anthology of Literature by Women,* Second Edition. New York: Norton, 1996.

Gilman, Charlotte Perkins. "The Yellow Wallpaper." 1892. In Sandra M. Gilbert and Susan Gubar (Eds.), *The Norton Anthology of Literature by Women,* Second Edition (pp. 1133-1144). New York: Norton, 1996.

Rich, Adrienne. "When We Dead Awaken: Writing As Re-vision" (1971). In Sandra M. Gilbert and Susan Gubar (Eds.), *The Norton Anthology of Literature by Women,* Second Edition (pp. 1980-1992). New York: Norton, 1996.

Washington, Mary Helen. *Black-Eyed Susans/Midnight Birds*. New York: Anchor, 1990.

Woolf, Virginia. "The Mark on the Wall." In M.H. Abrams (Ed.), *The Norton Anthology of English Literature,* Volume 2, Sixth Edition (pp. 1916-1921). New York: Norton, 1993.

______. "22 Hyde Park." *Moments of Being,* Second Edition. Jeanne Schulkind (Ed.). New York: Harcourt-Brace, 1985.

Chapter 7

Feminism and Film Studies

Karen Chandler

Because of its function as entertainment, film, especially Hollywood film, is commonly believed to lack seriousness or to bear only the most superficial meaning. Although more colleges and universities are offering courses in film, it has not lost its reputation as trivial. Popular film seems to offer a range of devices (such as glamour, exotic or absurd situations, grand spectacle, intrigue) designed to help viewers escape the responsibilities of their everyday lives rather than to know themselves and their world more fully. Film presents its share of social problems, of course, from marital infidelity and prostitution *(Indecent Proposal)* to the Holocaust *(Schindler's List)*. Yet many critics argue that these problems only function to excite or titillate viewers, rather than to challenge them to engage in profound thought. Indeed, some influential critics have argued that film desensitizes viewers to the problems of their immediate experience and of the world at large (Horkheimer and Adorno, 1989).

Although film can trivialize experience, it, like literature, can offer rich insights into life's trials and pleasures. It interprets lived experience in ways that call on viewers to evaluate, affirm, or challenge the values it conveys. Film calls on viewers to think about and question conventional ideas about individuality, family, community, gender, sexuality, race, class, and nationalism. Film is entertainment, but like most entertainment, it is also serious business. Analyzing film can yield important insights into American culture and history.

As a feminist critic, I am particularly concerned with the manner in which film defines gender, power, and race. My work leads me to analyze film acting, dialogue, music, editing, and individual shot design (the organization of objects, actors, and light within a frame of film), among other components. In addition, I research audiences' responses to film narratives. Both aspects of my work reflect my commitment to feminist theory and practice, which is concerned with the critical analysis of society (groups of people) and culture (the practices and beliefs that define them). *Critical* here does not necessarily mean negative. Though the results of feminist analysis of a social phenomenon might expose injustice, it might also expose heroism or beneficence by women and men. I use the term *critical* to stress that feminist analysis involves cautious evaluation or judgment of the evidence in question.

Feminist film criticism, which emerged as a serious, systematic endeavor in the 1970s, grew out of an interest in understanding the relationship between images of women on film and actual women's historical conditions in patriarchal societies. The Civil Rights movements of the 1960s and early 1970s inspired increased attention to women's and ethnic and racial minorities' portrayal in popular culture. Hence, early feminist studies of film tended to focus on the ways films recorded women's secondary social status. Indeed, the filmmaker Laura Mulvey (1977), one of the most influential feminist theorists, argued that the very structure of Hollywood films' plots caters to male viewers' deep psychological need to reinforce their power over women and to see men as superior. Women on screen served to satisfy men's pleasure in looking at beauty and in seeing any woman controlled by male protagonists. A distinct strain of feminist criticism by Linda Williams (1984), Ruby Rich (1985), Judith Mayne (1981), and others accepted Mulvey's assumption that much Hollywood film is sexist, but this criticism also resisted generalizing about all narrative films. These critics investigated the ways films made by different directors, in different genres, and at different times defined gender differently from the pattern Mulvey identified. Both lines of criticism were interested not only in examining the sexism in Hollywood film but also in discovering and analyzing films that either critiqued the Hollywood model or provided an alternative to its patriarchal ideology. Whereas some critics focused their energies on avant-garde films that arguably defied patriarchy, others examined the resistant strategies in mainstream narrative films.

Since the early 1970s, feminist criticism has become more attuned to both the history of film and the complexities of society. Much criticism is intent on understanding the place film has in particular audiences' experience and the roles film has played in debates over gender, race, ethnicity, class, and sexuality. If early feminist theory emphasized a hypothetical viewer, usually male, theory has broadened to encompass how persons from particular racial and ethnic groups, socioeconomic classes, age groups, regions, and time periods have connected with film. Complementing, testing, and challenging theories of viewership, demographic studies of how actual groups of people watch film have become important. One example is Jacqueline Bobo's (1995) research on black women viewers' interpretations of Steven Spielberg's adaptation of Alice Walker's novel, *The Color Purple.* Feminist scholarship has also focused on understanding how longstanding practices and changes within the film industry have shaped film production and, consequently, the messages about culture that film offers. Influential studies of film, for instance, have included Lea Jacobs' (1991) work on the ways industry-imposed censorship reshaped images of gender and power in the 1930s. Although theory has remained central to film study, it has increasingly been grounded in observations of the actual practices of the film industry, filmmakers, and film viewers. In many ways, these developments parallel the recent work of literary scholars interested in the relations between literature and its social and historical contexts. Attention to both text and context contributes to our understanding of the complex ways that film engages viewers, that viewers' values are recorded and challenged on film, and that the film industry seeks to exploit and shape viewers' tastes.

Feminist scholarship, as diverse as it is, continues to seek to explain how women (and men and children) are situated within society and how they learn the roles they are expected to play. Feminist analysis strives to explain what has become familiar or obvious without resorting to easy answers; it strives to apprehend the often hidden assumptions and myths that determine our social roles. When they turn to the film text, feminist critics look at how film presents female and male identity, often beginning by asking how a character's behavior and appearance reflect his or her gender and what the ramifications of the characterization are. Feminist film scholars also focus on other subjects in studying film. These include the nature and history of film production and distribution, the nature of genre films (westerns, musicals, maternal melodrama), the impact of stars' personalities, film's inevitable invitation to examine women's bodies (recall the films of Greta Garbo, Rita Hayworth, Marilyn Monroe, Jennifer Lopez, Halle Berry, Cameron Diaz, and Charlize Theron), the manner in which narrative is shaped by gender difference or inequity, and an audience's relationship to a film. My own work combines a number of these concerns, so let's take the book I am working on now, a study of melodramatic film from 1915 through 1940, as an example of feminist film criticism.

In one chapter of my book, I discuss two maternal melodramas, the silent film *Stella Dallas* (1925) and the early sound remake (1937), and examine what the heroine's victimization and triumph might have meant for audiences of women in the 1920s and 1930s. Each film concerns working-class Stella's effort to join a group of affluent, sophisticated New Englanders, an effort for which she is repeatedly punished because of her incapacity to mimic the social set's standards of decorum. As a young woman, Stella falls in love with the handsome young manager of the plant at which her father and brother work. After a short romance, the pair marry and encounter troubles when Stella proves less willing to imitate her husband's model of refined, restrained behavior than she has previously appeared to be. Stella sees her marriage to Stephen Dallas as a springboard into a better social class that she associates with leisure—elaborate clothes and access to a world of racing and country clubs and sophisticated people. Yet access to these experiences does not ensure Stella's full acceptance into the elite world of which they are part. Stella proves unwilling to conform to its staunch set of rules about personal decorum. Given to wearing garish, form-hugging clothing, to flirting with men, and to speaking and laughing brashly, she fails to fit in both with her husband and the elite world in which he comfortably operates. After they have a child together, the alienated Stephen leaves and she agrees to raise their child, Laurel, alone. Stella and Laurel develop a close personal relationship in spite of their very obvious differences: Laurel resembles the refined, elegant Stephen, but unlike him she adores Stella, accepting her mother's eccentricities with aplomb. As Laurel grows up, however, Stella's coarseness, particularly her apparent (but not actual) sexual openness, threatens to hurt Laurel's chances to find a place among the elite. When Stella realizes this, she withdraws from Laurel's life, thus facilitating Laurel's marriage to a man from a wealthy family. As both films end, Stella watches the wedding from the sidewalk outside Laurel's stepmother's mansion; she then walks away, apparently into social obscurity. As in many maternal melodramas, Stella sacrifices her happiness to ensure her child's social standing. (The recent Bette Midler movie, *Stella* [1990], is the latest version of this story.) The 1925 and 1937 films offer classic views of a woman's oppression by society, for in giving up her daughter, Stella subordinates her own desires to those of the more powerful social elites who judge her.

Some critics have argued that at the end of the films Stella is tragically cut off from everything she has ever wanted and, thus, appears to be merely a victim of the insensitive society that will not accept her. Yet the acting and shot compositions in both films emphasize Stella's moral superiority to the conventional people who oppose her and, consequently, these elements appraise Stella's fate in less defeatist terms. Both films suggest that Stella forsakes the world of class prejudice and personal insensitivity that cannot accommodate her human richness. The silent film, for instance, repeatedly isolates Stella in shots, lighting her softly and fully, while darkening her surroundings. Although such one-shots often emphasize women's status as sexual objects, the shot arrangements in *Stella Dallas* suggest that Stella transcends the environment others would confine her to. Rather than stressing one aspect of her humanity, her sexuality, these shots emphasize a fullness other characters in the film lack themselves and miss seeing in Stella. This fullness is conveyed by the expressive actress Belle Bennett's facial and body language, which suggests a range and depth of emotions missing from nearly every other character in the film. Similarly, the casting of Barbara Stanwyck as Stella in the 1937 film greatly reinforces the sense of the character's heroism, for Stanwyck was known for playing outsiders who fought against unjust systems. Stanwyck, like her contemporaries Bette Davis and Joan Crawford, was very popular with women viewers because of her characters' defiance of questionable social expectations.

Besides looking closely at the films' performances and shot designs, I have sought to test my interpretation of the films by exploring how contemporary viewers understood them. I have found glimpses of viewers' responses to the films in published and unpublished diaries and letters (often available for study only in rare book and film archives), in results of test screenings and surveys, and in magazine and newspaper reviews. Drawing on these and other sources has helped me understand the interpretations that may have been available to the large audience of women that made both films popular. I also have read histories of social experience and economic trends in the 1920s and 1930s to determine how the range of responses fit into the larger patterns of women's lives. This additional research has led me to speculate that Stella's rejection by her society's standard-bearers may have rung true for African-American women, whose appearance was also taken as a sign of intellectual and moral inferiority. Newspaper ads show that theaters catering to blacks showed the 1937 film beyond its original run, suggesting demand for the film was great. The story of Stella's limited class mobility and social isolation, however, may have resonated with working-class and middle-class women's experience in general. During the Great Depression, for instance, many women were restricted from taking jobs for which they were qualified to ensure that men would have access to the positions.

Feminist criticism of films such as *Stella Dallas* or more recent movies such as *Thelma and Louise, The Age of Innocence, Speed, My Best Friend's Wedding, Eve's Bayou,* and *There's Something About Mary,* can elucidate the social values that drive plot and shape theme and character. Such criticism exposes the illusion of any argument dismissing the importance of film to our culture. By looking at film from a feminist perspective, a person can gain entrée to a world of meaning that not only clarifies a particular film but also facilitates understanding of the world outside the film.

BIBLIOGRAPHY

The Age of Innocence. Directed by Martin Scorcese. Cappa, 1993.

Bobo, Jacqueline. *Black Women As Cultural Readers.* New York: Columbia University Press, 1995.

Chandler, Karen. "Agency and *Stella Dallas:* Audience, Melodramatic Directives, and Social Determinism in 1920s America." *Arizona Quarterly* 51(4) (1995): 27-44.

The Color Purple. Directed by Steven Spielberg. Amblin, 1985.

Eve's Bayou. Directed by Kasi Lemmons. Addis Wechsler, 1997.

Gledhill, Christine (Ed.). *Home Is Where the Heart Is: Studies in Melodrama and the Woman's Film.* London: British Film Institute, 1987.

Haskell, Molly. *From Reverence to Rape: The Treatment of Women in Movies* New York: Holt, 1973.

Horkheimer, Max and Theodor Adorno. *Dialectic of Enlightenment.* New York: Continuum, 1989.

Indecent Proposal. Director Adrian Lyne. Paramount, 1993.

Jacobs, Lea. *The Wages of Sin: Censorship and the Fallen Woman's Film.* Madison: University of Wisconsin Press, 1991.

Kaplan, E. Ann. *Women and Film: Both Sides of the Camera.* New York: Metheun, 1983.

Kessler-Harris, Alice. *Out to Work: A History of Wage-Earning Women in the United States.* New York: Oxford University Press, 1982.

Mayne, Judith. "The Woman at the Keyhole: Women's Cinema and Feminist Criticism." *New German Critique* 23 (1981): 27-43.

Modleski, Tania. *The Women Who Knew Too Much: Hitchcock and Feminist Theory.* New York: Metheun, 1988.

Mulvey, Laura. "Afterthought on 'Visual Pleasure and Narrative Cinema.'" In Christine Gledhill (Ed.), *Home Is Where the Heart Is: Studies in Melodrama and the Woman's Film* (pp. 75-79).

________. "Visual Pleasure and Narrative Cinema." *Screen* 16(3) (1977): 113-119.

My Best Friend's Wedding. Directed by P.J. Hogan. Tri Star, 1997.

Rich, B. Ruby. "In the Name of Feminist Film Criticism." In *Movies and Methods, Volume II* (pp. 340-358). Bill Nichols (Ed.). Berkeley: University of California Press, 1985.

Schindler's List. Directed by Steven Spielberg. Amblin, 1993.

Speed. Directed by Jan De Bont. Twentieth-Century Fox, 1994.

Stella. Directed by John Erman. Samuel Goldwyn, Jr., 1990.

Stella Dallas. Directed by Henry King. Goldwyn, 1925.

Stella Dallas. Directed by King Vidor. United Artists, 1937.

Thelma and Louise. Directed by Ridley Scott. MGM, 1991.

There's Something About Mary. Directed by Bobby and Peter Farrelly. Twentieth-Century Fox, 1998.

Williams, Linda. " 'Something Else Besides a Mother': *Stella Dallas* and the Maternal Melodrama." *Cinema Journal* 24(1) (1984): 2-27.

Chapter 8

Refusing to Close the Curtains Before Putting on the Light: Literature and Women's Studies

Lyndie Brimstone

In 1955 or thereabouts, Albert built an alcove cabinet with a gray Formica top and Perspex sliding doors to house *Encyclopædia Britannica.* He was a hard-working man who set great store by education as a means to self-improvement and, like George Eliot's Mr. Tulliver in *Mill on the Floss,* knew a good bit of binding when he saw it. A proud, cloth-cap man with a bicycle for work, a car and a suit for Sundays, he was never sick and took all the overtime he could get. On the same day each week, Albert handed his wages to his wife with the seal unbroken. Without need, Sadie wiped her hands on her apron and adjusted her glasses before taking them. Without sound, she counted, checked, and divided the money into pots on the sideboard. Debts were like head-lice: only dirty families had them, only slovenly women allowed them to spread. Sadie's weekly scrutinies, her hatred of waste, her hemming of school skirts to last for a lifetime, kept vice and vermin from our door.

The cabinet of exact proportions lived in the front room where three children sat firmly in the center of their designated seats. On good-mood days, my father remembered *Britannica.* I recall the weight of a volume placed in my lap, the coldness of the cover, the red mark the edge made at the top of a child's bare legs. "A good investment," he would say, "in the future." While the sales line pitched at the pride of an aspiring factory man had become Albert's own, Sadie saw it differently and the books went back in their numbered places the minute he left the room. Christmas annuals from aunts, thick-papered versions of *Heidi, Little Women, Black Beauty,* these were for children's hands.

I have no memory of Sadie or Albert with a book. At the end of their working, cleaning, cooking, fixing days, the television in the opposite alcove was enough. By the time my older brother, younger sister, and I reached the age when our fingers might have been trusted, *Britannica* had become so much a part of the unchanging furniture, so much a part of the polished doorstep we stepped over rather than on, we did not notice it.

Given that it is now more than twenty years since I last crossed that threshold, it was not immediately clear to me why, when preparing this chapter, these particular memories should intrude. How does this story relate to my present reality teaching literature in a women's studies degree program, and what relevance can it have for you, studying at a university at the start of a new millennium? I will return again and again to this question in the discussion that follows. First, some clarification of terms.

Academic women's studies came into being as a direct result of feminist action, and all our teaching and learning, materials, motivation, and method reflect this origin in myriad forms. This suggestion of multiplicity is entirely appropriate here since there never has been, nor should be, a single "grand theory" of feminism. What we have, instead, is a dynamic interplay of feminist approaches, with varying political priorities, converging and splitting on a range of issues. A broad, working definition, however, is helpful: feminism rejects the imposition of unequal relations of power based on assumptions of superiority and has focused especially on those that pertain between males and females. It operates as theory, that is, as a way of questioning, conceptualizing, and rethinking these relations, and as practice, a way of being and doing intended to bring about change.

With *change* as a keyword, the first priority in women's studies must be to create conditions that encourage active participation. This may well involve breaking form, doing things differently in order to draw attention to the taken-for-granted way that things are usually done. Since my autobiographical extract is hardly the standard way to start talking about an academic subject, I would at least expect your curiosity to be roused. You may have created pictures in your mind, made comparisons between the experiences described and your own, formulated questions about references and allusions that are strange to you. Importantly, you will have been alerted to the existence of an embodied speaker producing these printed words. You know that I was the middle child in a working-class British family and that I am now in my forties. Since there is no mention of racial identity, you also know I am white. Privileged identities have no need to declare themselves.

My parents, born around 1930, believed in the rightful roles of the sexes much as Mr. and Mrs. Tulliver, a century before them, had done. They knew about the importance of a sound education for boys and the trouble that would come to a girl "too clever for her own good" with "ideas above her station." Young, bright, passionate Maggie Tulliver with her willful hair made one dash for passion then went back to rue it for the rest of her truncated life. My chances were better than hers. With the accelerated shift from an elite to an open system of higher education during the 1960s and 1970s and the women's liberation movement gathering pace, the days of "Arthur's Education Fund" (Woolf, *Three Guineas,* 1977) were over. When I took up my place in 1981, women, many of them from working-class backgrounds, were entering higher education in unprecedented numbers. Without examples in our own families and communities, what expectations did we have? What did I imagine a degree in literature to be?

Most of us pick up the idea (although we would probably be hard pressed to locate just where or when we picked it up) that Literature—with its capital "L"—is a special kind of writing involving special kinds of people. For me it was a fearful tiger burning bright, Blake's angels, Wordsworth's daffodils, Shakespeare and Charlotte Brontë. Like *Britannica,* with its classical cream and burgundy binding, Literature meant status, value, improvement, durability, and privileged access. Received ideas like these, simply absorbed from somewhere, are very hard to dislodge.

Throughout my childhood, *Britannica* (and all the values and rules attached to it) was a part of "the way things were" and, unless something out of the ordinary has happened in the house to draw attention to it again, it is probably still there, in pristine condition. Objects, ideas, and practices that have been around for a while tend not be noticed. Once their actual or symbolic place is established, they are passed over, accommodated as normal, accepted as natural, right, proper, the way things are and seemingly always have been. They fit in so neatly, they may even cease to need naming. Many of the ideas, values, and beliefs that we hold in our all-too-familiar mental cabinets and emotional alcoves endure in this way.

In addition to a belief in the value(s) of *Britannica,* everyone on my street had white nets at the front window and drew the curtains before switching on the light. Sadie insisted on this proper order of things. Like most parents in the area, mine had been young adolescents when the Second World War broke out, their maturation forced in an atmosphere of nightly "blackouts" (a vital protection against enemy planes) and civic duty. Coventry, England, was especially badly hit, hence the new housing estate we lived on. More than a decade after the war, the curtain habit persisted, no longer consciously associated with its rational origins but linked, instead, to a set of values that distinguished good people from bad. I did not question the habit until I went to Amsterdam and saw not only prostitutes sitting in well-lit, street-level windows but elegantly furnished, canal-side houses displaying their front rooms all night. Once I had overcome a peculiarly British embarrassment at looking, it came to me that perhaps there was not a single "proper order" to life and things could be done differently.

This small illumination encouraged me to look at other received ideas and practices taken to be commonplace and helped me to understand how even the most seemingly "natural" of our feelings are orchestrated within a never fully articulated system of assumptions about "how life should be." The extent to which this kind of thinking will appeal, however, is likely to depend very much on our relationship to the status quo. As an undergraduate, I learned not only that we do not all read in the same way, but that no readings, including my own, are neutral.

Example One: A short, oral paper on Virginia Woolf's *Mrs. Dalloway.* I am fully confident that I am offering a rational, objective reading and that words on the page are all the proof that is needed. With numerous references to cite, I argue that the central concern of Woolf's novel is same-sex desire, the life-threatening impossibility of its social enactment, and the barren consequences of its denial. At the end there is silence. Books, pens, shoes, and noses seem suddenly to require attention. When discussion resumes, it is on a different aspect of the novel altogether.

Example Two: A lecturer who nurtures the romantic belief that poems, like people, have a unique essence and believes that great works can always be recognized by their inherent qualities. To prove the point, he gives the class an untitled, unsigned poem to read. It begins, "As virtuous men passe mildly away" and continues through nine stanzas without any female pronouns or identifiably female allusions at all. The poet asks his lover for secrecy because ordinary men would not be able to admit a love such as theirs, a love so "refin'd" even the lovers themselves "know not what it is." Although the poet feels their souls to be one, he will accept them as two in the same way as "stiffe twin compasses are two," one leaning as the other moves away and growing "erect" when it comes back. An exquisite love poem, I offer, to the evident delight of said lecturer, written by one man for another. No silence this time but a red-faced, frothing explosion: this is John Donne's "A Valediction: Forbidding Mourning" and my deviant reading has ruined, for him, one of the most beautiful expressions ever of love between man and wife. So much for the unequivocal purity of the great work.

The point of my examples is to illustrate the ways in which readings and value judgments are intimately bound up with the beliefs and experiences of the reader. Despite our best efforts to be rigorous, this is to some degree inevitable, and there is nothing actually wrong with it. Indeed, if we accept this, we can then do away with the pretence of neutrality and objectivity and engage, instead, in useful debate about the instability of language, the way apparent authority obscures ideological interests, and the importance of questioning all viewpoints, including our own. Excited by finding my own sexual concerns in a canonical text, I probably did overstate the case with *Mrs. Dalloway*. But that seminar was not about discussion or debate or even about Woolf. The lesson that day was about silence, negation, and the maintenance of power. Something Woolf knew a good deal about.

Situating myself throughout this piece, I remind you constantly that I am a particular writer, bringing particular experiences and insights to her subject rather than universal truths you are obliged to accept. In making myself audible and visible, I contribute, too, to the ongoing project of refusing social relations of power that privilege some identifications at the expense of others. Earlier I drew attention to the way that absence of information about race or ethnicity will be read as "white." The same is true for sexuality. The privileged identification is taken to be so normal, natural, right, "the way things are" that it does not need to be named. In the absence of other information, heterosexuality will be assumed.

Despite the examples given, the English department I was in as an undergraduate was more progressive than most. The more radical scholars and critics were gaining ground, and feminist literary criticism, while still regarded with considerable suspicion by many, could no longer be ignored. I cannot acknowledge sufficiently the debt I owe to the feminist scholars whose lectures and publications helped me to find the language I needed to bring myself (force)fully into being in an academic context. I read with incredible energy their incisive descriptions of misogyny and their painstaking analyses of stereotyping in the works of Great Men, women cast over and over as wife, mother, mistress, muse, virgin, temptress, and whore. I listened to debates about the formation of an alternative literary canon; witnessed the launch of women's journals, presses, and bookshops; and was enthused with the idea that feminist literary studies would be at the hub of a momentous cultural revolution. But change is never as neat or as even or as complete as that. Black women were far from confident that this particular feminist revolution would end expressions of racial discrimination far more threatening than a lyrical compass point, and there was little in this first important outpouring to challenge the heterosexual presumption. The boldness of the confrontation when it did appear was exhilarating. Among others were Jane Rule's *Lesbian Images* (1975), Lillian Faderman's *Surpassing the Love of Men* (1981), Ann Allen Shockley's "The Black Lesbian in American Literature" (1983), and Margaret Cruikshank's *Lesbian Studies: Present and Future* (1982). All these scholars took risks, naming themselves and refusing, as I was now doing in my institution, to close the curtains before putting on the light.

Light and shade are recurrent metaphors in writings by and about lesbians. In her 1928 lecture, Woolf spoke of "light[ing] a torch in that vast chamber where nobody has yet been," and the need to create "words that are hardly syllabled yet [. . .] some entirely new combination" to describe the hitherto secret relations between women that would be found there (*A Room of One's Own,* 1981, p. 80). She knew that this act of making visible, of bringing into language, would not be quick or easy. Even as she spoke, Radclyffe Hall's notorious novel, *The Well of Loneliness,* was being banned in Britain as obscene. Woolf's teasing, evocative comments again remind us that change does not come in straight lines or neat, clearly titled chapters. Although she expected that as a result of her published lecture she would be "attacked for a feminist and hinted at for a Sapphist" (*A Writer's Diary,* 1978, p. 146), it is still quite usual, half a century and numerous lesbian and feminist publications later, for Woolf to be taught without any reference to lesbian possibilities in either her life or her work. Silence and negation.

If a writer as revered as Woolf can be so selectively taught, which other known writers might there be whose lives and works are similarly distorted? Why is it that only the most unattractive representations of women loving and desiring each other get through: vampires, predators, and sad, sick spinsters? Take Lawrence's "corrupt" schoolteacher in *The Rainbow* or the couple in *The Fox* whose lives are so barren even their hens will not lay eggs. If we do not believe that all lesbians are tormented, physically repellant, and ultimately doomed, we must go on to ask what function (whose interests) these repeated characterizations serve. Lawrence has one woman in each of the above works restored to her "natural" role, sexually awakened by a potent man. He also has one woman punished, either by marriage to an industrialist or death under a falling tree. Discredited or destroyed, the message is clear: access to the female body is the inalienable right of the male. Again, these texts will usually be found on a standard syllabus. If there is no feminist engagement, the ideological implications that I have highlighted here will be overlooked.

Understanding ideology, the ways that ideas, beliefs, and values come to be commonly accepted, is central to feminist literary criticism and to my autobiographical piece. Your life, your background, and the scope of your knowledge and experience will inform your response to and interpretation of texts, including the one you are reading now. That the majority of students in a seminar group will like or dislike the same characters and share similar ideas about particular texts is no proof of rightness. Such agreement will signal the beginning of discussion, not the end.

BIBLIOGRAPHY

Cruikshank, Margaret (Ed.). *Lesbian Studies: Present and Future.* New York: Feminist Press, 1982.

Faderman, Lillian. *Surpassing the Love of Men: Romantic Friendship and Love between Women from the Renaissance to the Present.* New York: William Morrow, 1981.

Hall, Radclyffe. *Well of Loneliness.* London: Falcon, 1949.

Griffin, Gabrielle. *Heavenly Love?Lesbian Images in Twentieth Century Women's Writing.* Manchester: Manchester University Press, 1993.

Hobby, Elaine and Chris White (Eds.). *What Lesbians Do in Books.* London: Women's Press, 1991.

Loewenstein, Andrea. *The Worry Girl: Stories from a Childhood.* London: Women's Press, 1993.

Munt, Sally. *New Lesbian Criticism.* Hemel Hempstead, UK: Harvester Wheatsheaf, 1992.

Rule, Jane. *Lesbian Images.* Garden City, NJ: Doubleday, 1975.

Shockley, Ann Allen. "The Black Lesbian in American Literature: An Overview." 1979. In Barbara Smith (Ed.), *Home Girls: A Black Feminist Anthology* (pp. 83-93). New York: Kitchen Table—Women of Color Press, 1983.

Winterson, Jeannette. *Oranges Are Not the Only Fruit.* London: Pandora Press, 1985.

Woolf, Virginia. *A Room of One's Own. 1929.* London: Granada, 1981.

________. *A Writer's Diary.* 1929. St. Albans: Triad/Panther Books, 1978.

________. *Mrs. Dalloway.* New York: Modern Library [c. 1925].

________. *Three Guineas.* 1938. Harmondsworth: Penguin, 1977.

SECTION II: SOCIAL SCIENCES

"Rectification" by Marilyn Matthews

As the name implies, disciplines of the social sciences look at people or societies in a scientific manner. But, of course, that definition is much too simplistic. What does it mean that social scientists examine people? They look at individuals, individual behavior, groups of people or cultures, subcultures, occupations, smaller social units such as families or schools, people in the past, present, or future, trends among groups of people, interrelationships among people, foreign people, native people, young people, old people. In short, just about anything that focuses on a person or people and what they do is a legitimate object of study for social scientists.

How are social scientists, then, different from anyone else who lives and works around people? After all, just about everyone has to deal with other people and see what they are doing. Why is not everyone considered a social scientist? The answer has to do with the phrase "in a scientific manner." Social scientists examine things with scientific rigor and methodology; they set up experiments with people, they observe people, they count quantifiable trends or behaviors, and they observe people in groups of which they themselves are not normally members (what we call disinterested objectification). Then, they analyze people's behaviors to understand the various aspects of the larger trend, they test and retest their theories, they replicate experiments, and they deduce their theories based on general observations or experiments. In short, they conduct their studies with attention to logical, deductive thought, objectivism, theories, methods, and quantification of facts.

The umbrella term, social sciences, then, includes such disciplines as psychology, sociology, anthropology, history, communication, archaeology, education, linguistics, geography, economics, justice, and political science, as well as many others.

As you shall see in the following essays, much of that base of scientific methodology is beginning to be reconstructed in large part because of the ways in which feminist theories have prompted social scientists to reexamine the values of "scientific methodology." Moreover, the area of social sciences has recently experienced much new growth as it has become one of the central locations for newly conceived, interdisciplinary studies. Perhaps because social science originally incorporated both the scientific methodology of the natural world with the complexity of the social world, it has continued to be an appropriate place for further interdisciplinary inquiry. For example, social sciences cover women's studies, Pan-African studies, and foreign language and culture studies. This new growth and new interest in reevaluating the traditional, value-laden foundations make social science disciplines fascinating areas of study for students and teachers.

Eleven authors have contributed to the eight chapters that comprise this section. In the first, Barbara Burnell examines the traditional models and methodology of the study of economics and advocates for a more conscious recognition of women and women's influences on the marketplace. Second, Nancy Theriot states that most people have previously been taught to think that history is a set of facts, when in actuality history is a *story told by historians.* Theriot explains that feminist historians have broadened our ideas of what is considered historically significant. In a cogent look at the field of sociology, Cynthia Negrey also argues that feminist theories have influenced the kinds of things sociologists study: instead of limiting their studies to areas of occupations, politics, and class structures, sociologists are now more willing to examine issues of family life, mothering, reproduction, housework, and other more "womanly" topics. In an essay on the study of anthropology, Edwin Segal concludes that how we view the lives of people in our own cultures, views which usually exist in our subconscious, determines how we see people of other cultures; for example, if we are only interested in seeing the importance of men's roles in our society, then we may fail to recognize the importance of women's roles in other societies. Similarly, Mara Greengrass's essay on archaeology argues that how we view people lives in the present determines how we interpret the ancient artifacts of past civilizations and the lives of the people who made them. The sixth chapter, by Sharon Varallo, Pamela Tracy, Debian Marty, and Ashwini Tambe, describes the main areas of emphasis in the field of communication, including an observation that new technological inventions for communicating strongly need to be analyzed for the ways in which these inventions may actually reinforce harmful, traditional patterns of behavior, rather than helping to make our lives better or easier. Also in a study of language, Jessica Weinberg's essay on linguistics analyzes the fascinating similarities and differences between speech patterns of males and females. The final essay, Kathleen Kirby's essay on psychology, gives a moving description of the ways in which social stereotypes of gendered behavior can impede mental health.

These essays on the social science disciplines all draw attention to the connections between ourselves and our societies. As you read them, consider using these questions to help guide your reading and understanding. How has this discipline changed because of feminist influences? What do the kinds of models or methodologies these researchers use in their studies impact our view of women? How do the different fields perceive us in order to understand others? And how does our view of others implicate our understanding of ourselves?

Chapter 9

Using Feminism to Improve Economics

Barbara S. Burnell

The first time I taught the course "Women in the Economy" in the early 1980s, I began by telling my students that it was not going to be a "women's lib" course, that we were going to do "real economic analysis" of issues that were important to women. I cringe as I think back to that statement, but I also take great satisfaction from the evolution in my teaching of this course and from the changes that have recently occurred in the discipline of economics. Much of this change has occurred as a result of feminist theory and the development of women's studies programs. In this essay, I will discuss why feminists believe it is important to challenge the traditional work of economists, and I will suggest ways in which feminism has changed the discipline.

When I ask students in introductory economics courses for terms they associate with economics, the usual responses include "money," "markets," "inflation," and so forth. In some ways, these responses reflect a narrower focus than the usual textbook definition, yet in other ways, they are accurate indicators of the work of most mainstream economists. A standard economics textbook will define economics as a social science that studies how societies use their scarce resources to satisfy unlimited wants—that is, how they make decisions to produce, consume, and distribute goods and services. This definition seems to cover a broad range of activities, but historically most economists have focused on market activities. An introductory course in economics, then, will answer questions such as how firms decide how much of a product to produce, what price to charge, how consumers determine how to spend their money, and how the actions of all firms and consumers, considered collectively, will determine the level of economic activity for an entire society. All of these questions involve people coming together as buyers and sellers in markets; this suggests that my students' initial responses are on target.

Looking at these questions more closely suggests two important points, though. First, economics has a lot to do with people or entire societies making decisions, or choices; given this, we should be able to use economics to answer many questions about people's behavior, not just those involving the exchange of goods and services for money. In fact, many economists have studied behavior that falls outside the boundaries of market activity. Second, it appears that we should be able to use economics to answer questions of importance to women just as easily as we can use it to answer more general questions, especially with the broader definition of economics.

Both of these points are accurate. I use economics to answer such questions as what determines the wages women receive in the labor force, what kinds of jobs women hold, and should or should not the government subsidize child care services. These questions relate to the "narrow" definition of economics, since they partly involve markets and money. But I can also use economics to study other aspects of women's behavior, which historically have not been as closely tied to markets as has men's behavior. For example, economic tools answer questions about how much housework a woman does and how housework is divided among different members of a household. Since economics focuses on decisions and choices, it can also be used to understand marriage, divorce, and childbearing—certainly not aspects of behavior that fit into the narrow, market-based definition of economics!

Individuals' behaviors, and the ways in which they interact with one another to determine the course of an entire society, are complicated phenomena. Faced with such complexity, economists do what all scientists do—they simplify. Mainstream, or neoclassical, economists accomplish this simplification by constructing abstract models of individual behavior. This abstraction process has two important features.

First, when an economist constructs a model, she or he must make some assumptions about the motivations for people's behavior. Most economic models have four assumptions in common: people exhibit maximizing behavior; people behave rationally; people behave as individuals; and most important, we can observe people's behavior in the process of voluntary market exchange. The first assumption implies that people behave to maximize something—satisfaction, in the case of consumers, or profits in the case of firms—that is, more is always preferred to less. Rationality simply means that, once a person (or firm) has set such a goal, behavior will be directed toward reaching it. Individualism means that people are motivated by their own self-interest, and that they act in isolation from one another. People make choices to interact with one another based on a given set of preferences that is assumed to never change. The interaction between people occurs when they voluntarily come together as buyers and sellers, with each party improving their own position as a result.

The second important feature of the model-building process assumes that certain factors about a person or her or his environment are unimportant to the behavior being studied. This process of holding some factors constant is essential to the building of models. A model is useful for understanding or predicting people's behavior only if it allows us to simplify a very complex real world. If, for example, I wanted to build a model to understand why students were spending $25,000 a year to attend my college, there would be some things about them and their environment—their families' incomes and backgrounds and their high school records, for example—that would be important, while other characteristics that help to define them—eye color and height, perhaps—would be assumed to be unimportant. The tricky aspect of this part of the model-building process is deciding what we can safely or appropriately "assume away."

There is no question that the models constructed by economists help us to understand the behavior of individuals, business firms, and entire societies. Economists build models that capture the essential aspects of a situation, and then compare their results with actual experience or empirical evidence. If these comparisons indicate that the models do not "fit" the real world, the models are revised as necessary. Using this scientific method helps us to get a better idea of why people make the decisions they do and to better predict how they are likely to behave in the future. The desire to "predict what will happen" is something shared by all scientists, and economists as social scientists are no exception.

The methods used by mainstream economists and the models they build are not without problems, however. Two problems are especially relevant for using economics to analyze women's issues. First, the use of formal, abstract models often leads us to believe that the study of economics is scientific, objective, and value-free, and therefore the predictions we make using these models must be "right" or "true" in some sense. But we need to recognize the role that values play in the process of constructing a model, and also in the choice of issues that economists study. If the values of an economist, or even society at large, become embedded in a supposedly objective model, it will be difficult to determine what role they play in the analysis.

The second problem is the assumption that only the individual matters in an economic model, and this individual is usually assumed to operate in isolation from her or his social environment. If our individual has important connections to others, or there are factors in her or his social environment that influence her or his behavior that are excluded from the model or assumed away, then the model will not provide us with a good understanding of this person's behavior.

Some examples of how mainstream economic models have been used to study women will help to clarify these points. First, consider the fact that women as a group have very different jobs than men; economists refer to this as occupational segregation. Why does occupational segregation occur? The most popular mainstream economic explanation is that women have made free, rational choices to have jobs that are typically lower-paid and have fewer opportunities for advancement. Women end up in these jobs because of the investments they have made in their "human capital"—education and training that will provide them with skills for certain kinds of work. Mainstream economists argue that, since women have historically not spent as much time in the labor force as men and have interrupted their work to have children, it does not make sense for them to invest in education and training for highly paid, "fast-track" jobs.

But this explanation leaves out many factors that may affect the jobs that women "choose." Several questions are not answered: why do women interrupt their careers for childrearing? Are there cultural and social factors that are responsible for this? Do young girls receive subtle or explicit messages about what roles and jobs are "appropriate" for them as adults? Do these factors affect the choices they make about their education? I think that most people would agree that these things can play a role, but they are questions that the mainstream model cannot answer. Because the model assumes that women are born with a certain set of preferences, and because the importance of cultural and social institutions is assumed away, these factors cannot be considered as part of the explanation for why women have the jobs they do.

As another example, think about housework and who usually does it. Casual observation, as well as more formal evidence, indicates that most of it is done by women, and that this has not changed much even though so many women now work at paid jobs as well. Why is this the case? A mainstream economic model will explain it as follows. If a household wants to maximize its satisfaction, it will make sense for its members to engage in "specialization and exchange." That is, it is more efficient and productive for people to specialize in what they are "good at" and then "exchange" it for things produced by other household members. So, if we assume that men are "better" at market work, since their jobs pay more, and women are more productive at housework, then it is "logical" or "rational" for men to work outside the home and for women to do the housework and to share or exchange what each produces. Even as women enter the workforce, it is still "rational" for them to specialize in housework, given that they are more productive at it.

This model "works" in the sense that it gives us a reasonably good description of reality. But think about the hidden assumptions and the questions that are not answered by the model. Whose satisfaction is being maximized by this division of responsibilities? Why is it assumed that women are better at housework and men are better at market work? Are there reasons inherent in the sex of the individuals, or does this assumption reflect certain values about the "appropriate" gender roles for men and women? If we do not question the effect that these values and the role of social and cultural conditioning have on the model, we are left with the conclusion that this division of labor must be "right" since an "objective" model tells us that it is rational and logical.

These are just two of many examples that can be used to show that mainstream economic models often do not give us very good explanations of women's behavior or answers to questions about their economic status. Furthermore, because all of these models are "logical" and based on the notion of rational choice, they imply that women's secondary economic status is not a problem; the models can be—and often are—used to defend the status quo.

The fact that we can cite these examples means that feminism is having an impact on mainstream economic models. Feminist scholars are asking questions about how relevant and useful such models are for understanding women's experience, and they are beginning to transform economic models as a result. Feminist economists recognize that our conceptions of gender roles and of the discipline of economics are products of social forces, and that these forces interact in ways that exclude women and their concerns. Early feminist critiques focused on the relatively small number of female economists and the lack of attention given to women's issues in economic research. These critiques progressed to questioning the philosophical bases, methods, and assumptions of mainstream economics. Feminists argue that the definition of mainstream economics is too narrow and idealistic; they point out the limitations of mainstream models, and expose the notion that values are involved in the construction and use of economic models. Finally, feminists are trying to broaden the audience reached by these messages by bridging out to scholars in other disciplines.

The description of economics and its methods, and the applications to women's issues discussed above, have all been referred to as "mainstream." Using this term implies that this is economics that most economists think of as "good." We can define "good" economics as that which develops objective, abstract models of rational, individual free choice and tests these models using evidence or data to see if they correctly predict behavior. Anything that does not fit this mold is somehow "bad," if it is considered economics at all. But think about the words being used to describe good economics, and about how they relate to words that we often use to describe male and female gender roles in our society. Abstract, logical, objective, and individualistic are all terms that we associate with male gender roles. We also tend to think of these terms as somehow being superior to their "feminine" counterparts—warm, emotional, subjective, and interpersonal, which tend to be devalued or, at least, not thought of as "scientific."

What does this suggest about economics and women, as far as women's inclusion as practitioners and as subjects of serious study? If women are perceived as emotional and subjective, they are not likely to gain admittance to the inner circle of those who do "good" economics. This, in turn, is likely to affect the kinds of issues economists study, and the way they approach them. If women's experiences and ways of thinking about them are not considered legitimate sources of knowledge, then we will continue to use only the kinds of models discussed previously. Further, issues of particular concern to women are not likely to receive sufficient attention if most economists are men.

Part of the problem is that, when asked what motivates people's behavior, most economists respond by stating assumptions about rationality and maximizing behavior. What they do not include, as feminists have pointed out, is what effect such things as power, culture, and tradition have on behavior; they also do not recognize that not all people or groups make decisions in the same way. The narrow definition of most economic models that assumes individual free choice makes it impossible for economists to include such factors.

Feminist economists encourage us to broaden our definition of what economics is, and to change the standards for "good" economics. If we look back at our original definition of economics—a social science that studies how societies produce, consume, and distribute goods and services to satisfy wants—it is clear that there is more involved in this than an abstract model of individual choice. Thus, feminists have suggested that we become more flexible in our judgment of what constitutes good economic models, and in the methods that we use to develop and test them. Suggesting greater flexibility does not mean that there will be no standards applied to determine the validity of economic knowledge. Nor does it mean that we should throw out all of our economic models and testing and make economics subjective and "feminine." Flexibility means recognizing that mainstream models often leave out too many important determinants of people's behavior. Where appropriate, methods incorporating a wider variety of social and cultural factors and relying on people's experiences as important sources of information, should also be considered "good" economics.

Feminists also insist on examining the role of values in our economic models. Economists are products of social institutions. As such, economists bring to their work a set of values that affect the way they think, the problems they choose to study, the methods they use, and the way they evaluate the work of other economists. Incorporating values is not necessarily bad; in fact, there is no way around it. The problem occurs when economists claim that they are totally objective and that values do not enter their work; this problem is particularly important for feminists because the values being reproduced are those of a male-dominated profession and a market-oriented society.

Feminist economists argue against the concepts of detachment and objectivity as they are used—and idealized—by most economists. Acting on the beliefs that economists and those they study are totally detached from the world of which they are a part, and that it is possible to develop totally objective, value-free models to attain economic "truth" creates an economics that presents only a partial picture of the real world. We need to acknowledge the roles that values play in the work we do, and to recognize that the connections individuals have with one another are important aspects of their lives and economic behavior.

If economists take these suggestions seriously, I think several positive things will happen. First, we will see more meaningful studies of women's roles and experiences in the economy—meaningful in the sense that they can help us develop policies that will improve women's lives. If we acknowledge that the social and cultural contexts of people's lives matter, and allow our economic methods to be flexible enough to incorporate these where they are important, the predictions made by economic models will be more realistic and useful.

As an example, consider an economic analysis of welfare policies for single mothers. A mainstream economic model that analyzes a single mother's decision to work or to remain on welfare will focus on her comparison of the costs and benefits of working versus welfare; if the analysis shows that it is economically more beneficial for her to remain on welfare, it will have certain policy implications for the level of welfare benefits provided. Yet there is surely more involved here than a rational calculation of costs and benefits; in formulating policy, we need to look not only at the monetary aspects, but also at the social and cultural factors leading to a woman's "choice" to be on welfare in the first place, that affect her experiences as a single mother, and that affect her prospects for employment and for adequate care of her children. Although these factors will not "fit" into a mainstream model, they can fit into the broader type of model that feminists advocate.

Second, the possibility of doing more research that is meaningful to women's lives will hopefully attract more women into economics. Teaching economics to others and doing work that has an impact on policy is likely to be more attractive to women if they feel that the discipline is capable of doing a good job of addressing women's issues and concerns. And more women in the field will in turn provide new opportunities for critical discussion of economic methods within the discipline. Over time, such discussion has the potential to transform the discipline into one that is more receptive to a variety of perspectives on economic issues and methods for studying them.

Ideally, all economists will become more aware and self-reflective of the work they do. In fact, it is in this area that I think feminism has so far had the most significant impact on economics. Although feminist economists cannot claim all the credit, in the past several years there has been much discussion and critique of mainstream economic methods, and feminists have played a major role in focusing and directing the debate. If economists are going to change the way they work, they first have to be made aware that changes will improve the discipline as a whole. Discussions about the limitations of mainstream models and the role that values play in their development are a necessary first step in developing this awareness. These discussions have increased in both intensity and scope as feminist economists have begun working with one another and with those in other disciplines.

Feminism can be used to improve economics; hopefully, this essay shows that some improvement already has occurred. However, much remains to be accomplished. The majority of mainstream economists still consider feminist economists to be on the "fringes" of the discipline. Perhaps, when the next generation of economists begins to teach courses such as "Women in the Economy," they will be part of the mainstream and will not need to defend them as "not women's lib courses." We need to make economists more aware of the most important goal of the discipline—to understand how people and societies use resources to improve their lives.

BIBLIOGRAPHY

Blau, Francine, Marianne Ferber, and Anne Winkler. *The Economics of Women, Men, and Work.* Englewood Cliffs, NJ: Prentice-Hall, 1998.

Feiner, Susan (Ed.). *Race and Gender in the American Economy: Views from Across the Spectrum.* Englewood Cliffs, NJ: Prentice-Hall, 1994.

Ferber, Marianne and Julie Nelson. *Beyond Economic Man: Feminist Theory and Economics.* Chicago: University of Chicago Press, 1993.

Jacobsen, Joyce. *The Economics of Gender.* Cambridge, MA: Blackwell, 1994.

Nelson, Julie. *Feminism, Objectivity and Economics.* London: Routledge, 1995.

Chapter 10

What Is "Women's History"?

Nancy M. Theriot

In making small talk on airplanes and in waiting rooms, I have often been asked, "What do you do for a living?" If I feel like ending the conversation quickly, I reply, "I teach history." However, if I am feeling chatty and adventurous, I say, "I am a women's historian." The predictable next question or comment is, "What is 'women's history'?" or "How is that different from 'regular' history?" or "Oh yeah, Susan B. Anthony." Depending on how long the flight or the wait is, I launch into an explanation of women's history, an area of research that is almost thirty years old but still a surprise to most out-of-school adults. In this very short essay, I want to tell you a little about women's history and also about what it means to be a historian.

Most people think of history as a set of facts "discovered" by historians searching through the material left behind by previous generations. However, it is more accurate to think of history as a *story* told by historians. This does not mean history is made up by historians, but it does mean that historians actually create "history" by focusing their attention on some things and not on others. History is the interpretation of historians for events and developments they think of as important. Until recently, history was written by white, middle- or upper-class men who had a very specific idea of what counted as historically significant. In U.S. history, what was considered important were presidents and politics, broad economic developments, relationships with other governments, and the ideas of white male thinkers on a variety of subjects. As long as U.S. history was written primarily by middle- and upper-class white men, these were the "facts" seen as significant enough to compose the story of history.

By the 1960s, however, the pool of historians began to change. More African Americans, working-class white and black students, and women students of all races and classes were entering universities. Some became historians who, because of their class, race, and gender background, began to ask new questions about groups of people and types of experiences that had not been considered before by historians. Many of the women asked questions about women, sex, family, and gender. These women were keen on such subjects because they (we) were part of a generation challenging a variety of "ism's," including sexism. This new set of questions was the beginning of "women's history" as a field of study.

Because the new women's historians were educated by the "old-style" historians of the previous generation, the first questions many of them asked about women were questions that fit very well into a traditional idea of history. They asked about women leaders. Just as traditional historians concerned themselves with telling the stories of influential men in politics and society, the new women's historians looked at "great women" in political and social struggles, such as Elizabeth Cady Stanton, Jane Addams, and Rosa Parks. The new women's historians also asked other questions that followed a traditional line. They asked about women's exclusion from political power (from voting and from holding public office); they asked about women as wage earners (as workers in the traditional area of male employment); they asked about women's participation in the political struggles long seen as basic to United States history: the American Revolution and subsequent American armed conflict, the fight to abolish slavery, the labor movement, and the Civil Rights Movement. These questions were necessary and resulted in many excellent and important studies. Much work on women's history in the "public" domain necessarily filled in the women's names and women's organizations important in American political and economic life. However, most took for granted a very traditional view of history—that history is public, about politics or wage earning, about political movements, about war—and many saw women as victims of an oppressive male political structure. Although this victimization was certainly a "fact" of women's lives, there was more to women's history than this. The best women's history work on areas previously seen as "male" invited us to rethink "public" and "private" and also rejected the idea of woman-as-victim. An excellent example is Linda Kerber's *Women of the Republic,* a study of women's activities and ideas about women during the time of the American Revolution.

The next, but really overlapping phase of women's history scholarship focused on women's culture and the "private" sphere of family, sexuality, and sexual ideology. Beginning in the middle of the 1970s, women's historians wrote about concepts of "true womanhood" (Cott, 1977), the history of birth control (Gordon, 1977) and childbirth practices (Leavitt, 1986), and changing notions of the "model home" (Wright, 1980). Many women's historians began to suggest that these and other "personal" topics, thought by traditional historians as "not historical" or not worthy of historical attention, were the most significant areas of women's lives. Moreover, women's historians began to argue that these issues were central to understanding men as well as women. A description of slavery was incomplete if it only dealt with laws and sectional conflict; a description of slavery must also include the sexual politics behind white male masters raping black female slaves and white women holding black women responsible for mulatto children (Jones, 1985; White, 1987). In other words, women's historians began to assert that the personal, the private, the sexual, was indeed political and a significant part of the (hi)story of America.

More recently, women's historians have argued that gender itself should be considered a category of historical analysis (Scott, 1988). Instead of thinking in terms of public history and private history, we should recognize that gender relationships, ideas about gender, and constraints imposed by gender affect the public world of wage earning, politics, and economic structure just as profoundly as they affect more personal aspects of life. For example, gender inequality is the reason women in the 1990s make less than 70 percent of male wage earners' take-home pay. It is also the reason that almost 75 percent of American wage-earning women are working in "women's" jobs where the majority of workers are women, such as service positions, secretarial jobs, and elementary education. Because of gender, women in all job categories make less than men in the same categories and, likewise, constitute the vast majority of the adult poor

(Abramovitz, 1988; Gordon, 1994). Past and present gender discrimination accounts for the fact that women are underrepresented in the political structure of every modern democratic state. Women's historians have argued that applying gender as a category of analysis allows us to see how gender has shaped and continues to shape politics, economics, and national ideology as well as domestic, interpersonal relations.

Another concern of recent women's historians has been the differences among women. Instead of seeing gender as all-encompassing, women's historians have pointed out that race, class, and ethnicity affect gender relationships and also gender itself. For example, sexual ideology from the nineteenth century through our own time has been affected by the slavery of black women. Concepts of womanhood have been built on the idea of race and class, so that white women with no need of out-of-the-home employment have been seen as "real women," while poor women and black women regardless of class have been seen as unwomanly, promiscuous, and uncaring of their young. The very definition of womanhood in the United States has been determined by race and class (Carby, 1987; Solinger, 1992; Hine, King, and Reed, 1995). Likewise the necessity (and availability) of "women's work" has divided women's experiences, and therefore women's history, into many stories. Women's historians have written about the gendered nature of work, but also about the different cultures (beliefs, expectations, experiences) created by women's out-of-the-home work (Kessler-Harris, 1982; Peiss, 1986; Benson, 1988). The complex relationship of race, class, and gender continues to be a challenge for women's historians.

Although every women's historian in some way is interested in gender, some have focused on problematizing the concept of gender itself. It should not be surprising that gender would be interrogated, since the work of women's history has been to "de-naturalize" many ideas thought of as "natural," such as family, childhood, and sexuality. Some of the most interesting work done in women's history today begins by questioning what "gender" really is. This means that sex and body are not taken as "natural facts" of history, but instead are examined for their own history (Jordanova, 1989; Duden, 1991). For example, it may be surprising for many students to learn *that biological sex difference is itself a created fact,* just as most other things considered factual are instead created, interpreted, and communicated ideas; there is a history of biological sex just as there is a history of concepts of racial difference (Gallagher and Lacqueur, 1987). The body itself has a history. The sharp dichotomy we see dividing male and female was an *invention;* and even after the invention, dividing up the "masculine" and "feminine" traits was based on political economy and not on physical characteristics.

The idea that there is a history of sex—sexuality and sex difference itself—just as there is a history of political parties challenges traditional history. The challenge is not only that traditional history has left out significant developments because those developments were seen as natural and private, but also that the whole way we have been taught to view history is flawed. Women's history asserts that history itself is a self-interested narrative, a story told by someone who is personally interested in the story. This challenges the supposed objectivity of history by highlighting the fact that historians deal with issues they personally, subjectively, find interesting and important. There is no unified thing called *history;* there are only stories told by historians with individually limited assumptions, values, and questions. With more diverse people writing history, there will be a more complete and satisfying story; there is no one, true story. Women's history challenges traditional history at the very core of its boastful claims of universality and objectivity.

Finally, because women's history insists that history is a story told from a specific perspective, it is necessary for me, as a women's historian, to talk about my own assumptions and questions. In my writing and in my teaching, I let my readers or my students know my assumptive framework. The guiding assumption I bring to my present research on insanity and nervousness in the nineteenth century and to my classes is the idea that meaning is made by historical characters within constraints they neither choose nor control. In other words, I assume that people find themselves in material, political, and ideological situations they do not choose but cannot get beyond. These people are indeed trapped by their time, in that they do not choose and cannot control their situation. But within those constraints, people make their experiences meaningful; they make their own sense of the situation they are given; some of them make a contribution to changing the ideas and/or material conditions for the next generation. I see my role as a historian to narrate people's struggles in order to make life meaningful within constraints they do not choose. In providing this narration, this story, I am imposing my own ideas of "why" and "how" on history—ideas not necessarily stated by the people I am describing. My challenge is to tell the story the way I see it and acknowledge the historical characters' sense of the story (if they express one). Just as a literary critic strives to read the story in a way that acknowledges the author and the time, as a historian I want to read the past in a way that acknowledges both the self-perceived agency of the historical characters and the constraints of time, place, class, gender, and race that may not have been noted by historical characters. This sensitivity to "position" is due to the influence of women's history as a field of study and to my own place as a woman writing history.

All of this is very dense and serious, and I would like to end on a lighter note. Think of your own sixth birthday. In terms of traditional history, that event would not be important unless you ended up as someone politically famous, traditionally an appropriate historical figure, such as a president or secretary of state or assassin of an important person. In terms of women's history it can serve as a good example of the nature of historical discourse. If you were writing the history of your sixth birthday it would be a different story than the one your mother would tell or the one your older sibling would tell. Women's historians hold that all the stories are significant; one is not more true than another. Women's historians also believe that in order to talk about the event, we need to specify who we are and what our interests are; we need to identify the storyteller as the birthday-girl or the sibling, for example. Women's historians also assert that the culture of the "birthday party" is something important to study. It is a private family event governed by certain cultural rules. The rules vary in terms of race, class, section of the country, and sometimes gender. Private family events are significant because they teach us how to behave in the more public world. The sense of self we construct is based on these private-public events. Women's historians want to value and study events, perceptions, ideas, and structures that have seemed unimportant to traditional historians. We want to do this because we believe public and private are not separate, and all aspects of life are permeated with gender (and race and class).

Women's history assumes that all people's stories are important and that *all histories are stories.* Writing women's history and teaching women's history is a creative act of giving voice to hitherto untold stories, complaints, and possibilities.

BIBLIOGRAPHY

There are hundreds of works by women's historians I might have cited for this essay. These represent a very small sample.

Abramovitz, Mimi. *Regulating the Lives of Women: Social Welfare Policy from Colonial Times to the Present.* Boston: South End, 1988.

Benson, Susan Porter. *Counter Cultures: Saleswomen, Managers, and Customers in American Department Stores, 1890-1940.* Urbana: University of Illinois Press, 1988.

Carby, Hazel V. *Reconstructing Womanhood: The Emergence of the Afro-American Woman Novelist.* New York: Oxford University Press, 1987.

Cott, Nancy. *In the Bonds of Womanhood: "Woman's Sphere" in New England, 1780-1835.* New Haven: Yale University Press, 1977.

Duden, Barbara. *The Woman Beneath the Skin: A Doctor's Patients in Eighteenth-Century Germany.* Translated by Thomas Dunlap. Cambridge, MA: Harvard University Press, 1991.

Gallagher, Catherine and Thomas Lacqueur (Eds.). *The Making of the Modern Body: Sexuality and Society in the Nineteenth Century.* Berkeley: University of California Press, 1987.

Gordon, Linda. *Pitied but not Entitled: Single Mothers and the History of Welfare.* Cambridge, MA: Harvard University Press, 1994.

________. *Woman's Body, Woman's Right: Birth Control in America.* New York: Penguin, 1977.

Hine, Darlene Clark, Wilma King, and Linda Reed (Eds.). *"We Specialize in the Wholly Impossible": A Reader in Black Women's History.* Brooklyn, NY: Carlson, 1995.

Jones, Jacqueline. *Labor of Love, Labor of Sorrow: Black Women, Work, and the Family from Slavery to the Present.* New York: Basic, 1985.

Jordanova, Ludmilla. *Sexual Visions: Images of Gender in Science and Medicine Between the Eighteenth and Twentieth Centuries.* Madison: University of Wisconsin Press, 1989.

Kerber, Linda K. *Women of the Republic: Intellect and Ideology in Revolutionary America.* Chapel Hill, NC: University of North Carolina Press, 1980.

Kessler-Harris, Alice. *Out to Work: A History of Wage-Earning Women in the United States.* New York: Oxford University Press, 1982.

Leavitt, Judith Walzer. *Brought to Bed: Childbearing in America, 1750-1950.* New York: Oxford University Press, 1986.

Peiss, Kathy. *Cheap Amusements: Working Women and Leisure in Turn-of-the-Century New York.* Philadelphia: Temple University Press, 1986.

Scott, Joan Wallach. *Gender and the Politics of History.* New York: Columbia University Press, 1988.

Solinger, Rickie. *Wake Up Little Susie: Single Pregnancy and Race Before* Roe v. Wade. London: Routledge, 1992.

White, Deborah G. *"Ar'n't I a Woman?": Female Slaves in the Plantation South.* New York: Norton, 1987.

Wright, Gwendolyn. *Moralism and the Model Home: Domestic Architecture and Cultural Conflict in Chicago, 1873-1913.* Chicago: University of Chicago Press, 1980.

Chapter 11

Reconsidering the Missing Feminist Revolution in Sociology

Cynthia Negrey

Today, sociology is in many ways a different discipline from the one I first encountered as an undergraduate student almost thirty years ago. The basic theoretical and methodological foundations remain the same and largely unchanged by the feminist scholarship that has flourished over the same period. The discipline's contours have expanded, however, to include many new subspecialties—several the products of woman-centered approaches—and its theoretical core has shifted to a more critical, social-conflict centered perspective.

Before proceeding further with an evaluation of feminist transformation of sociology, however, I should define the nature of the discipline for the benefit of students who may not have encountered it in their studies. Most first-year college students are not familiar with sociology. Even when sociology is offered in American high schools, it is quite uncommon for teachers to teach sociology as a discipline with a theoretical frame and methodological rigor.

John Macionis, the author of one of the most widely used introductory textbooks at the college level, defines sociology as "the systematic study of human society" (1999, p. 2). Sociology's subject matter

---

The author thanks Dr. Barrie Thorne, Sociology Department, University of California-Berkeley, and Dr. Patricia Gagne, Sociology Department, University of Louisville, for helpful comments.

is the group—"society"—and the social interaction that results from humans' encounters with one another in groups. Taking the group as its unit analysis makes sociology different from psychology, for example, which focuses on the individual. Sociology's subject matter is far-ranging. It encompasses virtually any and all aspects of human life, including numerous subspecialties, some of which I will discuss later. Most important, sociology is a perspective. It is a way of viewing the social world that emphasizes the link between individual experience and the social forces that shape our lives (Mills, 1959). Sociologists analyze people in social contexts by seeing the general in the particular and the strange in the familiar (Macionis, 1999). For example, the sociological perspective distinguishes between suicide, which is an individual act, and suicide rates, which reveal patterns of the behavior across situations and segments of the population (Macionis, 1999). And sociologists study things that people take for granted, such as men's and women's "roles," and they help us understand that social behavior is not determined by nature. Sociology encompasses analyses of social structures and institutions (the "macro" level), interpersonal interaction (the "micro" level), and shared meanings as reflected in belief systems, symbols, and language (Thorne, 1998).

Sociology emerged as a distinct discipline in the late nineteenth and early twentieth centuries in the great cities and university towns of France, the United States, Britain, Germany, and a little later, Russia (Connell, 1997). R.W. Connell argues persuasively that sociology's origins lie in efforts to understand relationships between imperial countries and their colonies. Still, most sociologists continue to teach that sociology emerged in response to social changes associated with European industrialization, such as urbanization, mass production, and wage labor outside the home. Contemporary sociology's preferred methods of study include quantitative, statistical techniques associated with large-scale surveys and qualitative, interpretive techniques associated with in-depth observation and interviews.

Sociology's orienting assumptions and conceptual frameworks fall into three basic theoretical traditions: structural-functionalism, conflict, and interactionism. Structural-functionalism sees society as a complex system whose parts work together to promote cohesiveness and stability. This perspective is based on the idea that social structures, that is, relatively stable patterns of behavior, guide social life. Structural-functionalists think that these structures can be understood in terms of their functions, or consequences, for society. In this sense, society is similar to a biological organism—both are composed of interrelated parts with specialized functions that contribute to the maintenance of the whole. Society's primary functional parts are its social institutions, such as the government, the economy, families, religion, and education. Structural-functionalism emphasizes social balance and stability.

By contrast, the conflict perspective sees society as an arena of inequality that generates conflict and social change. Using the conflict approach, sociologists study how factors such as social class, race, ethnicity, gender, sexual orientation, and age are linked to the unequal distribution of money, power, education, and social prestige. A conflict analysis suggests that, rather than promoting harmony in society as a whole, social structures typically benefit some people while depriving others. Struggle between unequal groups in society sometimes preserves the status quo and sometimes generates greater opportunity for subordinate groups.

The third perspective, interactionism, sees society as the product of the everyday interactions of people. Thus, society is created, maintained, and changed by the social interaction of its members. Interaction occurs symbolically, through shared meanings associated with gestures, signs, rules, and language (Macionis, 1999). Students might distinguish the three theoretical traditions in the following simple terms. Structural-functionalism emphasizes harmony and consensus; conflict emphasizes unequal economic and political power; and symbolic interactionism emphasizes shared symbolic meanings among participants in social groups.

In the mid-1980s, Judith Stacey and Barrie Thorne assessed the feminist transformation of sociology after the first decade of such scholarship and declared a "missing feminist revolution" (Stacey and Thorne, 1985). More recently they reevaluated that conclusion in an article written for *Perspectives,* the theory section newsletter of the American Sociological Association. Traditional sociology spoke from and recorded the experiences of Western, white, upper-middle class, heterosexual men. Its "bedrock" assumptions required sociologists, at least in principle, to understand all social institutions and the experiences of their members, which in turn created the potential for including women and other groups in the analysis. In practice, however, the experiences of others, such as women and people of color, were too often ignored. Traditionally as well, gender-related issues were considered primarily in the subspecialties of family, population studies, and community studies, where women were so visible they could not be overlooked. Sociologists who studied occupations, politics, law, religion, formal organizations, and even social stratification and social movements virtually ignored women; they tacitly or explicitly assumed male experience as a norm without including gender as a category of analysis. The fact that gender was present in few subspecialties probably contributed to the initial ghettoization of feminism within sociology. Moreover, it is noteworthy that gender only became salient in studies of *women.* Men were assumed to be genderless (Stacey and Thorne, 1996). In other words, the male experience was considered universal, and when sociologists did study gender, they focused on women.

Feminist perspectives have helped correct male-centered biases in virtually all established areas of research in sociology, but especially in the study of occupations, criminology, deviance, health, and social stratification (Stacey and Thorne, 1996). Studies of mothering, housework, rape, reproduction, divorce, widowhood, and the life cycle have been revitalized by research undertaken by feminist sociologists who emphasize women's interpretations of their experiences in those realms (Stacey and Thorne, 1996). New areas of inquiry have been initiated as a result of feminist sociologists' attending to women's experiences, particularly regarding sexual harassment, battery, incest, sexualities, poverty, intimacy, conversation, emotions, and the intersection of family and employment (Stacey and Thorne, 1996). More recently, the gendering of organizations and the state have been fruitful areas of scholarship (Thorne, 1998). Perhaps feminism's greatest contribution to sociology has been the critique of the "public/private split" (Thorne, 1998), which fostered a redefinition and revaluation of unpaid work in the home as work. This redefinition allowed sociologists to analyze gender in a mutually reinforcing relationship of paid work outside the home and unpaid work within. The critique of the public/private split also established the groundwork for academic studies of domestic violence and the politicization of the phenomenon as a social problem. It did so by bringing violence in the home out from behind closed doors and into the arena of public discussion.

Feminists have been successful in pushing sociology's boundaries, first by challenging conventional interpretations of families and later the economy and the state, but until recently feminist scholarship in the discipline was isolated and segregated from the discipline's core. Although courses on sex roles, gender, and women are plentiful, sociology's dominant paradigms are relatively unchanged. For example, courses on sociological theory or methodology rarely include feminist literature or questions to rethink sociological canons (Stacey and Thorne, 1996; Stacey and Thorne, 1985). Joan Alway (1995) argues that sociologists see society as separate from nature. She argues that women are associated with nature and men with society. Moreover, she contends that sociological theorists remain uninterested in and resistant to feminist theory because an analysis of gender challenges these dichotomous categories—nature and society—that define sociology's boundaries and identity. Sociology's subject matter is society, yet gender exists at the intersection of nature and society. Further, according to Alway, feminism's central problematic of gender displaces sociology's traditional central problematic of modernity as related to the effects of industrialization and economic change.

Feminist scholarship has contributed to a rethinking of gender itself as a category of analysis. Twenty years ago sociologists had been greatly influenced by structural-functionalist theory, particularly as that theoretical perspective had framed the analysis of family life. Women and men were understood to exist in a harmonious, complementary relationship to one another that was the product of "natural" differences between the sexes. Women performed "expressive roles," that is, nurturing work in the home, and men performed "instrumental roles" as breadwinners and decision makers. Men and women were socialized from birth to perform those sex roles as adults (Parsons and Bales, 1955). Because men's and women's sex roles were perceived as complementary and natural, inequality between them was conveniently overlooked.

Since that time feminists have directed sociologists away from the functionalist view of gender. Today gender is understood as a set of patterned arrangements between men and women that generally subordinate women to men and can lead to conflict between them. What were once perceived as complementary roles are now understood as manifestations of unequal gender relations. Unequal gender relations in the home influence and are created by unequal gender relations outside the home, particularly in the world of paid employment. Women's responsibilities to care for the home, the children, the ailing, and the aging limit their employment options outside the home, and lower wages paid to women generally perpetuate their economic dependence on men.

Historically, the study of unequal social class relations has found a comfortable home in sociology, and appending race and ethnicity to analyses of social class was not especially difficult given sociologists' characteristically liberal bent. As a group, however, sociologists have less readily examined gender inequality per se perhaps because so many white men in the field benefited from their gender privilege. Feminists in the field, however, are increasingly successful in encouraging careful scrutiny of gender inequality as one of the basic organizing structures of human societies. Gender difference as measured by the variable "sex" has been quite commonplace in empirical studies that compare men's and women's job satisfaction, marital satisfaction, fear of crime, attitudes toward the death penalty, political attitudes, voting behavior, consumer preferences, leisure preferences, sexual behavior, and multitudinous other subjects. Feminist scholars seek to explain such differences by placing them in the context of men's and women's lives, which involves an understanding of their unequal political and economic power.

Defining gender as a dimension of structured social inequality has, in my view, elevated the status of the sociological study of gender relations to a plane equal to that of social class and race and ethnic relations. Social class and race have always been understood as inequalities "built into the system" rather than manifestations of biologically regulated roles, personalities, and identities. But gender too often is understood as just a matter of roles, personality, and identity. Efforts to encourage the development of an inclusive curriculum—in which racial/ethnic, class, and gender (including sexuality) inequality are attended to at their structural intersection and in all sociological subspecialties—reflect the elevated status of the study of gender.

In sociology, efforts to develop an inclusive curriculum have an increasingly powerful normative influence on the discipline. For example, since the fall semester of 1994, new sociology majors and minors at the University of Louisville are required to take a course entitled "Diversity and Inequality," which introduces students to race, gender, and social class as intersecting dimensions of structured social inequality. To date, however, relatively few sociologists have actually undertaken the laborious and time-consuming effort to revamp courses in their entirety to reflect this emerging norm of inclusiveness. The ideology of inclusiveness, however, is ever present as workshops on curriculum revision are routinely available. Further evidence is the recent receipt of an award from the American Sociological Association, the professional association to which most academic and non-academic sociologists belong, by the Center for Research on Women (CROW) at the University of Memphis. Scholars at CROW have spearheaded the movement for an inclusive curriculum in sociology. Yet gender, as an isolable sociological theory or perspective, remains outside the scope of theoretical canon (structural-functionalism, conflict, and interactionism) as it is conventionally taught. Thus, it is difficult to tell at this time whether the norm of inclusiveness is just a passing fad or whether it portends a fundamental paradigm shift in the discipline that will eventually transform its theoretical core.

Feminist sociologists initially queried, "What about women?" Those same feminist sociologists, now with women of color among their ranks, later asked, "What about women of color?" Out of this internal critique arose appeals for more sociological analysis of gender, race, and social class as conceptually distinct but intersecting dimensions of social inequality that include and affect not only disadvantaged groups in society but the privileged as well. With the attachment of gender to race and social class, feminism today potentially complements Marxism as the theoretical center of the conflict perspective. Indeed, feminism threatens to displace Marxism as the vantage point from which sociology itself is criticized. Historically, Marxism, with its emphasis on social class inequality, has offered the best theoretical framework from which to critique human society and the discipline that studies it. But an inclusive curriculum, inspired by feminist thought, promises to offer a more diverse and perhaps complete although currently fragmented critique. Such an enormous volume of gender-race-class scholarship is emerging in sociology today that few can genuinely call themselves sociologists without at least passing knowledge of this body of literature. At the dawn of the twenty-first century, American sociology is poised to take a leadership role in shaping public discussion surrounding multiculturalism as the American population becomes increasingly ethnically diverse. Feminists will continue to make their voices heard in that discourse.

BIBLIOGRAPHY

Alway, Joan. "The Trouble with Gender: Tales of the Still Missing Feminist Revolution in Sociological Theory." *Sociological Theory* 13(3) (1995): 209-228.

Anderson, Margaret and Patricia Hill Collins (Eds.). *Race, Class, and Gender: An Anthology*. Belmont, CA: Wadsworth, 1992.

Connell, R.W. "Why Is Classical Theory Classical?" *American Journal of Sociology* 102(6) (1997): 1511-1557.

Macionis, John J. *Sociology*. Seventh Edition. Upper Saddle River, NJ: Prentice-Hall, 1999.

Mills, C. Wright. *The Sociological Imagination*. New York: Oxford University Press, 1959.

Parsons, Talcott and Robert F. Bales. *Family, Socialization and Interaction Process*. New York: Free Press, 1955.

Rothenberg, Paula (Ed.). *Race, Class, and Gender in the United States,* Second Edition. New York: St Martin's, 1992.

Stacey, Judith and Barrie Thorne. "The Missing Feminist Revolution in Sociology." *Social Problems* 32(4) (1985): 301-316.

________. "Is Sociology Still Missing its Feminist Revolution?" *Perspectives, The ASA Theory Section Newsletter* 18(3) (1996): 1-10.

Thorne, Barrie. Personal Communication. August 15, 1998.

Chapter 12

Gender and Culture

Edwin S. Segal

When I first started studying anthropology, the teacher defined it as "the study of man," and this was the classic, well-accepted definition. Books had titles such as Kenneth Oakley's *Man the Tool-Maker* (1964). It never occurred to me then that there was any problem with this designation. Shortly after I left graduate school, a new compilation of work, *Man the Hunter* by Richard Lee and Irvin DeVore (1968), was published, and I do remember wondering slightly about the title. Looking back on it and reviewing those books, it is rather striking that, to the extent women were discussed at all, it was either in their role as gatherers of roots, nuts, tubers, and berries, or in association with the discussion of kinship, marriage, and the family. These were not necessarily seen as insignificant areas of cultural endeavor, but the possibility that women had wider roles in cultural life was not really considered. When women's roles that diverged from these domains were considered (for example, the roles of Ibo market women), the cases were seen as representing unusual instances. This vision of human life tended to minimize women's roles. The result was that many of the ways in which women's activities shape social and cultural life were overlooked until the last few decades.

Prior to academic developments of the 1970s, data on women from women's perspectives was not often included in anthropological research because these were not always considered to be important elements in a cultural description. The problem, as we currently understand it, rested in the fact that previous researchers were very much "culture-bound" (carriers of their own cultures) and therefore were not as objective or as detached as they thought. This means their judgments of what was important to include in their research of other cultures was biased by what their own culture considered proper or significant. Interpreting one culture's patterns through reference to another culture's values, or view of the world, is referred to as ethnocentrism. Anthropology generally tries to avoid ethnocentrism and to take a position of "cultural relativism," or the view that all human cultures should be accorded the same level of human dignity. (A word of caution is necessary here: cultural relativism does not mean that everything in a culture is approved.)

The contemporary anthropological perspective on the issue of ethnocentrism is that none of us can completely escape our culture; therefore, we need to learn to recognize our biases and blind spots, and to try to make them explicit. In doing so, we hope to recognize when we make value judgments about cultural significance, as well as our own roles in the cultures we study. The purpose of this essay is not explaining why or how our intellectual ancestors made mistakes. Rather, my goal here is to talk about how recognizing gender as an important factor in human life has enriched and strengthened anthropology and the knowledge it produces.

Anthropology has two major areas of investigation known as "physical" and "cultural." The first focuses on the biological aspects of human life, while the other emphasizes human behavior. Physical anthropology's central theme is the relationship between human physical characteristics and human culture. This portion of anthropology studies human evolution as well as human nutrition, genetics, biochemistry, and demography (population study) as these affect and are affected by human culture. In contrast, cultural anthropology is a comparison of differing ways of human life. Physical or genetic issues are less a focus here than the ways people behave. However, the distinction between these two areas of investigation begins to blur when we take into account the fact that human beings are an integrated organism, not particularly driven solely by either culture or biology.

Recognizing that human biology is everywhere exactly the same raises an important question about our cultural understanding of women, men, and their places in society. Human genetic biology is a constant; that is, no group of human beings is biologically different from any other. The variations we see, and sometimes emphasize, all result from the operations of the same genes. On the other hand, human cultures and the ways in which they construct the roles and positions of women and men vary greatly around the world. For example, in some cultures, women are thought of as physically weak; in others women are thought of as physically strong; in yet others, strength is conceived of as being relatively equal between the sexes. Women and men complete their various tasks according to their culture's gender expectations, which relate to their notions of physical strength. The essential point of comparing these cultural differences is that the constant cannot explain a variable; in other words, human biology cannot explain cultural constructions of gender traits.

Cultural anthropology, the comparative study of human ways of life, is enriched by a vision overtly recognizing that women are active participants in creating and sustaining human communities. In all cultures of the world, women and their labor are vital for societal survival. The variations in the roles and positions accorded women by their various societies are complex. For example, one of the earliest examinations of the relationship between women's roles as food producers and their roles as nursing mothers (Brown, 1970; Nerlove, 1974) found that the demands of farming or other work always take precedence over maternal activities. Such explicit examinations of women and their places in social and cultural life have led to these scholars' conclusion that human behavior is more strongly influenced by social and cultural needs than it is driven by genetics.

Likewise, physical anthropology's exploration of human biology has helped make it very clear that the old frame of reference opposing biology and culture in the "nature versus nurture" debate got us nowhere because it asked the wrong question: whether biology or culture was totally responsible for each trait being studied. Instead the question that will yield fruitful results (rather than stale arguments) focuses on the *interaction* of biology and culture. It asks how biology affects culture, and also how culture affects biology and biological functioning.

For example, human infants are born quite helpless. This trait does produce a biological need for some sort of group of people who will persist in relationship over the ten to fifteen years necessary for a human being to become more or less independent. Every human group does, in fact, fulfill this biologically based need. However, the resulting social and cultural systems differ, sometimes greatly, from society to society or from family to family. Thus, the idea of "universal human cultural characteristics" can only be phrased in very general terms. All human groups have a biological need for some form of family system. At the same time, the specific details of family systems vary from culture to culture. Similarly and perhaps more familiarly, all humans have a biological capacity for language use, yet languages differ among cultures.

Underlying the research objectives in each of these areas of anthropology is a shared interest in a full, holistic research methodology. Anthropology places a major emphasis on complete descriptions of entire cultures, what we call holism. The core of this methodology is participant observation, the study of a culture while living in it and being a part of its various events. Therefore, the knowledge gained of a particular people or region is based on personal experience. Although the aim of a total description is a sound one, up until the early 1960s, that description usually included data gathered mostly from male informants, who, of course, provided a man's perspective. The resulting bias was subtle, but very real. Anthropology's holism and its emphasis on understanding other cultures does direct the discipline toward issues involving women, children, and men, but if most of the data is not gathered from all participants being studied, then it is always likely that the informants do not possess the complete information the researcher seeks.

Every different description or explanation of a cultural phenomenon brings us a bit closer to that ideal, holistic (complete) description. Therefore, one of the important sets of voices to be heard is that of the people being studied. An anthropologist studying a culture and a person native to it are likely to have varied perspectives. Each will be different; both may be accurate, and so both need to be included in any final description. In contemporary phrasing: the greater the number and variety of anthropological voices that are heard, the closer we come to accuracy.

By employing a research methodology to obtain full, holistic description, anthropologists, some as early as the 1920s, began to listen to women's voices by tracing the importance of women's roles in different cultures. For fifty years, starting in 1921, Margaret Mead, a pioneer in the comparative study of women and men, was one of the world's most prominent anthropologists. We can also find other pieces of anthropological research focusing on women from a woman's perspective at least as far back as 1939 (e.g., Kaberry). However, it was not until the 1970s that a significant body of anthropological scholarship dealing with women had accumulated. More had been produced in the two and a half decades from 1974 to 1999 than had been produced in the preceding half century. These currents of anthropological thought began to produce new efforts at theoretical formulations as well as new textbook material. Growth in the literature of cultural anthropology directly examining and listening to women has not slowed down.

The decade of the 1970s and the increase of women in the field of anthropology brought exciting changes and developments when some scholars began to reformulate their research questions. The most important finding of anthropological research since the early 1970s argues that the biologically based explanations used throughout the first half of the twentieth century provide almost no understanding of the variation that exists. The things we thought we knew were either misinterpretations of the data or outright distortions based on a western European or North American vision of the proper place for women. Michelle Rosaldo and Louise Lamphere, in the introduction to their 1974 anthology posed a series of questions that virtually outlined a large-scale research program.

> Are there societies that, unlike our own, make women the equals or superiors of men? If not, are women "naturally" men's inferiors? Why do women in our own society and elsewhere accept a subordinate standing? How, and in what kinds of situations, do women exercise power? How do women help to shape, create and change the private and public worlds in which they live? (p. 2)

At the time, these were new questions, and they generated both considerable research and new explanations. Kay Martin and Barbara Voorhies (1975) set out to examine a large body of existing data, drawn from over a thousand cultures, to extract from it what we knew about the relative roles and positions of women and men, and to integrate those data with biological data. The result was a study producing new understandings of gender-based divisions of labor, and the social organizations of the ways in which food, clothing, and shelter are produced. Their study demonstrated that while biology is not destiny, a particular society's interpretation of its biological roles may be.

Another approach to the cross-cultural exploration of women and women's places in societies was Dorothy Hammond and Alta Jablow's 1976 survey, which demonstrated that women have different culturally defined places, depending on the specific circumstances and histories of their societies. Hammond and Jablow produced a descriptive survey of a number of cultural definitions of women and feminine attributes, and of the social institutions in which their lives take on meaning. This qualitatively oriented work detailed the difficulty in making the facile generalizations that were characteristic of earlier anthropological considerations of sex and gender. This same body of work also focused on some of the ways in which gender is only one part of the cultural equation defining a person's social location. Access to economic resources, age, kinship, and ethnicity are some of the other important intersecting variables.

In the late 1970s and early 1980s, other scholars, such as Nancy Tanner (1981) and Jane Lancaster (1978), combined approaches to consider gender through both a physical and a behavioral frame. Human hands and arms are highly specialized and adapted for manipulation and carrying. Human beings also live in groups and share many aspects of their daily activities. Tanner and Lancaster are concerned with the effects of carrying and sharing in shaping the context within which human evolution has taken place. The fact that human beings are neither strong nor fast puts a premium on cooperative behaviors as a major source of survival. Our ability to invent ever more elaborate devices for safely carrying loads (including children) has made it possible for us to ensure that more of our children survive and that we can produce and maintain adequate supplies for our physical requirements. Considering evolution and evolutionary pressures from a combination of physical and cultural perspectives yields a picture very different from that provided by studying "Man the Hunter."

Perhaps the best place to end this essay is with a reconsideration of man-the-hunter as a model for understanding ourselves. The essential features of the model are that men do the hunting, which means that men provide the food and that women (and children) are provided for. A major implication of this model is that women and children are passive and dependent and men are active. But what happens when we reexamine the model in a slightly different light? It is true that in most cultures in which hunting is a major part of subsistence, men engage in the activity most often and most regularly. However, if we start with an examination of the effectiveness of food producers, we discover that in about half of the existing foraging societies, women's activities provide most of the food. For these societies men's hunting provides food once a week or so. Yet, it is often the case that the results of a hunting expedition are loudly noticed by the group and accorded a great deal of prestige. The results of hunting gain prestige precisely because the activity does not provide a constant supply of food. The daily gathering activities that actually sustain individuals, and through them, the society, are not noticed because they are continual. Every day tasks simply are not as dramatic, but they are more important. Perhaps, then, our image of the brave, lonely hunter needs to be replaced by an image focusing on cooperation and sharing. Both the male hunters and the female food gatherers share the products of their labor. Contemporary anthropology sees sharing and cooperative effort as human characteristics par excellence.

Without the growth in the number of female anthropologists since the 1960s, anthropology would not have been able to make its contribution to the development of women's studies. We might still be thinking of hunting as the quintessential early human activity. We might still fail to recognize the significance of the daily activities that sustain societies, cultures and their members.

BIBLIOGRAPHY

Brown, Judith K. "A Note on the Division of Labor." *American Anthropologist* 72(5) (1970): 1073-1078.

Friedl, Ernestine. *Women and Men: An Anthropologist's View*. New York: Holt, Rinehart and Winston, 1975.

Hammond, Dorothy and Alta Jablow. *Women in Cultures of the World*. Menlo Park, CA: Cummings, 1976.

Kaberry, Phylis. *Aboriginal Women, Sacred and Profane*. London: Routledge and Kegan Paul, 1939.

Kessler, Evelyn S. *Women: An Anthropological View*. New York: Holt, Rinehart and Winston, 1976.

Lancaster, Jane B. "Carrying and Sharing in Human Evolution." *Human Nature* 2 (February) 1978, pp. 82-89.

Lee, Richard B. and Irvin DeVore (Eds.). *Man the Hunter*. Chicago: Aldine, 1968.

Martin, M. Kay and Barbara Voorhies (Eds.). *Female of the Species*. New York: Columbia University Press, 1975.

Nerlove, Sarah. "Women's Workload and Infant Feeding Practices: A Relationship with Demographic Implications." *Ethnology* XIII(2) (1974): 207-214.

Oakley, Kenneth P. *Man the Tool-Maker,* Third Edition. Chicago: University of Chicago Press, 1964.

Rosaldo, Michelle Z. and Louise Lamphere (Eds.). "Introduction." *Women, Culture and Society* (pp. 1-15). Stanford, CA: Stanford University Press, 1974.

Tanner, Nancy Makepeace. *On Becoming Human: A Model of the Transition from Ape to Human and the Reconstruction of Early Human Social Life*. Cambridge, NY: Cambridge University Press, 1981.

Chapter 13

"What Were Women Doing During the Ascent of Man?": Gender and Archaeology

Mara R. Greengrass

Archaeology, the study of the material remains of human life, is a subfield of anthropology, the study of human existence as a whole. Archaeologists learn aspects of how people lived in the past and what they did by carefully excavating the objects left behind as a result of human activity. For example, by looking at bones and seeds thrown away we learn what people ate, and by looking at the layout of building foundations and walls, we learn how people built their houses and allocated space within them. Although the methods by which we recover data from the ground are well established, how those data are interpreted changes rapidly. One of the newest interpretation methods is called engendered archaeology (Conkey and Gero, 1991) or feminist archaeology (Gilchrist, 1991). This chapter provides an overview of ideas generated and problems encountered by feminist

The author wishes to thank Richard J. Dent, Mark Leone, and William Leap for educating (and teaching) her. Special thanks to: Avi Fishman, Gail and Edward Greengrass, Tamar and Samuel Fishman, unindicted co-conspirators Jessica Weinberg and Jill Rappaport, and of course, Barbara Little, Lynn Jones, and Marian Creveling (my feminist archaeology role models). However, the author is sure they will all be happy to know they are not responsible for anything she has written.

archaeology, as well as the future of feminist archaeology. As a subset of anthropology, archaeology uses the word "culture" in a fairly specialized manner. Culture is often described as a shared web of beliefs, values, and actions. To be a part of a given society, one must know and practice these beliefs, values, etc. One part of culture is a society's ideas about gender, and every culture in the world develops its own ideas.

However, gender is not the same as sex—a person's biological traits, genitals, hairiness, etc.—even though many Western societies assume the terms to be synonymous. Many societies do not link the two terms as we do; indeed some recognize the differences between culturally determined gender and biologically determined sex. For example, anthropologists have documented a third gender in some Native American populations, a gender whose members are biologically male in some tribes and biologically female in others. Depending on which tribe they belong to, they may choose their gender identity for different reasons: some are guided to it by a vision, some show it by acting a certain way as a child, and some are chosen by shamans or other people of this gender. Members of this third gender (sometimes called berdache or, more recently, two-spirit people) play important roles in Native American society and have specific tasks that neither gendered men nor women perform in that culture.

Another important distinction to consider is between feminist and engendered archaeology. Although these two terms are sometimes used interchangeably, their definitions differ.

Feminist archaeology refers to archaeology specifically focusing on the place of women in societies and seeking to address the previous lack of interest in women's activities and lives. Engendered archaeology uses an understanding of the cultural construction of gender and the place of men, women, and others in society.

Feminist archaeology came out of the evolution of archaeological method and theory. By the middle of the nineteenth century, archaeology was emerging as an academic discipline in the United States. Archaeology was no longer a field of amateurs, but of professionals whose lives were spent studying the field. Artifacts in that century were sorted into groups by appearance and time period, and thus the peoples associated with the artifacts were also divided. Anthropologists and archaeologists became very interested in the theory of cultural evolution, the belief that human societies moved through a set of stages of organization before finally becoming "civilized" (i.e., like Europeans). With this theory, archaeologists hoped to determine the origins of human existence.

By the mid-twentieth century, archaeologists had decided they could not reconstruct a culture via artifacts or studies of prehistoric trade routes, and it was necessary to consider a society as a whole. Not just what kind of pottery people made, but how did they use pottery? What function did it serve and what part did it play in the structure of their society? The most enduring theories to emerge from this time are concerned with the effects of environment on native cultures. These were resurrected in an archaeological revolution known as the "New Archaeology."

The New Archaeology wanted to apply a scientific method to archaeology. The physical sciences had developed many techniques that could be applied to archaeological data. This scientific emphasis, called positivism or processualism (for its interest in processes), was spurred on by new methods to remotely sense a buried and lost site, new techniques for mathematical, statistical, and dating analysis, and new capabilities in chemical analysis. New Archaeology was dominated by a consideration of culture as a series of processes, not events, and archaeologists sought to understand the "laws" that governed the workings of societies. They believed that human behavior could be traced and finally predicted through the evidence of past behavior.

However, gender was not included since they believed it could not be easily proved in the archaeological record. In other words, what could not be seen by the naked eye could not be tested by archaeological hypotheses. Archaeologists could study the environment, foods, or population change, but religion and more ephemeral ideas were impossible to verify. However, in their eagerness to be scientific, certain unspoken (and often unconscious) assumptions were made about social structure. Foremost among these assumptions was that men did everything important. The New Archaeologists' concern with empiricism, hypothesis testing, and scientific fact let them believe that they were creating value-free, impartial interpretations.

> Processual archaeology was interested in the interplay between entire human societies and the environment and did not include detailed discussion of internal social structure except when evidence showed that it was shaped by environment. This distracted archaeologists from considering how men or women were reacting to or being affected by changes. (Wylie, 1992, p. 16)

After all, if societies were reacting as a group to external environmental pressure, there should *be* no difference between men and women, and no need to talk about them separately.

Several influences in the 1970s helped develop feminist archaeology: the shift to postprocessual thought, the resurgence of the women's movement, and increasing numbers of women who entered the field and questioned basic assumptions of archaeology.

A group of theories known collectively as postprocessual archaeology (sometimes jokingly called "The New New Archaeology") led to theories of feminist and engendered archaeology. Archaeologists such as Ian Hodder (1986) argued that processual archaeology had ignored the contributions of the individual to culture change. Another group (Shanks and Tilley, 1987; Leone, 1982) argued that the views we create of the past through archaeology are reflections of social relations of the present. Postprocessualism and feminist archaeology are so linked that Margaret Conkey and Joan Gero (1991) say that postprocessualism could not have occurred without the help of feminist archaeology, because "an engendered past replaces the focus on the remains of prehistory with a focus on the people of prehistory . . . " (p. 15). As eminent archaeologists struggled to explain what was missing from earlier archaeology, feminist archaeologists provided very real examples.

Alison Wylie believes the women's movement contributed because as we become aware of the "assumptions about gender that underpin *contemporary* sex roles," we realize these assumptions also affect how we describe the past (1992, p. 17). Thus, women recently empowered by the women's movement were more aware of gender creation in their own culture, and more aware that what was called "natural" was actually cultural.

Most early work in feminist archaeology was dedicated to pointing out the assumptions that male archaeologists made, and showing the androcentric (male-centered) biases. One example of androcentrism is the classic man-the-hunter image that pervades prehistoric work and popular culture. Most people believe that in hunter-gatherer societies, men provide food by hunting, and women gather plants and take care of the children. This is considered universal, and the basis for all other types of civilization.

The theories surrounding man-the-hunter contain several assumptions not supported by the evidence, but not questioned by archaeologists or anthropologists until the 1970s. Sally Slocum (1975) dissected man-the-hunter and found it based on three assumptions: hunting was the most important prehistoric activity, men did all the hunting, and tools we find were used for hunting. In fact, although meat is often highly valued, women in hunter-gatherer societies provide most of the food for their families, and women and children often hunt small animals. In addition, we have no proof tools were hunting weapons; perhaps they were used for gathering, making other tools, or cooking (Gero, 1991). The overemphasis on the importance of hunting in prehistory led to a de-emphasis of the actions of women, and too little attention was given to other survival skills for hunter-gatherer societies, such as raising children or gathering, preparing, and storing food.

Patty Jo Watson and Mary C. Kennedy (1991) broke new ground in their paper on the domestication of plants, the study of when and how humans switched from gathering wild plants to cultivating them in gardens and fields. Watson and Kennedy argue that archaeology rarely assigns an active role to women; that is, whenever women were involved, actions must either have occurred by themselves or men must have done it. Even though women are associated with the "passive" role of gathering plants while men were hunting, when it came time to decide who domesticated those plants, women were not considered for this "active" role. Instead, archaeologists developed convoluted theories about humans taking advantage of changes that were occurring naturally to the plants, or about shamans who used gourds for ritual purposes and might have tried to cultivate those plants. It makes more sense to assume that the people who gathered the plants (that is, the women) would most likely make plants more reliable for human use.

Another example of the effects of feminist archaeology is the work of Sharisse and Geoffrey McCafferty (1994), who reinterpreted evidence from a Mesoamerican site, Tomb 7 at Monte Albàn. The McCafferty's uncovered the bias of the original excavators at Monte Albàn, who designated Skeleton A of Tomb 7 as a man. The great wealth of artifacts associated with Skeleton A, along with Skeleton A's obvious high position in Mesoamerican society, meant "man" to male excavators. However, Skeleton A is associated with a jawbone that likely belonged to a female, and most of the artifacts are connected with weaving, an important part of women's lives in Mesoamerica. Thus, Skeleton A may be biologically female.

The McCaffertys' work leaves us unsure whether Skeleton A was biologically male or female, but they do show that Skeleton A was almost certainly gender female in their analysis of the surroundings of the tomb. This finding leads us to other new questions created by feminist archaeology. If Skeleton A was biologically female, how did she achieve high status? What role did she play in Mesoamerican society? If Skeleton A was gender female but biologically male, then even more complicated questions arise. Was it common for a man to be gender female? What did he/she do to become gender female? What role did he/she play? What implications did this have for the status of biological females? These new questions have few answers.

Donna Seifert conducted a study on women's labor in historic times in her comparison of working-class households and brothels in nineteenth-century Washington, DC. Different forms of women's work created distinctive patterns in artifacts; for example, brothels contained more lighting glass for nighttime work and more buttons, reflecting the necessity of buying clothing (1991). Seifert ably combines these data with historic research into the areas excavated and the ideas of the time about men's and women's activities. Especially interesting is how the ideals of gender roles conflicted with the reality of what was happening to labor as production moved out of the home and into the factory.

Feminist archaeology is still evolving. Most of the work done has been a tentative dip into the possibilities, questioning old ways of doing things, and thinking about how to proceed. To succeed, feminist archaeology must be on the cutting edge of archaeological research and work with other specialties. Elizabeth Barber says in order to throw light on women's activities and lives in the past, we must be willing to use every method at our disposal, even language. In her study of weaving in the ancient world, she "used such . . . etymologies as *tunic, shirt,* and *to ret* to throw light on the history of clothing and the processes of preparing fibers" (1994, p. 290). Chemical analyses can be used to trace raw materials, ethnology can "help determine the range of possibility and likelihood for what people did," paleobotany can tell us when and where certain plants appeared, and mythology may not be factual history, but it might provide details of daily life (1994, p. 289).

Archaeologists must work with anthropologists and historians because " 'women' is not a self-evident category . . . ; rather the construal of gender relations and of women must be in accord with specific histories and contexts" (Silverblatt, 1991, p. 155). Engendered archaeology could greatly assist anthropology and history by adding different dimensions of historic context and generating new ideas about what is happening in the present.

Barber recommends that archaeologists actually *try* the processes we are studying, whether that means learning to find clay and make pots, cooking with authentic tools, or spinning and weaving real cloth. This real experience benefits archaeologists because, as Barber argues, "[T]heories are kept on a sounder footing and new information gathered about the problems and limitations people faced in those days" (1994, p. 293). Studying work processes in context, or actually trying them, allows us to work back and decide what data might signal the presence of these tasks in history or prehistory (Brumfiel, 1991).

In order to create a truly engendered archaeology, gender must be integrated into every part of archaeology. This does not mean adding a section to every paper or report labeled "The Role of Women at . . . "; it means considering sex and gender throughout. How many archaeological site reports contain historical background listing John Q. Owner and his wife . . . where the wife never appears again? How on earth did John Q. Owner run a plantation/bar/lodging house/etc., without his wife's help? How often do archaeologists write about changes in prehistoric lifestyles in the passive voice, as if things just happened all by themselves? The default actor in archaeology should never again be only man. Conkey and Williams state that research must happen, "not just about women-as-subjects but into the cultural construction of gender . . . how gender roles and relations may have been defined, enacted, manipulated, enabled, or negotiated in varying sociohistorical contexts in the past" (1991, pp. 124-125).

The work of the McCaffertys points to a basically unacknowledged lack in current archaeology: an inability to acknowledge other systems of sex and gender than our own. No matter how remote in time and space, our interpretations of other cultures always seem to mimic our own two sexes and two genders.

Gender studies are not one technique or just a critique of archaeological theory. For an impact to be felt, archaeology must always consider the effects of gender, and question taken-for-granted topics such as the sexual division of labor and gender roles. The inclusion of women's contributions and women's experiences will thus allow archaeologists to create a fuller picture of human existence from prehistory until the present day.

BIBLIOGRAPHY

Barber, Elizabeth Wayland. *Women's Work, The First 20,000 Years: Women, Cloth, and Society in Early Times*. New York: W.W. Norton, 1994.

Brumfiel, Elizabeth. "Weaving and Cooking: Women's Production in Aztec Mexico." In Margaret Conkey and Joan Gero (Eds.), *Engendering Archaeology: Women and Prehistory* (pp. 224-251). Oxford: Basil Blackwell, 1991.

Conkey, Margaret and Joan Gero. "Tensions, Pluralities, and Engendering Archaeology." In Margaret Conkey and Joan Gero (Eds.), *Engendering Archaeology: Women and Prehistory* (pp. 3-30). Oxford: Basil Blackwell, 1991.

Conkey, Margaret and S.H. Williams. "Original Narratives: The Political Economy of Gender in Archaeology." In Micaela di Leonardo (Ed.), *Gender at the Crossroads of Knowledge: Feminist Anthropology in the Postmodern Area* (pp. 102-139). Berkeley: University of California Press, 1991.

Gero, Joan. "Genderlithics: Women's Roles in Stone Tool Production." In Margaret Conkey and Joan Gero (Eds.), *Engendering Archaeology: Women and Prehistory* (pp. 163-193). Oxford: Basil Blackwell, 1991.

Gilchrist, Roberta. "Women's Archaeology? Political Feminism, Gender Theory and Historical Revision." *Antiquity* 65(248) (1991): 495-501.

Hodder, Ian. *Reading the Past: Current Approaches to Interpretation in Archaeology*. Cambridge, NY: Cambridge University Press, 1986.

Leone, Mark. "Opinions About Recovering Mind." *American Antiquity* 47(4) (1982): 742-760.

McCafferty, Sharisse D. and Geoffrey G. McCafferty. "Engendering Tomb 7 at Monte Albán: Respinning an Old Yarn." *Current Anthropology* 35(2) (1994): 143-152.

Seifert, Donna J. "Within Site of the White House: The Archaeology of Working Women." *Historical Archaeology* 25(4) (1991): 82-108.

Shanks, Michael and Christopher Tilley. *Reconstructing Archaeology: Theory and Practice.* Cambridge, NY: Cambridge University Press, 1987.

Silverblatt, Irene. "Interpreting Women in States: New Feminist Ethnohistories." In Micaela di Leonardo (Ed.), *Gender at the Crossroads of Knowledge: Feminist Anthropology in the Postmodern Era* (pp. 140-171). Berkeley: University of California Press, 1991.

Slocum, Sally. "Woman the Gatherer: Male Bias in Anthropology." In R. Reiter (Ed.), *Toward an Anthropology of Women* (pp. 73-109). 1975.

Watson, Patty Jo and Mary C. Kennedy. "The Development of Horticulture in the Eastern Woodlands of North America: Women's Role." In Margaret Conkey and Joan Gero (Eds.), *Engendering Archaeology: Women and Prehistory* (pp. 255-275). Oxford: Basil Blackwell, 1991.

Wylie, Alison. "The Interplay of Evidential Constraints and Political Interests: Recent Archaeological Research on Gender." *American Antiquity* 57(1) (1992): 15-35.

Chapter 14

Feminism and Communication Studies

Sharon Varallo
Pamela Tracy
Debian Marty
Ashwini Tambe

Communication can be defined as the creation and exchange of meanings. Scholars investigate how we relate to others, express identity, and construct social rules through verbal and nonverbal practices. Traditional foci in communication have included the study of political speeches, stage fright, marital communication, telecommunication policy, and the effects of television on children. Other topics of research include studying the communicative components of music videos, dance, rituals, clothing, doctor-patient interaction, and intimacy. The field includes areas of study as diverse as mass communication, performance studies, journalism, argumentation, intercultural communication, organizational communication, political communication, and public relations. In this chapter, we address the increasing influence of women's studies on four areas of communication study: rhetoric, interpersonal, cultural/media studies, and telecommunication. Feminist efforts to include women in communication scholarship over the past twenty years have expanded the discipline's scope and revised fundamental tenets in each of these four areas.

For over two millennia, rhetoric has been conceived as the art of persuasion. Even today, rhetoricians continue to teach public speaking patterned after Aristotle's lectures on rhetoric, instructing speakers in how to become more effective advocates on behalf of their cause, client, or simply their own perspective. These speech standards, however, have been modeled after historically famous men able to claim the public spotlight in law, politics, and warfare. Since women generally have been excluded from public affairs, rhetorical standards precluded the possibility of studying women's speech. In response, feminist rhetoricians such as Karlyn Kohrs Campbell initially interrupted the Aristotelian tradition by searching for great women speakers, that is, those women who could meet the male-dominated standards of public address. The efforts of these scholars identified many women speakers, including anti-lynching activist Ida B. Wells in the nineteenth century and vice presidential candidate Geraldine Ferraro in the twentieth. The exclusive standards of public address, however, eliminated all but the most influential women from rhetorical consideration.

As a result, many feminist rhetoricians rejected traditional rhetorical standards. They looked instead to women's lives and their everyday use of rhetoric, and found compelling speech in women's storytelling, journaling and letter writing. These findings directed feminist rhetoricians like Sonja Foss and Karen Foss to extend their search beyond the conventional rhetorical forms of speech and writing toward women's nondiscursive expressions such as quilt making, gardening, and fashion. By investigating women's ways of communicating, feminist rhetoricians were able to redefine rhetorical standards to better represent women and women's verbal and nonverbal communication.

Feminist rhetoricians created new rhetorical criteria for recognizing women's speech and for critiquing public speaking standards. Through these efforts, they uncovered women's rhetoric from under the masculinist rhetorical tradition, both by identifying women as public speakers and by reconceptualizing rhetoric to accommodate women's experiences and expressions. Speech effectiveness, or persuading others to one's own point of view, is no longer the only standard for evaluating successful rhetoric. Cooperative dialogue and nondiscursive communication are now viable rhetorical endeavors.

The second category, interpersonal communication, refers to the process of interaction that takes place as people create meanings inside a developing or established relationship. Scholars in this area typically examine how verbal and nonverbal communication functions in establishing and maintaining relationships. For example, interpersonal communication research may focus on the role of communication in the development of romantic relationships, the effect of communication skills and abilities on student-teacher or doctor-patient interaction, the perceptions of sexual harassment in the workplace, and loneliness among committed couples.

Within the broad field of interpersonal study, relational and family communication typically has included women. Unlike other areas in communication, women often have been subjects in relational and family research, perhaps because intimacy and family life have long been considered women's domain. This stereotypic perception, however, arguably has misrepresented the female voices prominently featured in relational research.

Stereotypic constructions of the female or feminine voice have affected how interpersonal scholars evaluate communication in relationships, thereby fueling the feminist claim that the basic assumptions of interpersonal research are themselves gendered in nature. Atypically, interpersonal research has judged both female and male voices against a conventional feminine ideal rather than an invisible masculine norm. For example, same-sex friendships had for many years been evaluated according to how closely they embodied the intense emotional sharing that often characterizes women's friendships. Since men typically bond around shared activities, their friendships were categorized as lacking emotional substance. Interpersonal scholars Julia Wood and Chris Inman, who took seriously the feminist claim that gender is a profound socializing force, were among the first in the field to confront these gendered biases in friendship research by suggesting that men's friendships are different from, not worse than, women's friendships.

Although in the past the "feminine ideal" has colored scholars' conceptions of relationships, in other areas of interpersonal communication this is not the case. Similar to feminist scholars in other areas of communication study, feminist interpersonal scholars still work to uncover patriarchal gender biases that manifest as masculine norms against which women are judged negatively. Feminist interpersonal scholars investigate issues of perceived communication competence that influence hiring/promotions in the workplace—a competence that is based on behaviors most common to white, middle-class men—and of male domination as these issues appear in classroom climates that often unintentionally function to silence women.

Feminists argue that, when taken to an extreme, norms that silence others can promote or maintain violence, for example, in family environments wherein children are sexually abused and in heterosexual marriages where husbands are violent toward wives. Feminist interpersonal scholars work to provide more options for communicating through and about violence in relationships. Relational communication contexts are being reevaluated by feminist scholars in order to change gendered inequalities and to better understand communication patterns between and among women and men.

Scholars in cultural studies—the third area in communication—are interested in investigating the politics of everyday life. In doing so, they ask questions about how the power arrangements of daily living such as media practices, governmental regulations, and capitalism affect our interactions with others. Although power is understood as operating overtly in the form of laws, policies, and economic relations, these scholars are more interested in how power works in subtle, covert ways that shape our social belief systems or ideologies. In addition, cultural studies scholars challenge the assumption that people are completely passive and easily manipulated; therefore, these scholars are also interested in how people challenge and resist power.

A considerable amount of cultural studies scholarship in communication is devoted to the study of media: how media is produced, consumed and interpreted, and how media practices impact our daily interpersonal and social relations. They analyze how everyday activities such as shopping, watching television, or working are influenced by and influence media practices. Many times the relationship between these daily activities and the creation of media texts are taken for granted. For example, media depictions of working class men and women in advertising usually remain unquestioned precisely because their everydayness makes them seem natural or "just the ways things are." Left unquestioned, these representations impact workplace practices and how we interact with others. Thus, cultural studies scholars question the presumed normality conveyed by these media depictions as well as their effects on daily living.

By calling attention to the absence of the study of gender, feminist scholarship has shaped the direction of cultural studies work in a variety of ways. Early interventions by feminists such as Marjorie Ferguson and Ien Ang proceeded by analyzing what most cultural studies scholars overlooked, that is, feminine media texts—soap operas, women's magazines, romance novels—and women as audience members. Feminists were interested in understanding how women and girls were represented in the media, how they interpreted media texts, and how these textual interpretations impacted their everyday lives.

Because cultural studies research was primarily conducted in public arenas and settings, mostly inhabited by men and boys, feminists such as Angela McRobbie intervened by concentrating on how women and girls interacted with the media in their own spaces. They conducted research in the home, girls' bedrooms, and other places that women and girls occupied on a daily basis. This intervention called attention to the gendered ways in which society organized women's and men's lives, opened up new spaces to study communication practices, and enhanced our understanding of media impact on women's and girls' lives.

Feminist scholars also call attention to media representations of gender, race, class, and sexuality and how these depictions contributed to the construction of social inequities. Studying popular culture from girls' teen magazines to television programs such as *Melrose Place* and to musicians such as Madonna and Queen Latifah, scholars are particularly interested in how these representations work in subtle ways, contributing to the power relations taken for granted in our society. Focusing on media representations of the body, feminists look at how women are positioned in relationship to other women and men. For example, in advertisements, men are often placed on the page looking down at women, representing a more dominant stance. These scholars also analyze how men and women are shown using their bodies and how ideal body images are depicted. For instance, in women's magazines, desirable women are represented as uniformly thin, impeccably dressed, flawlessly made up, young, and almost invariably white. These images influence our beliefs about race, beauty and sexuality. Because these representations help to produce stereotypes that other institutions reproduce, scholars argue that these practices can affect women's everyday lives by supporting unequal pay for equal work, sexual harassment at work and school, and inadequate child care. By making women and girls more visible, feminists have expanded the study of power, culture, and media to include gender relations. Their efforts to unmask the reproduction of "normality" reveal the gendered practices shaping our everyday lives.

Telecommunication research, the fourth category, is concerned with how people communicate through electronic means across physical distance. Scholars study how different people use technologies, how producers present and promote technologies, and how and under what conditions technologies such as the telephone, interactive video, and computer networks develop. This relatively new focus in the field of communication has drawn much attention in the wake of the popularity of the Internet.

Feminists insist that technology is a gendered, and not neutral, process, expressing dimensions of inequitable relations between men and women. The development and marketing of telecommunication technology is shaped by the existence of a predominantly male usership. When technology is addressed to female users, it usually confirms conventional gender roles. Telework technology, for example, is promoted to women with the argument that it will help them stay at home for longer hours.

While individuals and households use technologies to fit their particular needs, usage styles generally reflect power differences. Feminist scholars have found that women and girls often are more inhibited in using new technologies. Rather than reflecting innate differences, this observation points out the differing expectations made of boys and girls. Feminists ask why technological inhibition—or incompetence—emerges and is considered acceptable and even "feminine." They note that girls are presumed to have a "natural antipathy" toward technology and are implicitly judged negatively against a masculine norm.

Some feminists argue that technology designed with male users in mind results in fewer women-friendly forms of technology. For example, the term "abort," which refers to ending a sequence in communication software, is an emotionally charged term which may not have been chosen if women users had been kept in mind. One can also find numerous examples of software developed exclusively for heterosexual male users, including, for example, the pornographic varieties of virtual reality software.

A key feature of new communication technology is the anonymity it offers to users. Interactive video games and forms of Internet correspondence that allow people to assume on-screen identities and interact with others in adventures of their own making are an example of technological design that not only inhibit women's technological use but often promote violent communication. Hiding behind their on-screen identities, male characters have reportedly harassed or even raped female characters. The defense of "It's just a game," obscures the harm of representing violence against women as entertainment. Under these male-dominated conditions, women's reluctance to use technology can be read as an expression of valid resistance rather than feminine inhibition or lack of know-how.

Some feminist telecommunication scholars such as Cheris Kramarae and Lana Rakow emphasize that technology can be adapted to take women's concerns into account. They hope that women's ways of communicating can be incorporated into technologies such as electronic mail newsgroups so that they can build networks with one another. Adapting technology to meet women's needs can be a complicated matter, however. Caller-ID, a device used to trace incoming phone calls, can serve some women as well as endanger others. In general, women have taken to this technology with enthusiasm because it inhibits anonymous and obscene phone callers. But the converse—that women callers can also be traced—presents a problem for some, such as battered women who are taking refuge in shelters. In public hearings over caller-ID technology, representatives of domestic violence, women's shelters argued to allow call-blocking technology to prevent abusive men from identifying the location of shelters.

Many telecommunication scholars view the development of new technologies as a neutral, unstoppable, and desirable force in the service of business, industry, and the military. Clearly, the technological "fix" that is used in so many domains today does not extend to resolving gender inequities; technology in fact often contributes to these inequities. New telecommunications technologies have facilitated shifts in the economy that characterize our age. Particular kinds of jobs are rapidly becoming the preserve of women: low-paying service jobs in the home, made possible because of networked computers. Feminists are becoming sensitive to problems of isolation that confront women whose entire lives are confined to the home. Many feminists therefore view their research as political, as a means of exposing power imbalances in the way telecommunication technology develops, so as to better serve women's lives.

In the four areas of communication study discussed in this chapter, feminist communication scholars have intervened to produce more gender-balanced scholarship. They have insisted on including women in the areas of study that previously ignored, negated, or deprecated their experiences. Part of the process of inclusion involved redefining assumptions and standards that had defined communication studies as an inhospitable discipline for women. As feminists continue their work in communication studies, our understanding of communicative difficulties and opportunities for both women and men should improve.

Feminists have paved the way for future inquiry into research practices, differences among women, and the evaluation of change. Already feminists have had a significant impact on how scholars study lived experience. They continue to raise important questions that challenge research practices, such as interviewing techniques and assumptions underlying who is studied and for what reasons. Feminists have asked for continued attention to merging academic theory with the practices of everyday life—finding ways that our work can positively impact society. In addition, feminists should be credited for contributing the most time and effort to the study of and recognition of differences. Feminist scholars provide the richest and most challenging discussions of how different identities such as gender, race, class, sexuality, and nationality (to name a few) intersect and impact our social policies and our interactions with others. In addition, as communication practices that supposedly engender greater freedom develop, a feminist eye becomes increasingly crucial for distinguishing their regressive from their potentially positive consequences on gender relations.

BIBLIOGRAPHY

Bowen, Sheryl Perlmutter and Nancy Wyatt (Eds). *Transforming Visions: Feminist Critiques in Communication Studies.* Cresskill, NH: Hampton, 1993.

Carter, Kathyrn and Carole Spitzacke (Eds.). *Doing Research on Women's Communication: Perspectives on Theory and Method.* Norwood, NJ: Ablex, 1989.

Foss, Karen A, Sonja K. Foss, and Cindy L. Griffin. *Feminist Rhetorical Theories.* Thousand Oaks, CA: Sage, 1999.

Rakow, Lana (Ed.). *Women Making Meaning: New Feminist Directions in Communication.* New York: Routledge, 1992.

Rothschild, Joan (Ed.). *Machina Ex Dea: Feminist Perspectives on Technology.* New York: Pergammon, 1983.

Taylor, H. Jeanie, Cheris Kramarae, and Maureen Ebben (Eds.). *Women, Information Technology and Scholarship.* Urbana: University of Illinois Center for Advanced Study, 1993.

Valdivia, Angharad. N. (Ed.). *Feminism, Multiculturalism, and the Media: Global Diversities.* Thousand Oaks, CA: Sage, 1995.

Wood, Julia T. (Ed.). *Gendered Relationships.* Mountain View, CA: Mayfield, 1996.

Chapter 15

Language and Gender Research: Not Just for Women Anymore

Jessica Weinberg

Linguistics is the study of language, including the structure of languages and how people use language in social contexts. Think of an engine: physicists and engineers study the engine's structure and how people use engines in their everyday lives in order to build a theory of how engines work, to determine what people need engines for, to fix engines, and to build better engines. Likewise, linguists study languages in order to build a theory of how language works, to determine how and for what purposes people use language, and even to fix language "problems."

Linguists interested in language structure study the "parts" of language, including sounds, words, and sentences, as well as larger chunks of language, such as conversations, lectures, poems, and news articles. Linguists may study how these parts work as well as how they interact. Linguists may also study how whole languages interact, when one person speaks more than one language or when speakers of many different languages live in the same geographic region.

How people use language is of great interest to sociolinguists, who study the relationship between language structure and such factors as situation and the identities of speakers and listeners. Any part of language structure, as well as the choice of language (for example, English, Spanish, or Navajo) or language variety (for example, African-American English, Appalachian English, or "standard" English), may be affected by these social factors. The area of sociolinguistics is central to one of the two branches of language and gender research.

Central to the other branch of language and gender research is language planning, or the solving of "language problems." Most linguists believe all languages change naturally through various social and cognitive processes. For example, some of the changes from the Old English of *Beowulf* to Modern English happened without conscious human interference, but some changes and lack thereof resulted from language planning. Language planning is the deliberate attempt to change, or to prevent from changing, some aspect of the internal structure of a language or the status of a language relative to other languages. It may also attempt to develop written resources for the study of a language, usually in response to some perceived problem regarding the language in question. The creation of a dictionary is language planning, as is the creation of a law dictating which language will be used for a country's official government business (a law the United States does not have).

The beginning of the field of language and gender research is generally credited to a 1973 article by Robin Lakoff, one of the first to call attention to the political implications of gender differences in language, in the newly emerging tradition of feminist theory. Previous research had not focused systematically on women's speech, and what little was written about women's speech tended to reproduce negative stereotypes about women. Lakoff intended to demonstrate the role of language in gender inequality, with evidence from women's speech and from the treatment of women in speech (1973). Lakoff's article encouraged an enormous amount of research into gender bias in language (talk about women) as well as gendered linguistic behavior (talk by women).

Early studies of gender bias in language, or linguistic sexism, focused on words in English that exclude women or deprecate and belittle women as compared to men. Linguistic sexism has long been a target, and in some ways a result, of the type of language planning that attempts to change the internal structure of a language, in English and in other languages. (See Hellinger, 1984, for a discussion of approaches to gender bias in several European languages.)

In standard English writing and formal speech, *he* (and *his* and *him*) may be used for either a male referent or an indefinite, or generic, referent, as in *A student should carry his books with him wherever he goes* and *Everyone should carry his books with him wherever he goes*. Likewise, *man* may be used to refer either to a human male or to all humans, as in *Some linguists believe that man's capacity for language separates him from other animals* and words such as *policeman* and *congressman*. Feminist linguists argue that the "masculine" meanings of *he* and *man* may subtly influence people to interpret girls and women as excluded from sentences with *he* or *man* even in their generic senses. Casey Miller and Kate Swift summarize research that suggests people do, in fact, interpret generic uses of *man* (for example, textbook chapter headings such as *Political Man* and *Social Man*) as including only males (1976). Donald MacKay summarizes research that suggests people also interpret generic uses of *he* (for example, *When a botanist is in the field, he is usually working*) as including only males (1983).

According to Ann Bodine, grammarians began prescribing the use of *he* over other third person singular neuter forms (*he and she* or *they*) in the mid-eighteenth century. In England, the prescription of generic *he* extended even to an Act of Parliament in 1850 (Bodine, 1975). Bodine argues that these language planning efforts were undertaken because of what she calls "an androcentric worldview" in which "linguistically, human beings were to be considered male unless proven otherwise" (1975, p. 133). Many linguists who claim gendered pronouns are simply a part of grammar with no sociopolitical influences or implications overlook this argument.

Alternatives to the generic use of *man* include *human* or *humanity,* as in *Some linguists believe the capacity for language separates humans from other animals*. For words such as *policeman* and *congressman*, alternatives include *police officer* and *member of congress* or *representative*. Many alternatives to the generic use of *he* have been put forth, including generic use of *she*, alternation between generic *she* and generic *he*, and use of *she and he*, *he or she* or *s/he*. Some writers try to avoid the issue by rewriting singular sentences into plurals or rephrasing in other ways, and some use *they* in generic sentences, even if the sentences are singular. At one time many writers, such as Jane Austen and William Shakespeare, used singular *they,* and many varieties of English still allow the use of singular *they* in speech (Bodine, 1975).

The "semantic derogation of women," according to Muriel Shulz, is evident in cases where words originally positive or neutral in meaning have acquired negative meanings (1975, p. 65). For example, *harlot* once meant a young person regardless of gender (p. 69), and a *hussy* was simply a housewife (p. 66). Various parallel pairs of words for women and men have asymmetrical meanings, with the term for women being insulting or trivialized. Compare, for example, *spinster* and *bachelor* and *slut* and *stud.* The first pair refers to unmarried adults, and the second to people who are presumed to be sexually promiscuous. However, in each pair the first term, which refers to a woman, has acquired negative connotations (pp. 66-69). It may be desirable to be a bachelor or stud, but not a spinster or slut. Even some pairs of terms with the same etymology have developed asymmetrically. A *governor,* who heads a state government, has much more prestige than a *governess,* who supervises the care of children (p. 65). The terms *master* (someone with specialized knowledge of a trade or discipline) and *prince* (a nice person) are complimentary, but *mistress* (a woman having a sexual relationship with a married man) and *princess* (a spoiled rich girl) can be insulting (p. 66). And although a woman can be a governor, a master *(Master of Arts* or *master artisan),* or a prince *(She's so nice, a real prince!),* a man cannot be a governess, a mistress, or a princess, even though men can fulfill these roles by taking care of children, by having an affair with a married woman or man, or by being spoiled and materialistic.

Feminist linguists, and those influenced by their work, have created many guides and dictionaries of nonsexist (and nonracist, nonantisemitic, etc.) usage in English, such as *The Bias-Free Word Finder* by Rosalie Maggio (1991). In addition, many governmental organizations, corporations, and universities have created language guidelines for official documents and correspondences. However, some researchers question whether such alternative usage actually solves the problems of the exclusion, trivialization, and deprecation of women, which begs the question of whether language reflects sociocultural attitudes or creates them. Many linguists believe that language and sociocultural attitudes create and sustain each other in a symbiotic way.

Some current research considers how women may reclaim words with negative connotations. For example, *Spinsters Ink* is a feminist publishing company, and according to Laurel Sutton's research, some younger women call each other *bitch* and *ho* as terms of endearment (1995, p. 288). Reclamation of negative terms, whether by women or other groups for whom derogatory labels exist, depends on context. Members of a group may consider it acceptable to call one another a particular term, yet be insulted if someone outside the group uses that term, and not all members of a group will agree about whether a particular term can or should be reclaimed (Sutton, 1995, p. 288). Another avenue of research centers on the subversion of gendered terms by people who do not easily identify with conventional gender roles. For example, Anna Livia (1997) examines the complex use of gendered terms in French by male-to-female transsexuals, lesbians, and gay men.

In her discussion of talk *by* women, or gendered linguistic behavior, Lakoff (1973) argued that "women's language," which she felt women are brought up to use, indicates uncertainty and a concern with trivial matters on the part of its speakers (pp. 49-57). She argued that women are in a catch-22; if they use "women's language" they are perceived as inept and superficial, but if they use "neutral language" (that is, men's language) they are criticized as unfeminine (p. 48).

In 1982, Daniel Maltz and Ruth Borker argued for a "two-cultures model" of language and gender (made popular by Deborah Tannen's 1990 bestseller *You Just Don't Understand: Women and Men in Conversation*). They argued that girls and boys learn behavior appropriate for their gender, including language behavior, by playing in sex-segregated groups and by engaging in gender-differentiated play activities. Maltz and Borker argued that this childhood socialization is the source of later miscommunication between women and men. They identified several areas of potential problems in conversational interaction between women and men, areas in which they felt women and men draw on differing rules of conversation, including the use of questions, topic shifting, and verbal aggressiveness.

Lakoff (1973) and Maltz and Borker (1982) agreed that gender differences in language use are caused by gender-specific socialization. In this sense, they were influenced by the feminist theory of gender as a social construction, which holds that gender, unlike biological sex, is not something we are born with; it is something we learn as we grow up, from adults, other children, and media images of women and men. However, Lakoff's and Maltz and Borker's theories came to represent two different views of language and gender within feminist linguistics, parallel to two different views of gender in feminist theory more generally. Maltz and Borker represented the "difference" view, which held that cross-gender miscommunication results from cultural differences between women and men rather than any intent by men to dominate women. Lakoff represented the "dominance" view, which held that women are taught to use powerless language, which is then used as an excuse to deny power to women.

In 1992, Penelope Eckert and Sally McConnell-Ginet argued that approaches focusing on differences between women and men and/or dominance of men over women depend on the existence of two categories of people, women and men, with little variation within each category. Such approaches also assume that although gender is socially constructed in that we learn how to be women or men, gender is relatively straightforwardly layered over biological sex. That is, people born with female anatomy become women and people born with male anatomy become men. Although Lakoff and Maltz and Borker suggested that certain groups, like gay men and "tomboys," might not fit well into the two-gender schema, for the most part they assumed the categories of women and men are cross-culturally universal. Eckert and McConnell-Ginet argued that people's gender identities cannot be predicted from their biology, and that particular linguistic forms are not automatically feminine or masculine or any other gender, nor are they automatically powerful or powerless. In fact, the same form may be interpreted differently if used by a woman than if used by a man. They argued that rather than assume that a community of women and a community of men exist, people simply learn how to talk like a member of one or the other, and that this happens in a similar way cross-culturally. Researchers should investigate the construction of "communities of practice" (p. 472). A community of practice is a group of people who engage in shared social activities, or practices, of which language is one. In fact, these practices create the group and the identities of people as members of the group.

Eckert and McConnell-Ginet provide a detailed example, in their 1995 article "Constructing Meaning, Constructing Selves," of a high school near Detroit in which students organized themselves into groups called *burnouts* and *jocks*. These communities of practice were defined by participation in certain activities, such as drug use for burnouts and participation in school sports for jocks, by the use of a newly emerging Detroit accent for burnouts and a more standard Midwestern accent for jocks, and by the labeling of themselves and one another as "burnouts" or "jocks." Gender and (class-based) burnout/jock identities interacted so that burnout girls participated in practices, such as being the most likely to use new pronunciations from Detroit, that differentiated them from burnout boys but also from jock girls. By attending to the construction of multiple identities, Eckert and McConnell-Ginet were able to notice subtleties in their data that would not be observed by simply comparing girls and boys in the high school. It is not that burnout girls necessarily had nothing in common with jock girls, but what the two had in common was perhaps not as significant for their identity as the practices that made them burnouts and jocks. Burnout girls identified with burnout boys more than with jock girls, but at the same time burnout girls were engaged in practices separate from burnout boys. In other words, these students were creating multiple identities simultaneously, as burnout or jock, girl or boy, but also as heterosexual (Eckert and McConnell-Ginet did not discuss students of other sexualities), and as youth. In addition, the students were actively creating and recreating norms of behavior as well as variously enforcing, complying with, resisting, and/or subverting those norms as they created communities of practice. For example, jock boys and girls collaborated in defining the jock norm as participation in boy's sports such as football, thereby constructing jock boys as the ultimate jock. Meanwhile burnout girls and jock girls constructed competing norms of femininity, such that they each defined the other as less feminine.

The importance of communities of practice may be easiest to see when people participate in communities that do not match their biology, such as when burnout girls and jock girls constitute separate communities of practice. However, Eckert and McConnell-Ginet advise researchers to investigate the construction of identities that do not diverge from the expected, or the norm, such as masculinity and heterosexuality, just as carefully as those that do. Many researchers have assumed that language and gender studies should focus primarily on women and how they deviate, or are perceived as deviating, from the norm. But Eckert and McConnell-Ginet (1992) argue that researchers must also study the norm in order to see how it becomes the norm and to challenge its status as the norm. This means studying men's use of language systematically, which very few studies have done (though see Johnson and Meinhof [1997] or current research on language and masculinity). Language and gender researchers have always studied heterosexuality. In fact, there has been little systematic study of language use by people who identify as lesbian, gay, bisexual, and transgender until very recently (see Leap, 1995; Livia and Hall, 1997), and studies which focus on women and men interacting with one another (whether through difference or dominance) tend to assume heterosexual identities for these women and men. However, researchers have not given much attention to the *construction* of heterosexual identities, nor to the construction of other such normative identities as white and middle class.

Women's studies as a discipline has benefited from collaboration with ethnic studies and sexuality studies, gaining insights into how gender interacts with ethnicity, sexuality, class, age, and many other identities, and how power interacts with all of these. Likewise, language and gender research has benefited from research on the complexity of identity and power. Future research must continue to account for this complexity and examine how individuals actively create their identities, as well as how they create and use power, on a day-to-day basis. According to Kira Hall and Mary Bucholtz (1995), one promising research direction is the investigation of linguistic stereotypes, for example of women's language and men's language, as resources for identity construction. For instance, Bonnie McElhinney (1995) examines how women police officers in Pittsburgh adopt stereotypically middle-class masculine linguistic practices to construct themselves as competent police officers in a job traditionally dominated by men. Kira Hall investigates how female and male phone sex workers employ stereotypically feminine linguistic practices to construct themselves as conventionally attractive, white, middle-class, heterosexual women to meet the expectations of male callers (Hall, 1995). Shigeko Okamoto (1995) explores how some younger women in Japan use stereotypically masculine linguistic forms to construct themselves as young, unmarried students, an identity previously unavailable to Japanese women. In each of these cases, women's power to create their own identities is tied to their power to control their own economic circumstances. Research on the practices of reclamation and subversion of gendered terms, which I mentioned above, also offers insights into the complexity of identity and power construction. As we approach the end of the third decade of language and gender research, it is no longer enough to focus our investigations solely on talk about women and talk by women. We must account for people's lived experiences as participants in multiple communities of practice, in which gender is one identity inseparable from many others.

BIBLIOGRAPHY

Bodine, Ann. "Androcentrism in Prescriptive Grammar." *Language in Society* 4(2) (1975): 129-146.

Eckert, Penelope, and Sally McConnell-Ginet. "Think Practically and Look Locally: Language and Gender As Community-Based Practice." *Annual Review of Anthropology* 21 (1992): 461-490.

________. "Constructing Meaning, Constructing Selves: Snapshots of Language, Gender, and Class from Belten High." In Kira Hall and Mary Bucholtz (Eds.), *Gender Articulated: Language and the Socially Constructed Self* (pp. 469-507). New York: Routledge, 1995.

Hall, Kira. "Lip Service on the Fantasy Lines." In Kira Hall and Mary Bucholtz (Eds.), *Gender Articulated: Language and the Socially Constructed Self* (pp. 183-216). New York: Routledge, 1995.

Hall, Kira and Mary Bucholtz (Eds.). *Gender Articulated: Language and the Socially Constructed Self*. New York: Routledge, 1995.

Hellinger, Marlis. "Effecting Social Change through Group Action: Feminine Occupational Titles in Transition." In Cheris Kramarae, Muriel Shulz, and William M. O'Barr (Eds.), *Language and Power* (pp. 136-153). Beverly Hills: Sage, 1984.

Johnson, Sally, and Ulrike Hanna Meinhof (Eds.). *Language and Masculinity*. Oxford: Blackwell, 1997.

Lakoff, Robin. "Language and Woman's Place." *Language in Society* 2(1) (1973): 45-80.

Leap, William (Ed.). *Beyond the Lavender Lexicon: Authenticity, Imagination, and Appropriation in Lesbian and Gay Languages*. Buffalo, NY: Gordon and Breach, 1995.

Livia, Anna and Kira Hall (Eds.). *Queerly Phrased: Language, Gender, and Sexuality*. New York: Oxford University Press, 1997.

MacKay, Donald G. "Prescriptive Grammar and the Pronoun Problem." In Barrie Thorne, Cheris Kramerae, and Nancy Henley (Eds.), *Language, Gender, and Society* (pp. 54-68). Rowley, MA: Newbury House, 1983.

Maggio, Rosalie. *The Bias-Free Word Finder: A Dictionary of Nondiscriminatory Language*. Boston: Beacon, 1991.

Maltz, Daniel N. and Ruth A. Borker. "A Cultural Approach to Male-Female Miscommunication." In John Gumperz (Ed.), *Language and Social Identity* (pp. 196-216). Cambridge, NY: Cambridge University Press, 1982.

McElhinney, Bonnie. "Challenging Hegemonic Masculinities: Female and Male Police Officers Handling Domestic Violence." In Kira Hall and Mary Bucholtz (Eds.), *Gender Articulated: Language and the Socially Constructed Self* (pp. 217-244). New York: Routledge, 1995.

Miller, Casey and Kate Swift. *Words and Women: New Language in New Times*. New York: Anchor, 1976.

Okamoto, Shigeko. "'Tasteless' Japanese: Less 'Feminine' Speech Among Young Japanese Women." In Kira Hall and Mary Bucholtz (Eds.), *Gender Articulated: Language and the Socially Constructed Self* (pp. 297-328). New York: Routledge, 1995.

Shulz, Muriel R. "The Semantic Derogation of Women." In Barrie Thorne and Nancy Henley (Eds.), *Language and Sex: Difference and Dominance* (pp. 64-75). Rowley, MA: Newbury House, 1975.

Sutton, Laurel A. "Bitches and Skankly Hobags: The Place of Women in Contemporary Slang." In Kira Hall and Mary Bucholtz (Eds.), *Gender Articulated: Language and the Socially Constructed Self* (pp. 279-296). New York: Routledge, 1995.

Tannen, Deborah. *You Just Don't Understand: Women and Men in Conversation*. New York: Ballantine, 1990.

Chapter 16

Gender Jail: A Look at Psychology and Gender

Kathleen M. Kirby

Psychology is the scientific study of why people do the things they do. Because we are complex, multifaceted human beings, there are many areas of study within this discipline, including how humans and animals are motivated and influenced; how they learn, think, communicate, make decisions, form meaning, and take action; and how others can intervene to help individuals make sense of their thoughts, actions, and inner being. Applied psychology—the areas of clinical and counseling psychology—helps people change distressing thoughts or behavior. As practitioners of the art of healing, psychologists are ethically bound to guide their clients toward health and wholeness. They do so by choosing therapies based on psychological principles, which are scientifically derived and proven effective in remediating specific symptoms and behaviors.

A few decades ago, psychologists assumed that there was no difference between women and men, so only men were studied. Practitioners used this research to guide their clinical interventions with women and, for many women, these scientifically supported approaches did not work. "Perhaps women did not try hard enough or were being difficult," therapists mused; they decided to study women to see what worked. Until recently, this was the status of the field of psychology. Soon women psychologists, aided by their feminist allies, began questioning theory and research after recognizing that true equality between the sexes occurs when women are acknowledged for their unique characteristics and talents rather than being considered, defined, and measured psychologically as men.

Clinical psychologists generally work with those people who have very serious mental health problems. Counseling psychologists are taught to work with normal individuals who are experiencing developmental stresses, most notably in the areas of career, relationship, or self image. As a counseling psychologist, I know that women and men often choose different career paths, have different work values, accentuate different relationship issues, and may feel misunderstood by the "opposite gender." Through the work of women such as Mary Belenky (1986), Nancy Chodorow (1978), Carol Gilligan (1982), Judith Jordan and Janet Surrey (1986), Jean Baker Miller and Irene Pierce Stiver (1997), and Anne Wilson Schaef (1985), I have come to realize the many ways women were being held to a standard developed for men. As my feminist therapist colleagues and I struggle to become effective agents of change and powerful tools for clients' use in their journeys toward personal fulfillment, we continue uncovering many ingrained prejudices and stereotypes about gender we might inadvertently reinforce. Happily, many nonfeminist psychologists now recognize that understanding gender difference and women's ways of knowing, acting, and being is important in perfecting our art of psychotherapy.

Gender is the concept that society holds about how a female or male should act depending upon their biological sex. Society is split along gender lines. Parents speculate about the sex of their unborn child long before medical tests can establish it. Most parents express hopes and expectations based upon the basic category to which the child will be classified—female or male. Their dreams often echo characteristics society deems valuable for success of boys/men and girls/women: masculine equals strong, driving, emphatic, leading, winning, and successful, while feminine equals soft, caring, submissive, agreeable, and gentle. These are, in a sense, unspoken equivalents of gender.

"If it's a boy, I hope he will have his dad's big shoulders and my brains; if it's a girl, I hope that she inherits my small bone structure, her father's smile, and his pleasant way," many an expectant mother has been heard to say. "Strength and intelligence are important for a male to succeed in our society; daintiness, beauty, and a pleasant personality were [sic] the most important characteristics to ensure a female thrives in our culture. I'll do everything I can to help my children be well adjusted and happy members of society." Some individuals plan to defy "tradition" and dress their children in blue and pink as opposed to one specific gender color.

Inadvertently, this mother-to-be was categorizing her soon-to-be-born child and locking her or him into "gender jail." She held different expectations regarding the positive or negative physical and emotional traits of her offspring depending upon gender. Parents, caretakers, relatives, friends, and society in general will communicate these expectations verbally and nonverbally throughout the lifetime of the child. They will shape parental decisions about room decor, clothing apparel, toys, books, television and movie viewing, hobbies, activities, sports, lessons, and cultural enrichment. The subtle and not-so-subtle approval a mother gives her child impacts her or his formation of self-image, likes and dislikes, expectations, life goals, and achievements. It appears likely this woman's child will resist some peripheral norms (girls wear pink; boys wear blue) but subscribe to the larger and more basic societal norms of selective behavior according to gender.

Almost all forms, like job, loan, or school application forms, ask us to check MALE or FEMALE. Subtly, the either/or dichotomous nature of this category is communicated by expectation of and reactions to such signals and markings as posture, speech, clothing, voice tone, stance, walk, manner of moving, and so forth. Even when performing identical acts, males will be perceived as more powerful, in charge, privileged, strong, and capable of leadership while females will be perceived as followers, dainty (weaker), compliant (needs direction), and vulnerable (must be protected). Certain attitudes and actions will be associated with each characteristic and labeled as appropriate behavior for males or females, commonly referred to as gendered behavior (Goodwin, 1987).

When individuals exhibit characteristics of the opposite gender or category, that is, when a man appears overly emotional or a woman exceedingly outspoken or dominant, society becomes uneasy. These individuals are not acting true to "type" or "category." The basic structure of society—dichotomous and different, male and female—

is blurred; someone is breaking out of gender jail. Societal sanctions will be evoked using the very powerful mechanisms of embarrassment, harassment, guilt, and shame. The message: Shape up and act right!

Until recently, these beliefs about gender so permeated our culture that no one questioned the fact that masculine traits and accomplishments were valued as the pinnacle of psychological development. After all, most psychologists and psychological researchers were male, as were most subjects of psychological experiments. The notion that females and males are physiologically different, act, think, communicate, and perhaps develop differently was not entertained. There was one "right" way to think, develop and be—the masculine way.

Even Freud, the father of psychoanalytic thought, was not immune to gender assumptions. He postulated that boys, and perhaps adult men, develop fantasies and fears because of dread of their father's anger. This anger was elicited because of the boys' physical and/or emotional desire for (or closeness to) their mother. A powerful father could easily eliminate this competition by castration (the Oedipus complex). Instead of drawing a parallel—such as little girls covet their fathers and, thereby, come into competition with their mother—Freud hypothesized that when girls became aware of the difference between their body and the male body, they instantly experienced their body as a lesser or inferior, mutilated form of the male. Girls pondered what "type" of a boy they indeed were and, discovering they were not and could not be male, experienced distress, disappointment, and penis envy. One wonders whether, if Freud had existed as a female in a less patriarchal society, her theory of human relational development might have included boys envying girls for their lack of external genitalia and their courage during bloodletting (menstruation). As Ellen Cook (1993) theorizes, power envy may be found in both women and men.

Carol Gilligan (1982), on the other hand, analyzed such gender assumptions, recognizing differences in thought, attitude, and values between women and men and questioning the universal timelines for psychological and moral development established by males based upon research data collected from men. Gilligan noted girls appear to be as or more assertive, intellectual, demanding, and in charge as boys until age eleven or twelve, when girls "seal up" or begin to draw within and stop voicing opinions or thoughts for fear of jeopardizing their personal relationships. Since independence of thought and action is viewed as the ultimate masculine trait and epitome of psychological development, girls/women were once seen as stagnated or arrested in their development at an earlier stage of mutuality, collectivity, or dependency. Today, Gilligan and her colleagues continue to study the development of girls and women. They resist forming a "theory" of female development, as may be urged, without first generating longitudinal data such as listening to women's voices (Gilligan, Lyons, and Hanmer, 1990).

In contrast, Judith Jordan and Janet Surrey (1986) have postulated a new model of female development and identity based on a reinterpretation of current psychoanalytic theory. They believe women organize their sense of identity, find existential meaning, achieve a sense of coherence and continuity, and are motivated in the context of a relationship, whether with others or with oneself. This "self-in-relation" theory emphasizes development of mutual empathy in the mother-daughter relationship, which is believed to proceed more smoothly than the mother-son relationship, and facilitates the young girl's relational abilities, special investment, and comfort in the relationship. In this theory, women and men are viewed as different and complimentary.

According to psychologists such as Jean Baker Miller, Gilligan, Jordan, and Surrey, women tend to differ from men in their stronger need to affiliate with and care for others due to their highly developed relational ability. Women are reinforced by the dominant culture to value and nurture relationships such as marriage, family, and friendship. These psychologists theorize that because women's emotional ties are more central to their sense of self, women are more vulnerable to emotional stress (often experienced in the form of depression) when relationships are broken or lost. Many other researchers also attribute the fact that women are diagnosed as suffering from depression about eighty times more often than men to the imbalance of power between male and female in our patriarchal culture (Lerner, 1988).

Realizing that an imbalance of power can affect women, psychology, like medicine, is also now recognizing that current information about male responses to various medical interventions or psychological problems are not directly applicable to the treatment of women for the same ailment. Psychologists understand that issues surrounding gender pervade all relationships of life and must be considered important variables in the scientific experiments that guide practice. Today more care is given to include both genders, as well as representative samples of ethnic minorities, in subject pools for experiments, and to generalize the results of studies only to the population measured (such as African-American females, teenage girls, or white males).

Feminist therapists, however, realized that changing variables in scientific measurements was only the first step. An entirely new approach to therapy was needed and was created by feminist therapists who were concerned about the power of the therapist to reinforce societal norms without awareness of the possible detrimental effects on their clients and themselves. Feminist therapy recognizes and attempts to equalize, as much as possible, the power difference between client and therapist and to involve clients actively in therapy decisions. It obligates therapists to offer service to those in need by adjusting cost to the individual's financial ability to pay and to continue therapy despite financial difficulties. Feminist therapists engage in political activity to arouse public awareness regarding inequity issues from majority culture influences. Likewise, they encourage clients to follow suit as a final stage of healing. Although they may use other therapeutic theories, feminist therapists recognize and validate the positive and negative effects of majority culture in order to sensitize and reassure their clients while modeling personal growth and contributing to societal transformation (Cook, 1993).

Psychology is beginning to explore issues of gender and ethnicity in client-therapist relationships and to acknowledge differences in treatment strategies and client response to interventions. I was taught in my graduate schooling that women and men preferred male therapists because males are seen as more expert and powerful. Today, research shows the majority of clients prefer female therapists; they attribute to female therapists a greater capacity to understand, show empathy, accept emotion, embrace apprehension, tolerate fear, invite relationship, and celebrate change. Fortunately, more female/feminist therapists are now practicing and counseling. (Unfortunately, as with every field that women enter in great numbers, the starting salary for entry-level professionals has recently dropped.)

Recent enrollment statistics in schools of clinical psychology and counseling psychology show that the majority of new students are female, a radical change from 1980, when only about 10 percent of students enrolled in graduate schools in the various disciplines of psychology were women. As a university professor and clinical training director of my counseling psychology program, I am often asked about undergraduate preparation for becoming a psychologist. My best students have studied foundational psychology (social psychology, human development, statistics and methodology, abnormal psychology, and studies in learning, cognition, motivation, and emotion) as well as completed courses in philosophy, psycholinguistics, literature, and women's studies. Such preparation encourages students' awareness of societal issues that mold the attitudes and beliefs of both client and counselor, while sensitizing them to symbolism, the power of language, the inner turmoil, the outer expression of the psyche, and the influence of others. Women's studies often provides the melding of all of these fields into a coherent map of gender issues.

Feminist research and publication further clarifies issues of gender and generates interest in the field of psychology. Recent areas of importance include interpersonal influence between therapist and client, the development of girls, relational differences between friendships of women and men, same-sex relationships, intergenerational friendships, and general inquiry into the experience of women in various roles and relationships. As Mary Pipher advocates in *Reviving Ophelia* (1994), feminist therapists recognize society will change only when we understand the "why" of current circumstances and take action to change the present.

BIBLIOGRAPHY

Baron-Faust, Rita. *Mental Wellness for Women.* New York: William Morrow, 1998.

Belenky, Mary Field, Blythe Clinchy, Nancy Goldberger, and Jill Mattuck Tarule. *Women's Ways of Knowing: The Development of Self, Voice, and Mind.* New York: Basic, 1986.

Chesler, Phyllis, Esther D. Rothblum, and Ellen Cole (Eds.). *Feminist Foremothers in Women's Studies, Psychology, and Mental Health.* Binghamton, NY: The Haworth Press, 1995.

Chodorow, Nancy. *The Reproduction of Mothering: Psychoanalysis and the Sociology of Gender.* Berkeley: University of California Press, 1978.

Cook, Ellen Piel (Ed.). *Women, Relationships and Power: Implications for Counseling.* Alexandria, VA: American Counseling Association, 1993.

Freud, Sigmund. "The Dissolution of the Oedipus Complex." 1924. In J. Strachey (Ed. and trans.), *The Standard Edition of the Complete Psychological Works of Sigmund Freud,* Volume 19 (pp. 173-179). London: Hogarth, 1961.

Gilligan, Carol. *In a Different Voice.* Cambridge, MA: Harvard University Press, 1982.

Gilligan, Carol, Nona P. Lyons, and Trudy J. Hanmer. *Making Connections: The Relational World of Adolescent Girls at Emma Willard School.* Cambridge, MA: Harvard University Press, 1990.

Goodwin, Marjorie Harness and Charles Goodwin. "Children's Arguing." In Susan U. Philips, Susan Steele, and Christine Tanz (Eds.), *Language, Gender and Sex in Comparative Perspective* (pp. 200-248). Cambridge, NY: Cambridge University Press, 1987.

Jordan, Judith V. and Janet L. Surrey. "The Self-in-Relation: Empathy and the Mother-Daughter Relationship." In T. Bernay and D.W. Cantor (Eds.), *The Psychology of Today's Woman: New Psychoanalytic Visions* (pp. 81-104). Hillsdale, NJ: Analytic, 1986.

Kaplan, Alexandra G., Jean Baker Miller, Judith V. Jordan, Janet L. Surrey, and Irene Pierce Stiver. *Women's Growth in Connection: Writings from the Stone Center.* New York: Guilford, 1991.

Kaschak, Ellyn. *Engendered Lives: A New Psychology of Women's Experience.* New York: Basic, 1992.

Kupers, Terry A. *Revisioning Men's Lives: Gender, Intimacy and Power.* New York: Guilford, 1993.

Lerman, Hannah. *Pigeonholing Women's Misery: A History and Critical Analysis of the Psychodiagnosis of Women in the Twentieth Century.* New York: Basic, 1996.

Lerner, Harriet Goldhor. *Women in Therapy.* New York: Harper & Row, 1988.

Miller, Jean Baker. *Toward a New Psychology of Women.* New York: Brunner/Mazel, 1976.

Miller, Jean Baker and Irene Pierce Stiver. *The Healing Connection: How Women Form Relationships in Therapy and in Life.* New York: Beacon, 1997.

Pipher, Mary. *Reviving Ophelia.* New York: Putnam, 1994.

Schaef, Anne Wilson. *Women's Reality: An Emerging Female System in a White Male Society.* San Francisco: Harper & Row, 1985.

Tannen, Deborah. *You Just Don't Understand: Women and Men in Conversation.* New York: Morrow, 1990.

SECTION III: NATURAL SCIENCES

"DaVinci's Daughter" by Kimberly Burton

The natural sciences have enjoyed a strong academic position since the European Renaissance, which was in fact based on people's pursuit of new knowledge of the natural world. Characterized by a focus on the factual aspects of nature, natural scientists try to discover the facts of the earth, space, human life, animal and plant life, and chemicals—in other words, the things that occur naturally. In contrast to the social sciences or the humanities, these sciences are much less concerned with the way humans behave socially or the way people think artistically and creatively than they are with the ways things—including human bodies and cells—work. These disciplines include such areas as chemistry, biology, physics, anatomy, medical fields, geology, aeronautics, as well as the history of these fields. Usually other "factual" disciplines such as mathematics are included under the term of quantitative reasoning because they examine the facts of abstract thought rather than concrete facts of nature. However, for the purposes of this volume, we have included some of these essays in this section, partly because the natural sciences need the formulas and theorems of quantitative reasoning to determine their own facts (for example, a statistical analysis of a cellular reaction), and partly because both types of disciplines—reasoning and natural sciences—try to determine facts.

Deep within these disciplines lies a strong belief in the knowability of facts. Scientists typically believe that facts exist in isolation to the people who try to know them. Such a belief underlies the techniques scientists use: observation, microscopic examination, and experimentation. This belief that things exist outside of ourselves and that we can know them—called objective positivism—has until recently failed to account for the ways in which we interpret facts. As you shall see in the following essays, feminist influences have changed the way scientists "interpret" facts. They now see that act of interpretation as being subjective, an act that may change those very facts that scientists sought to know. The following essays highlight much of these new influences and the current changes that these disciplines are experiencing.

In the first essay, about gender and medicine, Laura Shanner looks at the feminist contributions to ethical theory, reproductive issues, and nonreproductive issues of the health field. She further challenges our traditional ideas of health and disease and medical research. In their discussion of the field of physics, Barbara Whitten and Juan Burciaga describe three initiatives to transform their field: to demonstrate the roles of women and people of color in science and in physics, to document and eliminate ongoing discrimination in the field of physics, and to change the way physics is taught to make it a more inclusive area of study. Gwyneth Hughes, in her discussion of science and chemistry, gives an overview of the relationship between feminism and science that, although at times still uneasy, has helped to focus attention on the contributions of women scientists. Hughes asserts, however, that the curricula of physical science, in particular chemistry, have not changed significantly to accommodate women's perspectives of science. Julianne Lynch, Gilah Leder, and Helen Forgasz examine inequities in mathematics education. They emphasize the necessity of pluralistic approaches in mathematics classrooms, as well as inclusive classroom interactions that stress affirmation rather than competition. In the final essay, Amy Sue Bix gives a fascinating account of the role of women in the history of sciences, uncovering a multitude of ways in which women have shaped that study for centuries, usually without the fame and recognition that was accorded to work and discoveries made by male scientists.

As you read these essays, consider the ways in which the study of science shapes your life. How do you use science and scientific discoveries in your everyday life? How has an attention to feminist issues shaped the way these fields understand the world? How has feminism changed the ways scientists work? How has feminism changed the way science affects your life?

Chapter 17

Feminist Contributions to Bioethics

Laura Shanner

The field of bioethics brings together scholars from philosophy, law, health care sciences, theology, and the social sciences who seek to understand and resolve ethical dilemmas in health care and biomedical research. As rapid advances in technology allow us to alter our bodies or extend our lives, a bioethicist asks whether and how we *should* use them. Treatment decisions and research priorities involve much more than just biological science; the values we hold personally and collectively, the meanings we attach to life and death, and conflicts between individual and collective interests are constantly involved. Birth, death, illness, suffering, and the hope of recovery are the most profound of human experiences, and any intervention that deeply affects our bodies and life prospects requires careful ethical consideration. Medical interventions may even reshape entire societies: life-extending technologies have lengthened our average life span and revised our attitudes toward aging. Are these changes for the better? These are not easy questions, and the answers are seldom clear.

Because bioethics is a multidisciplinary field, and one that asks complicated questions about the intersections among our bodies, our beliefs, and our social structures, it can share substantial overlap with women's studies. Feminist contributions represent the cutting edge in bioethics theory, reproductive ethics, and nonreproductive health care issues. The full impact of feminist thinking has not yet become clear, and the overlap between women's studies and bioethics promises exciting developments.

In ethical theory, a distinction should be made between "feminist" and "feminine" ethics (Sherwin, 1992). Feminist approaches typically identify gender differences in the matter at hand and seek to eliminate inequalities in power and privilege. "Feminine" approaches, such as an ethic of care, seek to incorporate typically feminine perceptions and moral reasoning patterns into the canons of ethical theory. Although feminine approaches are usually feminist, not all feminists support a feminine approach. In addition, it is important to note that a feminine ethic is not intended to be gender specific or for women only; it is intended to balance overly abstract, male-dominated ethical models, allowing both sexes to make better moral decisions.

Feminist approaches to bioethics reveal further deep theoretical disagreements (Tong, 1996); women clearly do not speak with a single voice any more than men do. On one hand, *liberal feminists* emphasize the rights of rational agents to act freely, as long as their actions do not violate the equal rights of others. Accordingly, legal or social restrictions on personal decisions should be minimal. Reproductive rights, for example, would include not just access to abortion and infertility treatments, but also the right of rational agents to trade or sell ova, sperm, embryos, and gestational services. Further, since elderly men can still father children, equal liberty for women would entail a right of access to post-menopausal infertility treatment. On the other hand, *radical feminists* are more likely to suspect that all reproductive interventions involve patriarchal attempts by men to control women's lives, and may reject the activity of reproducing at all.

Social feminism seeks to restructure social and cultural institutions to suit feminine lives and life cycles. For example, current educational and business structures make it difficult for women to achieve economic security while also having children when it is healthiest and easiest to do so. Technology allows older women to become pregnant after delayed childbearing, but social feminists would advocate restructuring social institutions to make such delays unnecessary. *Marxist feminists* and other economic theorists call our attention to the unpaid economic value of women's experiences: women provide the vast majority of at-home care for ailing relatives, and labor and delivery are usually ignored in economic discussions of productive labor.

A principle-based approach (Beauchamp and Childress, 1994) is the most widely-known ethics framework in bioethics. Four principles are the most common: *Autonomy* is the capacity by which rational moral agents make choices about their lives, bodies, and personal information. *Beneficence* is the duty to do good by preventing harm, relieving distress, or promoting welfare, and *nonmaleficence* is the principle of doing no harm, in the tradition of the Hippocratic oath. *Justice* is a principle of fairness, equality, or equity, which most often arises in medicine as problems of resource allocation.

Most feminists would not completely reject principles, recognizing that some of the most important advances for women involve appeals to justice and respect for women's autonomy. However, feminists and others note that there is no apparent resolution for conflicts among the principles, nor clear direction for applying abstract principles to concrete cases. Feminists also frequently challenge the ways that the principles themselves are defined. For example, the word "autonomy" frequently conjures images of isolated and independent individuals, ignoring the fact that most of our "autonomous" desires and expectations, not to mention our moral duties and conflicts, arise from the interactions we have with others. Some concepts of justice portray individuals as interchangeable entities, but strict impartiality may lead us to ignore our moral obligations to certain individuals that arise from relationships in families, communities, and institutions. Social justice is often taken for granted in discussions of distributive justice, but it will not do to offer equal resources or liberties when underlying inequalities in power remain masked.

The feminine "Ethic of Care" (Carse, 1991; Sharpe, 1992), widely discussed in feminist philosophy and nursing ethics, is increasingly recognized as an important alternative that challenges standard interpretations of the principles approach. Contrary to the abstract, universal perspective adopted in most ethical theories, in the care ethic the moral agent is perceived to be embedded in specific moral situations and relationships. Genuine equality among individuals is rare, as people tend to differ in political power, resources, and physical strength; such inequalities are typical in relationships between children and adults, between sick and healthy individuals, and between patients and health care providers. Those with greater resources have a duty to ensure care for weaker or more vulnerable people by responding to need and by creating strong, nonabusive relationships that prevent abandonment or neglect. Health care decisions thus are not negotiations among equals, nor do they pit patient autonomy against caregiver paternalism, but are attempts by those with greater knowledge and strength to enable more vulnerable individuals to feel secure and to achieve their own goods as much as possible.

Women's contributions are especially impressive in reproductive topics, which should not surprise us; the fact that women and not men become pregnant makes it vitally important to ask, "What does this technology or policy mean for women?" (Overall, 1987; Purdy, 1996; Shanner, 1998). While extensive debate has focused on the status of embryos or fetuses, feminists are the only consistent voices asking whether reproductive research or interventions might pose harm to women's (and their children's) interests. Feminists are also unique in exploring the motives for women to undertake treatments that are often expensive, risky, invasive, painful, unsuccessful, and objectifying. Pervasive "pronatalist" beliefs linking femininity and mothering, along with a network of social barriers to success in nonreproductive contexts, create enormous pressures on women to bear children. Images of women as reproductive vessels or machines are commonly considered, as is the fear that the social importance of reproducing "high quality" offspring will lead to coercive genetic testing, invasive birth management, and restrictions on pregnant women's activities.

The rancorous public debate over abortion usually emphasizes the moral and legal status of a fetus. However, the debate can be avoided by noting that even if fetuses are considered full persons with a right to life, such a right cannot justify continued use of a woman's body without her consent. Judith Jarvis Thomson (1971) imagined the case of an adult with a severe metabolic disorder who needs to be attached to someone else's body temporarily to survive. While supporting someone else's life if you can is always a good thing, it hardly seems morally *required* to sacrifice one's own body to do so. Carol Gilligan (1982) further observed that both abortion and adoption fracture the mother-child relationship, and that adoption is therefore not necessarily the least-worst option in an unwanted pregnancy, as many suppose.

Unique to a woman's perspective is detailed attention to what it is like to *be* pregnant. Fetal imaging techniques look *through* the woman to see the fetus, but no technology shows the woman and the fetus together. Understanding pregnancy as a lived phenomenon reminds us that there simply is no such thing as a fetus without a pregnant woman sustaining it, and that women's experiences must not be ignored. Women's insights help us understand the reasons behind abortion, the despair of infertility, our common revulsion at pregnancies maintained in the bodies of clinically dead women or in (future) mechanical wombs, and the ambivalence that is common in both wanted and unwanted pregnancies. "Surrogate mothering" is controversial not just in practice, but also in name, as the word "surrogate" seems to devalue the pregnant person's experience; "contract pregnancy" would be a better term.

The researchers who develop contraceptives and fertility drugs, the fertility specialists who "create" babies, the geneticists who test embryos and fetuses, the obstetricians who "deliver" the babies, and even the doctors who perform abortions, are predominantly male. When these male-dominated medical professions exist in a community with male-dominated religious and political structures, it is difficult to see how women are really gaining greater control over reproductive processes. Further woman-centered reflection on reproductive interventions is thus crucial.

The most intriguing challenges from woman-centered scholarship concern the topics that bioethicists choose to discuss. The traditional emphasis on doctor-patient relationships has often ignored the roles and duties of nurses, social workers, physical therapists, and other (predominantly female) health care providers who work in a deeply hierarchical health care system. Virginia Warren (1992) points out that most bioethics topics are "crisis issues," such as when to turn off a ventilator, rather than "housekeeping issues," such as the relationships and communication among health care providers, patients, and families that would prevent most crisis issues from arising in the first place.

The exclusion of women's perspectives from medical and social policy assumptions can lead to devastating but unnoticed consequences for women. Releasing patients from the hospital "sicker and quicker," so that their recovery can continue at home, is often suggested to reduce health care costs. There is a hidden injustice, though: women provide an estimated 70 to 90 percent of unpaid home care for relatives, but the unequal economic, social, and physical impact on women is rarely considered in analyses of early discharge. Social expectations must also be considered carefully in the debate regarding assisted suicide (active euthanasia). Since women's roles tend to emphasize passivity and self-sacrifice, there is concern that women will disproportionately request assistance in dying because they wish not to "burden" others or they feel they do not deserve to live.

Women have recently made great strides in reversing the accepted norm of excluding women from medical research trials (Dresser, 1992; Baylis, Downie, and Sherman, 1998). New drugs and procedures must be proven to be safe and effective before they can be widely used. If the study group is homogenous, it is easier to tell when the intervention being tested (rather than sex, age, race, or body size) is causing any observed difference. Researchers also fear accidentally causing birth defects by exposing fetuses to dangerous chemicals. The results of exclusion for women, though, can be disastrous. The differences between women's and men's bodies—the ones that that might confuse the data—mean that treatments that work well in men may be ineffective in women, may require different dosages, may fluctuate in effectiveness during menstruation, or may cause different side effects. Even basic research into disease processes and healthy body functioning tend to focus on male bodies. AIDS and cardiovascular disease both progress differently in women than in men, for example, but neither disease is well understood in women. Does an aspirin a day protect women from heart attacks as well as it does men? Nobody knows.

Feminist challenges to male-focused research have created astounding policy shifts in the 1990s, as substantial investments were finally made in research into breast cancer, cardiovascular health, and other nonreproductive women's health matters. Further, in 1994, the U.S. government required the National Institutes of Health and other federally funded health research bodies to ensure that females were appropriately represented in all studies. Although such advances redirect research toward the interests of those whose needs usually do not dominate the research agenda, further care needs to be taken to ensure that oppressed or marginalized groups are not exploited for research purposes. The extensive testing of contraceptives in developing countries is an example of the way that women, poor or non-white persons, and other less powerful groups may be placed at risk for the benefit of others.

Misdiagnosis of women's conditions may also arise through questionable definitions of "disease." Recent advances in hormone replacement therapy challenge our perceptions of normal aging: is menopause a disease of hormone deficiency or a natural stage of female development, more like puberty? In psychiatry, "hysteria" (from the Greek *hyster* or uterus) has largely disappeared from the official diagnostic manual, and women are less likely than in previous decades to be given addictive tranquilizers for "nerves," but two new provisional diagnoses have been introduced. "Premenstrual Dysphoric Disorder" is severe premenstrual aggression and irrationality, and "Self-Defeating Personality Disorder" is a predominantly female struggle with abusive partners, low-status employment, and nonassertive behaviors. Stereotypically feminine passivity is pathologized, but so is female aggression or anger. Paula Caplan (1995) wonders why there is no corresponding "Dominating Delusional Personality Disorder" or "Macho Syndrome" for men who are violent, domineering, competitive, and unable to identify and express emotions.

Plastic surgery has received substantial attention in women's studies, as women apparently "need" more facelifts and tummy tucks than men do. Silicone breast implants are still widely used to treat "micromastia" (small breasts) and "ptosis" (drooping breasts) despite the implants' tendency to leak and become painfully hard and lumpy. Ethical analysis of elective cosmetic enhancement draws substantially on women's studies' analysis of appearance, sexuality, and social role expectations.

Although bioethics itself is a young and developing field, the voices of women are already having an important—and growing—influence. Women's studies are offering not just different perspectives on medical issues but are also challenging the very types of questions that are asked in bioethics and the theoretical approaches taken to resolving them. Bioethics is beginning to profit from the multidisciplinary attempts in women's studies to understand how social forces, economics, power differentials, and language affect our expectations and practices regarding our bodies. Recognizing that medicine itself is an institution within a social context offers new horizons for addressing the many ethical dilemmas that arise when we try to alter our lives and deaths. The future for contributions to bioethics from women's studies is bright and truly exciting.

BIBLIOGRAPHY

Baylis, Francoise, Jocelyn Downie, and Susan Sherwin. "Reframing Research Involving Humans." In Susan Sherwin et al. (Eds.), *The Politics of Women's Health: Exploring Agency and Autonomy* (pp. 234-259). Philadelphia: Temple University Press, 1998.

Beauchamp, Tom L. and James F. Childress. *Principles of Biomedical Ethics*, Fourth Edition. New York: Oxford, 1994.

Caplan, Paula. *They Say You're Crazy*. Reading, MA: Addison Wesley, 1995.

Carse, Alisa. "The 'Voice of Care': Implications for Bioethical Education." *Journal of Medicine and Philosophy* 16(1) (1991): 5-28.

Donchin, Anne and Laura Purdy (Eds.). *Embodying Bioethics: Recent Feminist Advances*. New York: Rowman and Littlefield, 1998.

Dresser, Rebecca. "Wanted: Single, White Male for Medical Research." *Hastings Center Report* 22(1) (1992): 24-29.

Gilligan, Carol. *In a Different Voice*. Cambridge, MA: Harvard University Press, 1982.

McCarrick, Pat M. and Martina Darragh. "Feminist Perspectives on Bioethics: Scope Note 30." *Kennedy Institute of Ethics Journal* 6(1) (1996): 85-103.

Overall, Christine. *Ethics and Human Reproduction: A Feminist Analysis*. Boston: Allen and Unwin, 1987.

Purdy, Laura M. *Reproducing Persons*. Ithaca: Cornell University Press, 1996.

Shanner, Laura. "Procreation." In Alison Jaggar and Iris Marion Young (Eds.), *A Companion to Feminist Philosophy* (pp. 429-437). Malden: Blackwell, 1998.

Sharpe, Virginia A. "Justice and Care: The Implications of the Kohlberg-Gilligan Debate for Medical Ethics." *Theoretical Medicine* 13(4) (1992): 295-318.

Sherwin, Susan. *No Longer Patient: Feminist Ethics and Health Care*. Philadelphia: Temple University Press, 1992.

Thomson, Judith Jarvis. "A Defense of Abortion." *Philosophy and Public Affairs* 1(1) (1971): 47-66.

Tong, Rosemarie. "Feminist Approaches to Bioethics." In Susan Wolf (Ed.), *Feminism and Bioethics: Beyond Reproduction* (pp. 67-94). New York: Oxford, 1996.

Warren, Virginia. "Feminist Directions in Medical Ethics." In Helen Bequaert Holmes and Laura M. Purdy (Eds.), *Feminist Perspectives in Medical Ethics* (pp. 32-45). Indianapolis: Indiana University Press, 1992.

Chapter 18

First Steps Toward a More Feminist, Multicultural Physics

Barbara L. Whitten
Juan R. Burciaga

At the end of the twentieth century, the physics community remains one of the most homogeneous of all the sciences. In 1991, the National Science Foundation reported that 92 percent of full-time college physics instructors were male and 86 percent were white; African Americans, Hispanics, and Native Americans together constituted less than 5 percent of physics faculty.

This homogeneity is not accidental; resistance to the inclusion of others has been strong. Richard Feynman, who was to become possibly the best theoretical physicist of his generation, was denied entrance to Columbia in 1936 because of the Jewish quota. When he applied to graduate school at Princeton, his ethnicity again became an issue because, according to the department chair, of the "difficulty of placing them." His undergraduate mentor at MIT assured the Princeton faculty that his personality was more attractive than that of most Jews.

In 1933, Robert Millikan, a very prominent American physicist, wrote to the president of Duke University to advise against hiring a German-Jewish woman physicist, on the grounds that she was not as talented as Lise Meitner, one of the foremost physicists in the world. It is highly doubtful that there were many faculty anywhere as talented as Meitner. Ironically, her success made it more rather than less difficult for other women to follow in her footsteps.

Most cruelly, these informal (and even formal) policies of exclusion were not recognized by the majority of physicists. Most regarded the physics community as a meritocracy and attributed the dearth of women and people of color to their lack of ability.

Eradicating this legacy of discrimination and opening the physics community have been the focus of feminist and multicultural critiques of the field over the past twenty years. This initiative requires a three-pronged effort. First, we must recognize that despite all the formal and informal barriers, despite the constant harassment and lack of recognition, women and people of color have always been part of science. They refused to be discouraged by the most blatant discrimination, hid in closets to listen to lectures so they would not upset the "real" students, performed experiments in carpenter shops because they were not allowed in laboratories, and worked for little or no pay. They worked for love of science and succeeded in making major and minor contributions. We must rescue these people from obscurity, honor their extraordinary lives, and appreciate their contributions. We can at the same time recognize and honor those people of character on the "inside" who recognized talent and worked to include and encourage "others."

The second part of this project is to document and fight the discrimination that still exists. The physics community has worked hard in the past decade or so to become more welcoming, but the discrimination described above, though rare, does persist. For example, in 1996 Gordon Freeman wrote, in a letter to the Forum on Physics and Society, that encouraging more women to enter physics is responsible for the woeful lack of jobs. It would be better for physics and society as a whole, he says, if women again stayed home and looked after their families. Most physicists dismiss Freeman's arguments, but he continues to teach and influence students.

More important than these isolated instances of discrimination are more subtle problems. The overwhelming homogeneity of the physics community discourages many who are different. Nearly alone in classes composed almost entirely of white males, women and students of color are deprived of role models and a supportive community; they often report feeling isolated and stigmatized. This "chilly climate" is a significant factor in discouraging women and students of color.

Margaret Rossiter (1982), a historian of science who wrote a two-volume study of American women scientists, showed that women's colleges have a long tradition of producing and nurturing women scientists far out of proportion to the number of women they educate. Minority students succeed in physics in schools where they are not in the minority. Project Kaleidoscope reports that historically black colleges and universities produce 45 percent of the African-American bachelor's degrees in mathematics and physical sciences, and Puerto Rican colleges and universities produce a large proportion of the Hispanic-American physical science graduates.

Nor is it necessary for women and minority students to attend entirely different institutions. At Berkeley, Uri Triesman has directed a program to help minority students with introductory calculus. The program is designed to familiarize students with campus culture, provide a supportive environment, and encourage them to work together in study groups. It is not a remedial program; the problems assigned are more rather than less challenging. This program has lowered the failure rate for black students in calculus from 60 percent to 4 percent.

Even in the absence of blatant discrimination or a chilly climate, other factors make it unnecessarily difficult for women and students of color to succeed in physics, so the third major challenge is to change the way we teach and practice physics. In the past decade, physics instruction has undergone a miniature renaissance; Priscilla Laws (1991), Lillian McDermott (1991), and others have developed innovative approaches to the teaching of physics. These programs differ but typically include an emphasis on collaborative rather than competitive learning, a shift in the teacher's role from authority to facilitator, an awareness of differences in learning styles, a recognition of the value of personal experience, a greater appreciation for the context and historical development of physics, and a more inclusive view of the history of physics.

A traditional introductory physics class is a survey that covers all the big ideas of physics. The development of concepts is logical; the historical or social context of the physics is rarely discussed. Class begins when the teacher, almost always white and male, assumes his role at the front of the classroom. He lectures for about an hour, illustrating key ideas, solving sample problems, and exploring the "big picture." Questions are allowed but are infrequent in this inhibiting format; excessive questions are discouraged because this would slow the pace of the lecture, causing the class to get behind.

In an innovative classroom, the role of the instructor has changed dramatically. Rather than saying, "I am here to teach you," she (we speak hopefully, though most physics teachers are still white men) begins the course with "I am here to help you learn." She lectures for about ten minutes, briefly setting questions about today's subject in the context of the historical and conceptual development of physics. Then she poses a series of questions. Students gather in groups of three or four to pursue activities suggested by the questions. The instructor wanders from group to group, listening to the students grapple with concepts and their mathematical models. Occasionally she asks a provocative question or offers a brief explanation. Toward the end of class, the instructor calls the students together to test and reinforce their understanding. She briefly describes the assignment for tomorrow—a context-rich problem that applies students' new understanding.

This kind of instruction is most amenable to small classes, but variations are being tried in large (100+) university classes. Sue Rosser (1990), a zoologist who studies feminist pedagogy in the sciences, has shown that many of these techniques have feminist roots. The emphasis on cooperation rather than competition, the inclusion of the historical and social context, and the appeal to different learning styles make physics more attractive to a broader range of students.

Changing physics instruction as described above will make the classroom less forbidding to women and students of color and (we hope) will increase the diversity of professional physicists. But physics has come under feminist criticism in ways that have much more serious implications for our practice.

Physics, among the sciences, has a special role. It is the most theoretical and quantitative of all the sciences, partly because we deal with either relatively simple systems (e.g., atoms and molecules) or with simple aspects of complex systems (e.g., the orbital motion of the planets in the solar system). Other sciences have often aspired to model Newtonian mechanics, and some philosophers of science have judged the maturity of a science by how closely it comes to that theoretical structure. Stephen Jay Gould, an evolutionary biologist and well-known science writer, speaks of "physics envy," which leads scientists to oversimplify complex questions such as intelligence in hopes of achieving the quantifiable nature of physics. Many traditional scientists (and nonscientists) believe that the "truths" of science are value neutral, objective, and rational; they also believe that the conclusions of science do not depend on the time or place or culture of the scientists who discovered them.

In contrast, feminist theory derives much of its analytical strength from the claim that values, institutions, and practices of human beings are socially constructed and cannot transcend culture. Feminist critics of science have made a great deal of progress in showing that science is in fact socially constructed knowledge, that is, knowledge that grows out of a particular time, space, and culture. These concerns are mirrored by scientists who come from ethnic backgrounds where people have trouble with the reductionist philosophy of physics. But these questions strike at the very root of the cultural assumptions of the physics community and are difficult for traditional physicists to accept.

Feminist critics of the social and biological sciences have shown, in many examples, how the cultural and gender biases of scientists have led them astray and how the inclusion of women scientists has led to better science. But the analysis of the physical sciences is just beginning. Evelyn Fox Keller (1985) and Karen Barad (1996), both feminists trained in physics, have subjected the philosophical underpinnings of quantum mechanics to feminist analysis. And Sharon Traweek (1988), using the methods of feminist anthropology, studies the social organization of a large research laboratory in high-energy physics.

Finally, feminism has profoundly changed our society and how people live, and physics, as part of society, has been affected. A traditional scientist devoted virtually all his (traditionally, scientists were men) time and energy to scientific research, publishing, and teaching. His wife was responsible for raising their children, keeping their household running, and managing their social life. This scenario has changed in the past generation; now most American women work outside the home and both partners are expected to share in the upbringing of their children. But nontraditional families still receive little social support. Working parents rarely have flexibility to fulfill their family responsibilities, and public schools and other social institutions assume a stay-at-home mom is available. A woman seeking to become a scientist faces formidable pressures. Society and family expect her to maintain her role as the primary nurturer in the family, while the scientific world expects her to maintain the same (or often greater) productivity as her male colleagues. Scientists from cultures that expect extensive involvement in their family and community experience similar conflicts.

We have described at some length the first tentative steps proposed by feminist and multicultural critiques to change the way we teach and practice physics. It is logical now to ask what is the eventual goal of our journey—what might feminist, multicultural physics look like? This vision may be many generations away, but it is good to have an idea where we are going.

In an ideal future, reforms based on feminist philosophy, multicultural critiques, science education, and computer networking have combined. The science community is now much larger than before; in addition to Nobel laureates in established research programs, it includes graduate students, K-16 students, and laypersons pursuing their own studies and questions. The lines between scientific disciplines are blurred in this future, and the distinction between science and non-science is much less clear. It is often possible to readily identify a person and say "This is a Scientist!" but it almost impossible to find someone who is not now, or has never been, engaged in scientific inquiry. Science is well respected, and there are few science phobes in this best of all possible worlds.

The public has a healthy understanding of the fundamental paradigms of science, its methods, and its history. Most have retained their childhood sense of curiosity and wonder about the natural world. An informed and skeptical public sometimes makes it harder to fund large-scale scientific endeavors, but when commitments are made the projects are carried out, regardless of the cost and time involved. Normally these large-scale projects are believed to be necessary for the health and well-being of humanity or our world. Sometimes, though, projects are approved that will help answer key questions about what used to be called pure science. Smaller amounts of money for small-scale projects tend to be readily available.

But how do we get there? What can we do today? Unfortunately, the answer right now is "Do your best to hold on." The hard-won social and educational innovations of the past few decades are under fire. Continued change will require the participation of people inside and outside the scientific community.

If you are not a scientist, you can contribute by educating yourself about science and science policy, by refusing to be intimidated by the jargon of scientific "experts," and by talking to your scientist friends about their work and their attitudes about science. If you are a practicing scientist, you can organize your research group along less hierarchical lines and begin to think about your work in its social context. You can learn about feminist and multicultural critiques of science and join that discussion. And you can talk to your nonscientist friends about their attitudes toward science. If you are a student, you can treat other students as allies in learning rather than as competitors. You can believe that your questions are as valid as those of others, and you can give free rein to your curiosity. If necessary, you can go beyond the classroom to discover the history and context of the science.

Feminism and multicultural critiques will continue to reshape our practice as researchers and teachers. But possibly the most important contribution of feminist philosophers has been to remind us that our hallmark as physicists is not the objectivity we bring to our field but rather our passion for understanding and our delight in the wonder of the universe. It is good to be out in the open.

BIBLIOGRAPHY

Barad, Karen. "Feminism and the Social Construction of Scientific Knowledge." In Lynn Hankinson Nelson and Jack Nelson (Eds.), *Feminism, Science, and the Philosophy of Science* (pp. 161-194). Dordrecht, Netherlands: Kluver, 1996.

Freeman, Gordon. Letter. *Physics and Society: Newsletter of the American Physical Society Forum on Physics and Society* 25(1) (1996): 4.

Keller, Evelyn Fox. *Reflections on Gender and Science.* New Haven, CT: Yale University Press, 1985.

Laws, Priscilla. "Calculus-Based Physics without Lectures." *Physics Today* (December 1991): 24-31.

McDermott, Lillian C. "Millikan Lecture 1990: What We Teach and What Is Learned—Closing the Gap." *American Journal of Physics* 59(4) (1991): 301-315.

National Science Foundation. *Women, Minorities, and Persons with Disabilities in Science and Engineering.* NSF Report #NSF-94-333. November 1994.

Project Kaleidoscope. *What Works: Building Natural Science Communities.* Washington, DC: Project Kaleidoscope, 1991.

Rosser, Sue V. *Female-Friendly Science: Applying Women's Studies Methods and Theories to Attract Students.* New York: Pergamon, 1990.

Rossiter, Margaret. *Women Scientists in America: Struggles and Strategies to 1940.* Baltimore, MD: Johns Hopkins University Press, 1982.

Traweek, Sharon. *Beamtimes and Lifetimes: The World of High Energy Physicists.* Cambridge, MA: Harvard University Press, 1988.

Chapter 19

Science and Feminism: Partners or Rivals?

Gwyneth Hughes

This essay gives an overview of the uneasy relationship between feminism and science that has evolved over the past two decades. I shall explain that although women's studies has helped to put the contributions of women scientists on the map, more fundamental challenges to science have had less of an impact. Women first began to look more closely at gender and biology in the 1980s following the work of the women's health movement that criticized medical experimentation on women's bodies and the poor treatment women often experienced. More recent interest has focused on computers and information and communication technologies with a determination that women will not be left behind in new virtual worlds. As well as drawing from these areas, I have chosen to draw from examples in chemistry to assess how far feminist ideas have impregnated the world of scientists because chemistry is rarely mentioned in women's studies. I shall argue that the sometimes hostile dialogue between science and feminism has meant that transformation of science and its subdisciplines has begun, but there is still a long way to go. Mainstream science now acknowledges the contributions of once-obscured women in science, but physical science in particular has not taken this further to include the much more sophisticated analyses of science produced in women's studies. This essay has been informed by many years of teaching and researching in science and an assimilation of a range of feminist viewpoints, and I hope this will provide a forum for continued discussion of some of the points I raise. Throughout the account, I shall consider science mainly as presented in education, but will also refer to science in an industrial and global context.

The idea that women have a contribution to make to the world of science and technology is not a new one; recent histories of science show that women have participated in scientific enterprises from antiquity until the present day. Feminist historians have collected evidence that women throughout the world have for centuries been healers, midwives, and herbalists, and women's contributions to Western mathematics, astronomy, and chemistry are moderately well documented. For instance, the name Lavoisier, associated with achievements in chemistry such as the naming of oxygen, represents the work of both Marie and Antoine Lavoisier. It is not possible to separate the contributions made by each member of this husband and wife team, although it is the male partner, Antoine, who is usually given full credit. Although this example is not yet widely known, biographies of women scientists such as Rosalind Franklin, whose work on a proposed DNA structure has now been acknowledged, or Rachel Carson, the renowned ecologist and author of *Silent Spring,* are beginning to enter the mainstream.

Much of this effort to uncover the lives and contributions of famous women scientists from the past has taken place only recently and there is now, at least in feminist circles, understanding of how such contributions became lost as historians left women's names out of their accounts, or did not credit women's activities as scientific. There is also some recognition now that the historical evidence we have documents the lives of the educated and wealthy, and does not acknowledge the inestimable contributions to science made by those in far less privileged positions.

Over the past two decades, equality campaigners have also studied the position of women in science in some detail. As well as rewriting sections of the history of science from a feminist perspective, they have focused on the gender imbalance in numbers of persons working in, or studying, sciences today. Concern over women's dropout rate in science education and careers, particularly in physical sciences, engineering, and technology has led to a range of responses from employers and educationalists in an attempt to achieve greater equality. These include revising of teaching methods and resource materials to encompass what is considered to be a more female-friendly approach, and improving career advice and support for women scientists. However, while a range of equality campaigns such as Women into Science and Engineering (WISE) in the UK have been instrumental in promoting science, technological, and engineering careers for young women, the physical and applied sciences continue to be male-dominated areas in many parts of the world.

Although in some areas the numbers of males and females in science are approximating parity, much still needs to be done; feminists and other critics have examined how science itself might be gendered. Critics of science and related technologies point out that science is directed and funded by military or capitalist concerns that do not support most women's interests, or the interests of humanity as a whole. Environmentalists and eco-feminists have documented the damage to the environment arising from shortsighted technological developments that place life on the planet at a very low priority compared to wealth and power. Arguments used to challenge contemporary science are often linked to gender, with the destructive, exploitative aspects associated with a masculine science contrasting with a more feminine, caring, and in-harmony-with-nature approach taken by some feminists and environmentalists. Historically, science evolved with a fundamental belief in symbolically masculine rationality and control over a symbolically feminine natural world. The predominant masculine side of science and technology is now exemplified by military developments such as the atom bomb while the feminine side has been associated with social and environmental concerns. However, it is not only feminists who advocate such views on science; indigenous people in countries such as Australia uphold an environment-centered approach and associate destructive aspects of science with Western imperialism. So it is problematic to reduce a critique of science to gender polarities without acknowledgement of these parallel and overlapping views.

Despite these criticisms, the above work does represent a shift from appropriating gender simply as representing two categories, male and female, to attempting to understand gender as a collection of complex, all-pervasive, culturally constructed phenomena that shape our understanding of what science is. But debate on the relationship between gender and science has been dismissed by those who continue to claim that science itself is neutral and it is only the uses or abuses of technological application of science that involve social or political factors.

The gender analysis of science outlined above has developed alongside a related accusation that scientific research, particularly in biology and medicine, is gender-biased. This has included the uncovering of medical trials that have tested drugs on males and then generalized the results as being applicable to both males and females without taking possible different responses into account. Critics, encouraged by a now well-established women's health movement, have challenged Western medicine's accounts of women's biology with its pathologizing of the female body and overemphasis on hormonal problems. Debates have emerged over whether these are examples of bias in science that can be eliminated if proper scientific procedures are adhered to, or whether these are inevitable symptoms of a deeper, more sinister nature of science as a product of a dominant masculine or patriarchal culture. Science, in this case, is a political tool fashioned by the most powerful for exploitation and control of women's bodies. A group of international feminists, FINRRAGE (Feminist International Network of Resistance to Reproductive and Genetic Engineering), has used this argument to oppose development and use of reproductive technologies such as surrogacy and in-vitro fertilization. They argue that such practices offer few opportunities for poor women from the West and the developing world who experience fertility control on the one hand or exploitation in surrogacy cases on the other. This view that science reflects culture and all of its inequalities parallels fundamental challenges to the status of so-called scientific knowledge that have emerged over the past decades. Philosophers and sociologists of scientific knowledge propose that science is more of a fiction created by humans, closer to a story or a novel than a true account of the natural world. This story is told by the most powerful to maintain the status quo and is therefore difficult to oppose.

It is not surprising, then, that most of these debates on connections between gender and science do not circulate in the mainstream of science or science education except perhaps in very limited forms that are not too challenging. There is even hostility to some of the ideas suggested, particularly those that link science with sociology and politics.

The initial aims of equality campaigners to increase the numbers of women in science, engineering, and technology to achieve gender parity have achieved mainstream status, and this is now a widely recognized issue, even if gestures to take action may be mere tokens and equality still seems a long way off. As I indicated earlier, in both industry and education, action programs to encourage more women into scientific fields are well established, and physical sciences and engineering are promoted as suitable careers for women. Feminist work on rewriting the history of science has been noticed; in schools the names of female scientists such as Rosalind Franklin are slipped into the curriculum. Nevertheless, although this work continues with partial success, little examination is made of the nature of the science in progress. So science curricula, particularly in the physical sciences, have not changed significantly to accommodate women's perspectives of science.

This is certainly the case in chemistry. Chemistry is widely perceived as the study of the transformation of chemical substances into new ones with large-scale industrial applications in pharmaceuticals, petrochemicals, and the synthesis of a range of chemical compounds from fertilizers to household detergents. The study of chemistry tends, by most accounts, to emphasize understanding chemical processes at the molecular and atomic levels with little attention paid to the wider political, environmental, and social implications of these processes. Nor is there any consideration of how chemical ideas might be a product of our contemporary culture rather than a true explanation of the natural world. For instance, the very language used in chemistry is steeped in masculine war-like imagery: species *attacking* molecules, molecular *bombardment.* Realizing this, it is a small step then to question whether all chemical concepts must inevitably reflect the cultural values of the persons who constructed them. However, a perpetuation of the myth that sciences such as chemistry are somehow immune from culture means such issues are rarely, if ever, discussed by chemists. Women's studies as a discipline emphasizing the pervasiveness of gender into all aspects of humanity has much to offer science, but at present is not being taken seriously enough. Unfortunately, there are those who are content with the status of their discipline and do not feel that they need to listen to other voices, particularly from women.

In biological sciences, particularly in the areas of health, medicine, and the environment, there has been more progress. It is difficult, if not impossible, to separate contributions by feminists from those of socialists, environmentalists, anti-racists, or ethicists but, nevertheless, the long-established tradition of feminist work in the field of biology means it has closer links to the environment and social and political worlds than do the physical sciences. For example, eco-feminists have drawn parallels between gender exploitation and environmental damage and have raised ethical issues. Questions surrounding medical ethics, biotechnology, and genetics as well as environmental protection are now frequently raised in both education and politics and it is no longer assumed that the public does not need to understand science and technology. Bodies such as the AAAS (American Association for the Advancement of Science) and PUS (Public Understanding of Science) in the UK encourage contemporary debate, even if on scientists' own terms. In addition, the inferior status of women has been compared to the inferior status of animals, meaning that questions of gender may well be relevant for contemporary arguments over the uses of animals in laboratory experiments. However, in many of these and other areas, the aims of some feminists, and those of scientists in medicine or industry and their supporters, may be directly opposed, such as in the areas of new reproductive technologies (NRTs). Here complex debates have arisen between those who argue for choice, and therefore support technological developments in fertility treatment, and feminists, who see the context of NRTs as motivated by profit and patriarchal control over women's reproduction.

Chemistry also touches on environmental areas that have human consequences, for example, in monitoring the release of chloro-fluoro-carbons (CFCs) and the ozone-depletion situation. Here it would seem difficult not to bring in the industrial and political complexity resulting from global CFC bans, CFC substitutes, and so on. But the scientist frequently sees his or her role as providing the technical solutions to technical problems rather than social and political solutions to social problems. Thus, while the chemist looks for ozone-friendly substitutes, questions of who profits from these, and the unequal distribution of resources between the West and the developing world, are conveniently left off the agenda. There is much potential for science education and public debate to include more consideration of these topics and once more a feminist perspective could be very important, but as yet this potential is underrealized.

I have indicated that social and political context is not generally something that receives the attention of physical scientists, and this highlights another gender dimension to science for our consideration. Bringing in the human is a complex and messy business, with problems of ethics and environmental protection breaking up the smooth maintenance of detached masculine rationality. It is rationality and objectivity that supposedly gives science its special status in relation to other "softer" disciplines, such as humanities. Those working in scientific fields may not be prepared to relinquish their elevated position. It therefore seems quite likely that in physical and applied sciences, resistance to change and desires to protect masculine strongholds may well be fiercer. Thus, it is not difficult to understand why contributions made by feminists to debates on science and some of its social and political connections are at best deemed irrelevant and at worst greeted with derision. While concern for numbers of women scientists including chemists is now on the agenda, and attempts are being made to dispel the man-in-a-white-coat image of chemistry, there seems to be little evidence of a revaluation of the nature of chemistry as a discipline in terms of gender. The study of gender and the study of chemistry seem worlds apart.

The partnership between women's studies and mainstream science seems superficial, but once explored in any depth, uneasiness and potential rivalry arises. In physical sciences, this partnership has barely reached the first date! Feminists have made fundamental contributions to the social studies of science and technology, but scientists have largely ignored these contributions. In biology, where social questions have been less easily brushed under the carpet, there does seem to be some influence by feminists and other groups, particularly in the areas of women's health and environmental awareness, but the physical sciences continue to operate at the abstract level. Scientific knowledge is kept apart from the social and political concerns so that there is little room for feminist critiques of the more patriarchal and destructive aspects of science. But this artificial boundary set up between the abstract and the social becomes ever more difficult to maintain as resistant groups, including feminists, come knocking at the door of a reductionistic, socially detached science, and demand to be let in and heard. Meanwhile, there are growing numbers of people who wonder how much longer the door to this masculine fortress can remain locked.

BIBLIOGRAPHY

Alic, Margaret. *Hypatia's Heritage: A History of Women in Science from Antiquity to the Late Nineteenth Century*. London: Women's Press, 1986.

Birke, Lynda. *Feminism, Animals, and Science: The Naming of the Shrew*. Milton Keynes, UK: Open University Press, 1994.

Bleier, Ruth (Ed.). *Feminist Approaches to Science*. Oxford, UK: Pergamon, 1988.

Harding, Sandra. *Whose Science? Whose Knowledge?: Thinking from Women's Lives*. Milton Keynes, UK: Open University Press, 1991.

McNeil, Maureen (Ed.). *Gender and Expertise*. London: Free Association Books, 1987.

Rose, Hilary. *Love, Power, and Knowledge: Towards a Feminist Transformation of the Sciences*. Cambridge, UK: Polity Press, 1994.

Tuana, Nancy (Ed.). *Feminism and Science*. Bloomington: Indiana University Press, 1989.

Wajcman, Judy. *Feminism Confronts Technology*. Cambridge, UK: Polity Press, 1991.

Chapter 20

Mathematics: A Dilemma for Feminists

Julianne Lynch
Gilah C. Leder
Helen J. Forgasz

Usually when asked the question "Are you good at math?" or "Did you get a good grade in math?" you are not being asked about an ability or knowledge that is accessible to and used by all. Rather than the mathematics we all practice in everyday life, these questions refer to a mathematics with a capital M, a mathematics that is *found* in textbooks, classified into topics, and examined in schools. This version of mathematics, the type that is available through a formal education, has acquired an international status and value beyond its usefulness purely as mathematics. The question "Did you get a good grade in math?" is primarily a query into an individual's status. *Carrying* a "good grade" in mathematics is comparable to carrying a form of currency, in that it gives you power to do things, such as enrolling in certain university courses and pursuing certain careers, that those without it do not have.

Formal mathematics learning is currently the route to many high-paying, high status occupations, such as engineering and other science- and computer-related occupations. In many cultures, success in mathematics is associated with intelligence and ability in other areas and is used to screen students for nonmathematical higher education courses. Consequently, individuals who discontinue their mathematical studies are cut off from a significant number of educational and occupational options and the financial independence and prestige that comes with them.

Inequities in mathematics education tend to mirror the gender and cultural inequities in society and education in general. Internationally, mathematics and related occupations have been identified as male domains. Statistics in the United States (Bureau of the Census, 1997) and elsewhere reveal that women and minorities are underrepresented in the most advanced mathematics courses and in related professions. Even at the high school level, the most demanding mathematics subjects are more likely to be taken by males. In industrialized countries, these trends persist despite the removal of formal barriers preventing women from pursuing an education in mathematics. As a rule, these patterns are exaggerated in less-developed countries (Graham-Brown, 1991).

Occupations that use or require mathematical aptitude, such as engineering or astronomy, were traditionally considered male pursuits. Until the 1970s, in Australia and other developed countries many subjects at the high school level were explicitly targeted at either girls or boys. This is most obvious for subjects such as sewing and metal work; however, timetabling was often such that girls were forced to choose between mathematics and subjects that seemed more appropriate and more able to provide them with financial independence, such as secretarial skills. This is only one example of the many barriers to mathematics education that arose from a combination of formal and attitudinal structures.

Although most of the formal barriers have now been removed as a response to legislation, vestiges of "attitude" remain. Attitudes and expectations of parents, teachers, peers, and students themselves may still lead to students choosing traditionally sex-typed subjects and the career paths seen as being appropriate for them, without considering other options. Furthermore, it has been reported that those individuals who do choose to follow a path traditionally appropriate for the other sex still encounter obstacles, such as peer pressure and parental suspicion, because of their choices (Milligan, Thomson, and Ashendon, 1992).

Stereotyped attitudes toward gender and mathematics are best understood with reference to the history of mathematics and education.

Traditionally, mathematics was formally studied by men only. The great figures in the field were all men: Euclid, Descartes, Euler, Newton, Leibniz. The problems to which mathematics was applied, such as those concerning laws of the physical world, were considered men's business. However, in North America in the 1970s, feminist educators and historians began to investigate the previously unacknowledged contributions of women to various fields. As a result, the lives of a few exceptional women, often the wives and daughters of notable men, were documented and their contributions, against all odds, to the field of mathematics supplemented the main (male) story of the development of mathematics. These women included Hypatia, Mary Somerville, Louise Hay, and Linda Rothschild.

One commonly cited example of a woman mathematician is Sophie Germain (Perl, 1978). Germain, born in 1776 in Paris, was the daughter of a wealthy merchant. She was self-taught, using books from her father's library. Her family did all they could to discourage this inappropriate pursuit, going so far as depriving her of heat and light at night so she could not study. At the age of eighteen, she obtained lecture notes for several courses at L'Ecole Polytechnique by taking a male pseudonym. Using this name, she submitted an end-of-term paper that so impressed the professor (Lagrange) that he wanted to meet with her. This was her informal introduction to the all-male circle of prominent mathematicians of the day.

This focus on exceptional women mathematicians has since been criticized because it paints a picture of a mathematics that is accessible only to women who are in some way unique, gifted, or privileged and who suffer hardship or sacrifice other aspects of their lives to pursue mathematical studies. By the early 1980s, in North America, Britain, and Australia, the weaknesses of focusing solely on exceptional women were realized and moves were made to promote mathematics to women as something useful and accessible to all, rather than to the exceptional few. At this time, the liberal movement was having an influence on many areas of social justice in developed countries through the promotion of individual rights, particularly the right to education. This understanding, married with the belief that mathematics education was a desirable pursuit, led to the premise that equality in education is reflected in the participation of representative proportions of different demographic groups. In other words, in an equitable society, the same number of women and men would study mathematics at all levels, as would proportionate numbers of minorities. This liberal understanding of a just society provided much of the stimulus for the directions taken by women's liberation movements and has been dubbed by some as the first wave or generation of feminism. It was a time when women sought equality with men in terms of equivalent participation in all realms of society.

Most gender-oriented research into mathematics education during this period, continuing to the present, focused on determining the differences between females and males in participation rates and learning outcomes. Intervention programs addressed these differences by aiming to bring girls up to the same level as boys. For example, *Multiplying Options & Subtracting Bias* (Fennema, Becker, Wolleat, and Pedro, 1980), a U.S. government-funded series of workshops and videos, was designed to achieve increased participation by females in math. Statements such as, "Until females recognize the importance of studying mathematics to keep career and life options open, mathematics education equity will not exist" (preface, p. ix) and "It seems that women who have hit stumbling blocks while learning mathematics have been reluctant to remove them, leading to a pattern of avoidance that has been hard to shake" (p. 16) point to the focus of this program on raising females' awareness of the importance of mathematics and its connection to other life choices.

This approach to mathematics educational reform has since been criticized by feminist educators because it assumes a male norm and identifies women and girls as being deficient. References made in government documents, such as " . . . we suggest a number of strategies which we believe may contribute to improvement in the mathematical performance of girls" (Cockroft, 1982, p. 64) implied that females were lacking. They unquestioningly assume that mathematics, and the way it is taught in schools, is appropriate for girls and that, if girls would only overcome their incorrect beliefs about and fear of mathematics and realize what harm is incurred by avoiding it, they too could be successful.

Many of the intervention projects that are in place today can be criticized as reinforcing the belief that girls have difficulty with mathematics. These interventions do not recognize the possibility that girls and women make informed decisions not to continue with mathematics because they prefer other subjects and see them as more welcoming and more relevant to their long-term plans (Noddings, 1998). Feminist researchers have challenged the assumption that all women and men have similar learning characteristics and should strive for similar educational goals.

Theorists (Rogers and Kaiser, 1995) argue that we are currently in a transition between perceiving women as needing to change in order to reap the benefits of mathematics education and perceiving mathematics education and mathematics itself as having developed within a monoculture (white, middle-class, male) that does not address the lives, experiences, and preferred learning styles of women and other groups. Practices consistent with the latter understanding have not yet found their way into mainstream curricula and classrooms. An example of an intervention program that acknowledges the dangers of emphasizing a lack in females and promoting a male norm as desirable for all is a North American program called SummerMath (Morrow and Morrow, 1995).

SummerMath is a three-week residential program that aims to create a learning community in which young women are encouraged to take control of their learning in a cooperative, supportive environment where people and their individual understandings are valued as the source of mathematical learning. This approach links two ideas about how we learn: first, by building on our own experiences and ways of understanding, and second, by communicating these ways of understanding and by connecting with others. This program is delivered in a single-sex setting outside of the more competitive and hierarchical environment of mainstream mathematics classrooms, an environment that has been found to alienate and disempower many female students.

When equality in mathematics education is approached with a focus on women, rather than on the mathematics that men do, as it is in the SummerMath program, we no longer argue that females need help so they can better participate in mathematics education. Instead, we argue that traditional mathematics, the way it is taught and the way it is assessed, needs to change. Gender-oriented research in mathematics education challenges the meek acceptance of the male norm, identifying this norm as being culturally and historically determined, established at a time when women were excluded from mathematics education.

When we recognize that mathematics and modes of instruction and assessment are culturally specific practices, we are better able to understand why some individuals and cultural groups do not experience success in traditional mathematics classrooms. The tendency for particular groups to discontinue mathematics education is better understood by looking to the cultural practices and knowledge of the particular group than by focusing on the poor performance of the group in traditional mathematics education. By valuing other ways of teaching and learning, and the strengths of others' mathematical knowledge, we can better accommodate women and other groups. However, this approach needs to be applied in an inclusive manner to avoid essentialism, or the risk that formulations and interventions aiming to value *female* characteristics will present these characteristics as innate in women and, therefore, alienate those women who do not have them. This approach also risks perpetuating traditional gender stereotypes without necessarily elevating images of women in mathematics to a position equal to that of men in mathematics.

Indeed, the characteristics of learning environments, such as that created at the SummerMath program, are not characteristics that benefit women only. Ideally, mathematics education would be reconstructed to include us all, regardless of ethnicity, class, age, gender, or other social demarcations, by being more flexible, inclusive, and affirming. By making the link between mathematics and what we do in everyday life explicit, we make the transition from a fear or an awe of mathematics to a confidence in our own ways of learning, a respect of others' ways of learning, and an ownership and sharing of our own mathematical knowledge.

Both the field of mathematics and the mathematics classroom will benefit from more pluralistic approaches that speak to women and other groups, and from more inclusive classroom relationships and interactions in which competition and authority are tempered by affirmation and caring. Although these ideas have not yet permeated mainstream mathematics education practice, theorists in this area have begun to acknowledge the value of different ways of knowing and doing and the harm that has been done in the past, both to individuals and to larger societies, by denying diversity. These new ways of approaching mathematics education have the potential to transform and enhance learning, not just for women and girls, but for all students.

BIBLIOGRAPHY

Bureau of the Census. *Statistical Abstract of the United States.* Washington, DC: Bureau of the Census, 1997.

Cockroft, Wilfred. *Mathematics Counts.* London: Her Majesty's Stationary Office (HMSO), 1982.

Fennema, Elizabeth, Ann DeVaney Becker, Patricia Wolleat, and Joan Daniels Pedro. *Multiplying Options and Subtracting Bias.* Published with a grant from the U.S. Department of Health, Education, and Welfare, Office of Education. Madison, WI: University of Wisconsin. 1980.

Graham Brown, Sarah. *Education in the Developing World.* New York: Longman Publishing, 1991.

Milligan, Sandra, Karen Thomson, and Ashendon & Associates. *Listening to Girls.* Australia: Australian Education Council, 1992.

Morrow, Charlene and James Morrow. "Connecting Women with Mathematics." In Gabrielle Kaiser and Patricia Rogers (Eds.), *Equity in Mathematics Education: Influences of Feminism and Culture* (pp. 13-26) London: Farmer Press, 1995.

Noddings, Nel. "Perspectives from Feminist Philosophy." *Educational Researcher* 27(5) (June/July, 1998): 17.

Perl, Teri. *Math Equals: Biographies of Women Mathematicians + Related Activities.* Menlo Park, CA: Addison-Wesley, 1978.

Rogers, Patricia and Gabrielle Kaiser (Eds.). *Equity in Mathematics Education: Influences of Feminism and Culture.* London: Farmer Press, 1995.

FURTHER READING

Burton, Leone (Ed.). *Gender and Mathematics: An International Perspective.* London: Cassell Educational, 1990.

This collection provides insights into questions that are relevant to different cultures.

Chipman, Susan, Lorelei Brush, and Donna Wilson (Eds.). *Women and Mathematics: Balancing the Equation.* Hillsdale, NJ: Lawrence Erlbaum, 1985.

This is an earlier collection of research articles, focusing on gender issues and mathematics learning.

Fennema, Elizabeth and Gilah C. Leder (Eds.). *Mathematics & Gender.* St. Lucia, Queensland, Australia: University of Queensland Press, 1993.

This collection of chapters from both Australia and the United States are of interest to both research and classroom practice.

Forgasz, H. J. (Ed.). Special issue. "Gender and Learning Settings." *Mathematics Education Research Journal* 9(3) (1997).

A range of issues are explored including: single-sex learning settings, adult vocational education, encouraging women into engineering courses, "ways of knowing" mathematics, and the interaction of gender and ethnicity.

________. *Society and Gender Equity in Mathematics Education.* Geelong, Victoria, Australia: Deakin University Press, 1994.

This book explores the links between the development of equity issues in society and those in mathematics education for women.

Grevholm, Barbro and Gila Hanna (Eds.). *Gender and Mathematics Education.* Lund, Sweden: Lund University Press, 1993.

These are the proceedings of a special study held under the auspices of the International Commission on Mathematical Instruction in Höör, Sweden, 1993.

Leder, Gilah (Ed.). Special Issue. "Mathematics and Gender." *Educational Studies in Mathematics: An International Journal* 28(3) (1995): 195-333.

The papers in this special issue reflect a diversity of approaches to addressing issues concerned with gender and mathematics learning.

Leder, Gilah C., Helen J. Forgasz, and Claudie Solar. "Research and Intervention Programs in Mathematics Education: A Gendered Issue." In Alan J. Bishop, Ken Clements, Christine Keitel, Jeremy Kilpatrick, and Colette Laborde (Eds.), *International Handbook of Mathematics Education* (pp. 945-986). Dordrecht, The Netherlands: Kluwer Academic, 1996.

This chapter offers an international perspective on gender issues and mathematics education.

Morrow, Charlene and Teri Perl (Eds.). *Notable Women in Mathematics: A Biographical Dictionary.* Westport, CT: Greenwood, 1998.

This dictionary of 59 women who have left their mark in mathematics includes both contemporary and historical figures.

Rogers, Patricia and Gabrielle Kaiser (Eds.). *Equity in Mathematics Education: Influences of Feminism and Culture.* London: Falmer Press, 1995.

Many of the chapters in this book arose out of sessions organized for the International Organization for Women and Mathematics Education as part of the Seventh International Congress on Mathematical Education, held in Québec City, Canada, in 1992.

Secada, Walter, Elizabeth Fennema, and Lisa Adajian (Eds.). *New Directions for Equity in Mathematics Education.* Cambridge, UK: Cambridge University Press, 1995.

This book explores equity issues. The second part focuses on feminism and mathematics.

Taylor, L. (Ed.). "Gender and Mathematics: Multiple Voices." *Focus on Learning Problems in Mathematics* 18 (Special issue) (1996): 1-3.

Articles cover a range of themes: developing mathematical voiçe and connections, individual development, feminist perspectives on gender issues, gender differences, and gender equity programs.

Chapter 21

History of Women in Science and Technology

Amy Sue Bix

Scientists and engineers have, naturally enough, often been intrigued by the historical origins of their professions. Over recent decades, history of science and technology has become established as an important academic discipline, enjoying rapid growth and scholarly recognition. Early studies commonly centered on the lives and work of such famous individuals as Galileo, Isaac Newton, Charles Darwin, and Thomas Edison. Since the 1970s, an increasing number of historians have branched out from "great men and their ideas" to explore new intellectual directions. Science and technology, after all, do not evolve in a vacuum. Researchers have linked the history of science and technology to other disciplines, including social history, economic history, labor history, popular culture, and notably, women's history. Although intellectual history and the study of prominent men should by no means be discarded, adding extra dimensions has transformed history of science into a richer, more complete narrative. Once researchers broaden their focus to include gender issues, new questions suddenly leap to the forefront.

As an instance, Ruth Schwartz Cowan transformed history of technology with her 1979 essay, "From Virginia Dare to Virginia Slims: Women and Technology in American Life." Scholars needed to reach beyond familiar studies of steam engines, automobiles, and airplanes, Cowan suggested, to examine "uniquely female technologies" such as household appliances. Early twentieth-century manufacturers promised that electric refrigerators and washing machines would give housewives hours of free time. Such leisure failed to materialize; as Cowan explained, new technologies actually brought "more work for mother" (1983). Modernization increased expectations; cars created the job of family chauffeur, and Americans began automatically throwing clothes into the laundry after a single wearing. The history of home technology thus ties in with broader perspectives on family life, advertising, and economics.

When I challenge students (or virtually any group) to name a female scientist or engineer, most people promptly think of Marie Curie and then get stuck. In reality, through the centuries, many, many more women have contributed to the realm of knowledge and deserve to be remembered. True, the early history of women's intellectual achievements is complicated by uncertainty. The life of philosopher-mathematician Hypatia of Alexandria, who lived around 400 A.D., has been entangled in mythology about her supposed beauty and martyrdom. Much evidence has simply disappeared over time; although we know that women participated in the philosophical schools of Pythagoras and Socrates, their writings have been lost.

Once we move into later periods of European civilization, women's participation in scientific life becomes undeniably significant. In the 1700s, the Marquise Emilie du Chatelet first translated Isaac Newton's *Principia Mathematica* into French, promoting acceptance of the new physical theory by adding her own notes to help readers follow difficult arguments. Another Frenchwoman of that period, Sophie Germain, taught herself mathematics despite her parents' objections and proceeded to work on both pure and applied problems, including Fermat's last theorem. In Italy, Laura Bassi taught anatomy, mechanics, and experimental physics at the University of Bologna.

A lingering suspicion that advanced formal education was inappropriate or unnecessary for females made life difficult for many intelligent women. Scientific societies often hesitated to recognize women's discoveries; physics and other disciplines took root in all-male universities. Social obligations and family demands ate up women's time, further hindering their access to knowledge. Research required leisure, space, money for books, and equipment. Caroline Herschel began astronomical work in the 1770s as an assistant to her brother William, helping him make telescopes and record observations, all the while struggling to make time for her own research. Eventually, Caroline was credited with identifying eight new comets and honored as a talented astronomer in her own right.

The twentieth century brings still more numerous examples of women who made a difference in science. Of course, Marie Curie deserves to head the list. Her explorations of radioactivity earned her Nobel Prizes in two different disciplines (physics in 1903 with husband Pierre, chemistry in 1911 independently). Crystallographer Rosalind Franklin played a major role in discovery of DNA's double helical structure, and marine biologist Rachel Carson aroused public environmental awareness with her 1962 book, *Silent Spring,* criticizing pesticide overuse. Barbara McClintock startled the scientific community in the 1950s by announcing experiments that showed genes shifting position between generations. As Evelyn Fox Keller (1983) has noted, McClintock's colleagues found such an idea too radical to accept until other investigators confirmed her "jumping gene" theories, bringing McClintock a Nobel Prize in 1982.

In one case, female researchers reshaped an entire field, primatology. Jane Goodall's work with chimpanzees, Dian Fossey's with gorillas, and Birute Galdikas' with orangutans changed both scientific methodology and fundamental notions of primate behavior. Instead of chasing animals through the woods, these women began living closely with a population to discern individuals' behavior patterns over long periods. Critics dismissed this approach as female sentimentality, but results proved too astounding to ignore. Goodall witnessed chimps using twigs to pry insects from cracks, revolutionizing ideas about tool use in nonhuman species. The three women also became involved with wildlife conservation and served as role models, encouraging other women to take up science.

The list of female scientists and engineers whose work deserves recognition includes Lise Meitner, Lillian Gilbreth, Irene Joliot-Curie, and many others. Beyond "big names," historians have begun to demonstrate how many women of lesser fame also participated in scientific activity over the centuries. The 1600s and 1700s have been called the age of the "scientific lady," when an amateur interest in science became fashionable among upper-class women. Fancy telescopes became popular accessories, while books such as *The Ladies'*

Diary and Jane Marcet's *Conversations on Chemistry,* brought math, astronomy, and physics to a female audience.

Finding women in the history of science and technology is often a matter of simply knowing where to look. A search for female students or professors at Yale or Princeton in the 1800s will get you nowhere. American women instead found opportunities at Oberlin, at state land-grant colleges such as Cornell, Wisconsin, and Michigan, and especially at the "Seven Sisters." Wellesley's founder encouraged the establishment of a science curriculum, building what was then only the second student physics laboratory in the entire country. Maria Mitchell headed Vassar's observatory and almost single-handedly trained a generation of women astronomers, while Florence Bascom did the same in geology at Bryn Mawr.

Women found certain niches in science, especially in new subfields where research just underway remained relatively open to female investigators. In the late 1800s, about half the students and researchers at the Woods Hole (Massachusetts) Marine Biological Laboratory were female. In the early 1900s, leading figures in crystallography expressed a willingness to accept female students, drawing women into that area (which then was criticized as too female-dominated and disparaged as "intellectual knitting").

In other instances, women carved out their own space. In the 1870s, when Vassar graduate Ellen Swallow wished to continue her study of chemistry, MIT admitted her on condition she work in a separate lab from men. Her interest in applied research helped establish a new profession of "domestic science," blending chemistry, biology, engineering, and economics. Many high schools and colleges soon set up home economics courses and began conducting fruitful research on nutrition, family management, and household technology. Such programs allowed graduates to secure good jobs in institutional management, corporate research and development, or academia. At the same time, home economics amounted to a separate "women's curriculum"; female students who expressed an interest in pure science might be channeled into this "more appropriate" area.

Such instances highlight an important point made by Margaret Rossiter (1982). Even when women won the right to pursue degrees in science, the battle was not over; graduates still faced the challenge of locating employment in a system stacked against them. During the late 1800s and early 1900s, many ended up performing what Rossiter called "women's work" in science, subordinate, tedious, and low-wage jobs such as cataloging museum collections. At the Harvard Observatory, director Edward Pickering hired a number of women to analyze star photographs and perform complex calculations; these skilled female "computers" (as they were known) have been referred to as "Pickering's harem"!

Women found it difficult to overturn that professional marginalization before World War II. The wartime manpower shortage temporarily opened positions for female scientists in universities and on military projects (including development of computers and the atom bomb). With peacetime, that window of opportunity closed, again pushing women aside. For years, university antinepotism rules prevented physicist Maria Geoppert-Mayer (who went on to win a Nobel Prize in 1963) from being hired for a proper academic job.

Although it would be nice to suppose that such discrimination is safely confined to the past, analysis of women's current status in science and engineering raises doubts. Through the 1980s, many female scientists and engineers were still underpaid, underemployed, and marginalized. Episodes of discouragement and classroom bias continue, though often in more subtle forms than before. Too many girls who start off performing well in science and math "drop out of the pipeline," losing confidence in their ability as they move through the educational system.

To correct that, numerous individuals, schools, and organizations (including the American Association for the Advancement of Science and the National Science Foundation) have recently undertaken special efforts to encourage girls to pursue science and engineering. The Girl Scouts have introduced badges rewarding achievement in computer literacy and environmental study. Many colleges have designed mentoring programs, matching female science and engineering majors with "role model" professors or professionals. Although valuable, such efforts offer no panacea. The female share of scientific and technical degrees jumped impressively after the 1960s, but these professional gains have more recently started to level off, leaving women significantly underrepresented.

Some feminists have taken this analysis a step further, raising questions about the very nature of modern science and technology. While practitioners may idealize the "scientific method" as the ultimate means of getting at truth, some skeptics have questioned whether real-world science proves so perfectly neutral. Objectivity, feminist critics suggest, can be complicated by the politics of science and by assumptions about gender. Over the centuries that women have worked to find places in science, their sex has simultaneously made them objects of scientific study. "Expert" pronouncements on female physiology, psychology, and socialization provided authority to dictate a woman's "proper" social role. Back in ancient Greece, Aristotle's writings decreed that active and rational males were inherently superior to passive, emotional females. His writing referred to man as the ideal human form, to woman as a lesser-developed, "mutilated male." The idea of females as a biological "monstrosity" remained authoritative through much medieval thought. As Anne Fausto-Sterling (1985) has indicated, much modern research into hormones or brain structure still tends to exaggerate sex differences or to assume female inferiority. Carol Tavris (1992) calls this tendency "the mismeasure of woman," arguing that our science still improperly judges females against male norms.

Sandra Harding (1986) and other philosophers have highlighted sexist and racist aspects of the scientific enterprise, not with the intention of destroying science, but with the hope of correcting such faults. Science can become more accurate, they suggest, when researchers identify and compensate for unintentional gender biases. A 1994 conference on "Evolutionary Biology and Feminism" pointed out that although biologists had long described egg production as a huge drain on female resources, some only recently thought to ask whether sperm production imposed similar costs on males. In science, the answers you get depend on the questions you ask; observers of one jaybird population looked for and failed to find the expected male hierarchy—while ignoring female birds.

In analyzing technology, again, finding women's place requires knowing where to look. While female inventors received less than .5 percent of all patents issued in the nineteenth century, they accounted for 25 percent of all patents on dishwashing machines, as Autumn Stanley (1993) has documented. Moreover, the record sometimes obscured women's inventions in nontraditional areas, as when the patent office mistakenly classified Harriet Strong's design for Colorado River dams and reservoirs as kitchen equipment.

Technology is shaped by human choices, and the evolution of various machines, from the typewriter to the microwave oven, reflects (among other things) ideas about gender. As Virginia Scharff (1991) has noted, automakers touted clean electric cars (with their limited driving range) as more "suitable" for women than dirty, dangerous gasoline motors. Not all women, however, accepted limitations on their use of technology; during World War I, middle-to-upper class French, British, and American women (including Gertrude Stein and Alice B. Toklas) drove trucks and ambulances to carry supplies, rescue the wounded, and evacuate refugees. Other adventurous women mastered the strange, new world of aviation; Amelia Earhart was only one among dozens of female pilots racing for distance and speed records in the 1920s and 1930s. During World War II, the Women's Airforce Service Pilots flew every type of plane in use, ferrying aircraft between factories and bases, towing gunnery targets behind their planes so anti-aircraft units could practice shooting (with live ammunition!). Soviet women aviators saw actual combat in World War II, earning the nickname "Night Witches" for their devastating bombing raids. When the WASP program was disbanded, airlines offered the women jobs—unfortunately as stewardesses.

To the extent that science and technology remain central to our modern world, it becomes important to ask gender-related questions. Genetic engineering and new medical technologies raise both practical and ethical issues, especially about reproduction and birth control. The information age brings up vital issues about girls' access to computers and women's place in cyberspace.

The number of studies investigating such questions has exploded in recent years, contradicting any stereotype of history as a static field. Thanks to groundbreaking work by Cowan, Rossiter, and many others, today those of us teaching the history of women in science can draw on a wealth of fascinating books and articles. Yet for all that progress, many gaps in our knowledge remain. The history of African-American and other minority women's involvement with science and engineering cries out for further investigation. Scholars have barely touched questions about the gender dimensions of science and technology in non-Western cultures. Only by continually broadening our sights to include such topics can we hope to keep our field a rich, exciting discipline.

BIBLIOGRAPHY

Abir-Am, Pnina and Dorinda Outram (Eds.). *Uneasy Careers and Intimate Lives.* New Brunswick, NJ: Rutgers University Press, 1987.

Alic, Margaret. *Hypatia's Heritage.* Boston: Beacon, 1986.

Angier, Natalie. "Feminists and Darwin." *The New York Times* June 21, 1994: C1.

Benditt, John. "Gender and the Culture of Science." *Science* 260 (April 16, 1993): 383-430.

Brush, Stephen G. "Women in Science and Engineering." *American Scientist* 79(5) (1991): 404-419.

Carson, Rachel. *Silent Spring.* Boston: Houghton Mifflin, 1962.

Cassell, Justine and Henry Jenkins (Eds.). *From Barbie to Mortal Kombat.* Cambridge: Massachusetts Institute of Technology, 1998.

Cherny, Lynn and Elizabeth Reba Weise (Eds.). *Wired Women.* Seattle: Seal, 1996.

Cowan, Ruth Schwartz. "From Virginia Dare to Virginia Slims: Women and Technology in American Life." *Technology and Culture* 20(1) (1979): 51-63.

________. *More Work for Mother.* New York: Basic, 1983.

Fausto-Sterling, Anne. *Myths of Gender.* New York: Basic, 1985.

Harding, Sandra. *The Science Question in Feminism.* Ithaca: Cornell University Press, 1986.

Hynes, H. Patricia. *Reconstructing Babylon.* Bloomington: Indiana University Press, 1990.

Kass-Simon, G. and Patricia Farnes (Eds.). *Women of Science.* Bloomington: Indiana University Press, 1990.

Keil, Sally. *Those Wonderful Women in Their Flying Machines.* New York: Rawson Wade, 1979.

Keller, Evelyn Fox. *A Feeling for the Organism.* San Francisco: W.H. Freeman, 1983.

Lear, Linda. *Rachel Carson.* New York: Henry Holt, 1997.

McGaw, Judith. "Women and the History of American Technology." *Signs* 7(4) (1982): 798-828.

Noble, David. *A World Without Women.* Oxford, UK: Oxford University Press, 1992.

Ogilvie, Marilyn Bailey. *Women in Science.* Cambridge: Massachusetts Institute of Technology, 1986.

Quinn, Sally. *Marie Curie: A Life.* New York: Simon & Schuster, 1995.

Rosser, Sue. *Re-engineering Female Friendly Science.* New York: Teachers College Press, 1997.

Rossiter, Margaret. *Women Scientists in America: Struggles and Strategies to 1940.* Baltimore: Johns Hopkins University Press, 1982.

Rossiter, Margaret. *Women Scientists in America: The Limits of Opportunity, 1940-1972.* Baltimore: Johns Hopkins University Press, 1995.

Rothschild, Joan (Ed.). *Machina Ex Dea.* New York: Teachers College Press, 1983.

Scharff, Virginia. *Taking the Wheel.* New York: Free Press, 1991.

Schiebinger, Londa. *Nature's Body.* Boston: Beacon, 1993.

Stanley, Autumn. *Mothers and Daughters of Invention.* Metuchen, NJ: Scarecrow, 1993.

Tavris, Carol. *The Mismeasure of Woman.* New York: Simon & Schuster, 1992.

Trescott, Martha (Ed.). *Dynamos and Virgins Revisited.* Metuchen, NJ: Scarecrow, 1979.

Tuana, Nancy. *The Less Noble Sex.* Bloomington: Indiana University Press, 1993.

Wajcman, Judy. *Feminism Confronts Technology.* University Park: Pennsylvania State University Press, 1991.

Wertheim, Margaret. *Pythagoras' Trousers.* New York: Times Books, 1995.

Wright, Barbara Drygulski (Ed.). *Women, Work, and Technology.* Ann Arbor: University of Michigan Press, 1987.

SECTION IV: PROFESSIONS

"Doorways" by Kimberly Burton

This section is different from all of the other sections, for it encompasses a range of professional fields: architecture, law, library science, sports studies, and education. These fields have been predominately occupied by men, and have only recently opened their doors to women. Some of these professional fields, however, continue to eye women suspiciously and make women's entry difficult. Even those that have allowed women to enter their hallowed halls often still fail to acknowledge women's contributions to their profession.

What determines a profession is a question that lacks a clear answer. Unlike the humanities, social sciences, or natural sciences, in which students ask certain kinds of questions and talk and write about their subjects in ways that reveal certain perspectives, the professions are unique in that each is a discipline within itself. The questions that an accountant may ask will differ greatly from the kinds of questions that a scholar of library science or a student of education will pursue. Likewise, an accountant's way of thinking, experiencing or investigating a subject varies greatly from an educator's way of experiencing or investigating a subject. Yet each is classified as a profession.

So what is a profession? The *American Heritage Dictionary of the English Language* defines a profession as "The body of qualified persons of one specific occupation or field." Most professions are categorized as such because members of the profession are part of a larger body whose entry is dependent upon passing some form of a test. For example, all American attorneys must pass a test, the American Bar Exam, in order to be considered a certified attorney. Once an attorney has passed this test, she or he becomes certified by the state and now belongs to an elite group of persons who have passed this exam. She or he also becomes a member of the American Bar Association. Thus, becoming a professional usually requires a postsecondary education and advanced study.

Although today in the United States increasing numbers of women are moving into traditionally male fields, in other words, into the professions, the American labor force is still largely segregated by sex, with women vastly overrepresented in certain lower-paying job categories: elementary schoolteachers, maids, secretaries, food servers, bookkeepers. In contrast, the majority of engineers, dentists, physicians, and lawyers are men. In a time when nearly half the workforce is female, the majority of women are still channeled into low-paying clerical, secretarial, and service occupations while men continue to dominate the high-paying professions.

Much of the wage gap between men and women is rooted in history. Before mass industrialization, most women and men worked at home, their joint labor sustaining the household. With industrialization, however, work became separated from home and was redefined as labor that had a paid market value. Because domestic labor was unpaid and largely invisible inside the home, it was not classified as work and, thus, women who worked as housewives inside the home were not considered valued workers.

Five scholars representing five professions have contributed chapters in this section. These authors describe efforts to reread their field's traditions to include women and women's perspectives. All of the authors also examine the trend of feminism in their field and question where feminism will go in the future. In "The Impact of Feminism on the Library Science Profession," Amy Begg DeGroff explores the inequalities that still abound in the field of library science although, traditionally, library science has been and still is considered a female-dominated profession. The adoption of feminist styles of leadership, DeGroff believes, including the rejection of a hierarchical structure of leadership and the encouragement of cooperation and collaboration, would greatly benefit the library science profession, if it were adopted uniformly by librarians and the library community. Haithe Anderson, in "Behind School Doors: Feminism and Education," discusses the history of education in the United States, and evaluates the kind of education girls/women have received in contrast to the kind of education boys/men have received. She questions these differences and the educational practices found behind school doors. The next step for feminists in the field of education, Anderson argues, is paying more attention to the intersection of outside social forces with inside educational practices. Likewise, in "Women's Place: Architecture and Feminism," Jeanne Halgren Kilde explores the historical assumption that men and women identify with specific spaces and that women have a special connection to domestic space while also examining how women have resisted the limiting gender ideologies embedded in the built environment. Thus, although women's studies and feminism have not yet transformed the field of architecture, they have certainly contributed an awareness of gender as a critical element in understanding the built environment. Moreover, Mary Childs discusses the profound and challenging critiques of legal theory and practice that feminists have made in her essay "Law and Feminism." Feminism and women's studies have given rise to new analyses of every aspect of law, from the most specific details of courtroom practice to the most abstract conceptual frameworks of law. Conversely, Dayna Daniels argues in "The Forgotten Discipline: Sport Studies and Physical Education" that although sport studies has started to acknowledge women's place in the field, a re-evaluation of sport studies as a discipline still is needed; even fields such as women's studies often fail to include sport studies as part of their curriculums. Daniels questions why sport studies is still devalued as a discipline.

As you read these essays, pay close attention to the definition of profession and try to determine what you think makes each field a profession. What is it about each field that has kept it closed to women for so long? How will the application of feminist philosophies and principles change each field? Perhaps your answers to these questions will lead you to a complete revisioning of the professions.

Chapter 22

Behind School Doors: Feminism and Education

Haithe Anderson

> Our high and mighty Lords . . . have denied us the means of knowledge, and then reproached us for the want of it.
>
> Pamela Mason, 1793

The quest for equal educational opportunities has occupied the minds of generations of American feminists. From the 1790s onward, women's demands for formal education opened school doors around this country. By the nineteenth century, providing a formal education for girls became a more widely accepted practice. Not every girl, however, attended school. Many girls from the freed laboring classes, for example, still had to work to support their families, and it was illegal to educate enslaved girls. Moreover, girls who went to school did not receive the same *kind* of education as boys. Indeed, girls from families wealthy enough to afford private schools had a variety of educational options. Some families preferred to send their daughters to fashionable finishing schools whose ultimate purpose was to train young women to be elegant and appealing to men. These schools provided some rudimentary training in grammar, composition and rhetoric, and languages, but focused mostly on the fine arts. Other families, who were critical of this kind of training, sent their daughters to single-sex academies that made more serious attempts to emulate the liberal arts curriculum found in private boys' schools. Many of these girls' schools, however, were underfunded and ill-equipped. Still other families, who believed a woman's education should make her more efficient around the house, supported schools that provided a thorough training in the "domestic sciences."

Despite the different kinds of education that private schools offered, all began with the assumption that a woman's place was in the home. Traditional gender expectations were shaped, in turn, by social assumptions about racial differences. After the American Civil War, when access to schooling began to improve for all girls, racial identity became increasingly central to the process of defining a girl's educational experience. American Indian girls, for example, were sent to federal boarding schools designed to obliterate their cultural heritage and assimilate them into European-American culture. Government officials thought that the most effective way to domesticate life on the reservations was to remove young girls from their families and teach them proper household management techniques. It was hoped that these young women, upon returning to their reservations, would reeducate members of their tribe. Many African-American girls, on the other hand, voluntarily left their homes to attend "industrial" schools that provided lessons in European-American domesticity. They were taught the skills needed to become servants and to occupy other domestic positions traditionally prescribed for black women in the South.

By the beginning of the twentieth century, children from all walks of life regularly began to attend schools. State after state adopted compulsory school laws, requiring school attendance. These laws, however, still did not guarantee that all girls would receive the same kinds of educational opportunities, nor did they guarantee that girls and boys attending the same school would receive the same kind of education. While the old-fashioned practice of having boys and girls enter the classroom through separate doors and hallways was disappearing, the equally old practice of teaching them to occupy separate and unequal roles continued. The focus of feminists interested in transforming educational opportunities for young women, as a consequence, shifted. Unlike their nineteenth-century counterparts, who fought to open school doors, feminists throughout the twentieth century have challenged the educational practices they found behind school doors.

During the first part of the twentieth century, feminist scholars focused on what they called "sex differences." They wanted to know if men and women, reared in the same environment, developed different intellectual abilities and personalities, as many people believed they did. Pioneering research in psychology and educational testing by Helen Thompson, Leta Hollingworth and Clelia Duel Mosher, and others, significantly undermined the notion that men and women had different intellectual capacities. Their work also raised serious doubts about the idea that there were inborn differences between racial groups. Other women in the social sciences, such as Jessie Taft, Elsie Clews Parson, Mary Roberts Coolidge, and Margaret Mead, challenged the notion of sex differences in other ways. Their research helped undermine the prevailing notion that differences between men and women were natural. If women and men appeared to be different, this research suggested that these differences were not inborn. Instead, they were the result of the different kinds of education women and men received.

During the latter part of the twentieth century, feminist research continued to undermine the notion that men and women were "naturally different" and, hence, required different kinds of education. In 1972, the U.S. Government finally passed legislation officially acknowledging that women and men were entitled to the same kind of education. The first clear policy statement supporting this idea was Title IX. This act made it illegal for schools to continue the overtly sexist policies that had previously excluded girls from classrooms or extracurricular activities traditionally reserved for boys. More subtle forms of sexism inside classrooms, however, proved to be much more difficult to overcome. By the late 1970s, the feminists who had worked hard to pass that legislation realized that the new law was not having the impact they had hoped for. Researchers were still finding that girls and boys, even if they were in the same classroom, were receiving different kinds of education.

What kinds of differences separate the educational experiences of boys and girls? To highlight the kinds of differences feminists in education have found, it is important to distinguish between two types of teaching content found in all classrooms—the overt curriculum and the hidden curriculum. The overt curriculum refers to the obvious subjects that teachers teach. For example, the lesson plans and the materials used to teach students are part of the overt curriculum. From the overt curriculum children learn to read, write, and do arithmetic. The overt curriculum at all levels of education has been criticized by feminists for being too androcentric (male-centered) and Eurocentric (focused solely on European Americans). During the 1970s, there were several studies by feminists that examined curriculum materials used at the K-12 level. In textbooks, readers, and biographies they found a world in which females were essentially invisible. Books used for reading, for example, were dominated by boy-centered stories about European Americans. When girls were present they tended to be passive—watching or helping boys. Adults in these stories, researchers found, occupied traditional roles with fathers going to work and mothers staying at home. If women did work outside the home they tended to be stereotypically portrayed as nurses and secretaries.

The implications of such school lessons are obvious. The overt curriculum of our schools was teaching girls that their primary role in society was to be the helpmates of men—either as their wives or secretaries. By teaching girls that their future roles were limited to a narrow range of options, the overt curriculum of schools reinforced the idea that women were and should be subordinate to men. Feminist research in education has contributed to the transformation of K-12 curriculum materials by making people much more sensitive to the overt sexism contained in textbooks. Increasingly, children are using textbooks and literature that reflect positive images of girls and women from all races and generations. Nonetheless, there is still much work to be done in creating gender-balanced textbooks. In addition, efforts to create unbiased textbooks do not guarantee that all schools will use these materials. Many poorer school districts simply cannot afford to buy new textbooks and have to rely on outdated materials. Moreover, many school libraries continue to be stocked with books that contain limited views of women's potential. In addition, feminists have found that much of the computer software used in well-funded schools continues to be dominated by male figures and stereotypical representations of women.

Feminists interested in higher education have also alerted us to the invisibility of women in colleges and university textbooks. In the 1970s and 1980s, researchers found sex bias in disciplines ranging from medicine to sociology. Women were either absent or represented in stereotypical ways. Despite the growing identification of sexism in education, a study of education texts in the 1980s revealed that only .5 percent of space in these books was devoted to helping teachers think about gender issues in the classroom. Changing the overt curriculum at every level has, in other words, been a very slow process. Nonetheless, students in colleges and universities will come across courses that more accurately reflect social diversity. Indeed, it is increasingly common to find colleges and universities requiring students to take at least one course that has culturally diverse content. In addition, many schools offer degrees in areas such as women's studies, African-American studies, Mexican-American studies, Asian-American studies and Native-American studies. Thanks to the efforts of feminists concerned with the overt curriculum at colleges and universities, we have seen many improvements.

Overcoming biases in the overt curriculum, although an ongoing problem, has been easier than overcoming biases in the hidden curriculum of schools. The hidden curriculum refers to aspects of the curriculum that are not part of the apparent lesson plan. To put it another way, we all learn lessons in classrooms that are not found in our textbooks. For example, students learn to respect authority, to accept and obey rules made by others, to be punctual, to value competitiveness over cooperation, to accept their place in a hierarchy of abilities, and so on. From kindergarten onward, we learn the kinds of behavior that will be expected of us in the workplace. If a teacher tells a student she is smart, she learns to expect a place at the top of the job ladder. If a teacher tells a student she is dumb, she learns to accept a place on the bottom rung of the job ladder. Recent feminist research in education has transformed our understanding of the hidden curriculum and its influence on girls. After spending countless hours observing classroom interactions, feminists have concluded that hidden curriculum often teaches girls and women, in very subtle ways, that the bottom rungs of all ladders are reserved for them.

What we have learned over the past twenty years from feminist scholarship is that teachers, female teachers and male teachers, from preschools to universities, interact more with males than they do with females. The implicit message is that girls' intellectual development comes second. The problem, unfortunately, is bigger than this. The quality of interaction that girls and boys receive is also different. The quality of the teacher-student interaction is vital because it contributes to students' self-confidence. David and Myra Sadker spent years studying patterns of teacher-student interaction in K-12 environments. (See *Failing at Fairness: How Our Schools Cheat Girls,* 1995.) Their research, and other research like theirs, has transformed our understanding of how the hidden curriculum works to discourage and even dismiss girls. For example, in a study of over 100 fourth-, sixth-, and eighth-grade classrooms, the Sadkers found that boys not only received more teacher attention, but they also received the most positive and helpful attention. In an eighth-grade sample, boys were eight times more likely to shout out answers to teacher's questions than were girls. Teachers, in turn, were much more likely to critically respond to boys' answers and encourage their thinking. The typical response to girls who shouted out answers was to remind them that they needed to raise their hands. The Sadkers also found, as did others, that boys are much more likely to receive praise and the precise attention needed to overcome academic weaknesses than are girls. Further, research has shown that teacher and student interaction is influenced by the race of the student. What limited research is available suggests, for example, that both girls and boys from African-American backgrounds receive less teacher attention than do European-American students. What is more, teachers often treat African-American girls in ways that cause them to doubt their academic ability.

In classrooms unfriendly to girls' voices, girls of all races become silent. Girls who sit quietly in classrooms and obey classroom rules tend to become invisible to teachers. This does not mean that girls are not learning. Girls who enter kindergarten full of confidence and with high self-esteem often exit high school with low self-esteem. Too many girls, in other words, have internalized the overt and hidden lessons found in school curriculums. Their intellectual development, they are subtly taught, counts less than that of their brothers. Schools also reinforce the idea that girls and boys are different and that those differences matter. For example, teachers often use gender as a basis for organizing classroom activities. They may assign different chores to girls and boys, divide girls and boys into same-sex groups, and make children sit with children of the opposite sex as a form of punishment. Interestingly, girls and boys self-select into same-sex groups. Although girls and boys in homes and in neighborhoods often play together, it is rare to find them playing together on school playgrounds.

Unfortunately, the patterns of interaction that highlight differences by promoting the silencing and invisibility of girls in K-12 environments are replicated on college and university campuses. Throughout their educational careers, men tend to dominate classroom discussions. For example, research has shown that professors interact more with men, that they interrupt women more than men, and that they allow male students to interrupt women. Some feminists interpret women's silences inside college classrooms as forms of resistance to an overt and hidden curriculum they perceive as sexist. Others argue that women's silence is imposed upon them by the presence of men in the classroom. Ironically, in the nineteenth century, feminists unhappy with the kind of education that women received in single-sex schools, felt that coeducation was the best way to improve educational opportunities for girls and women. As we come to the end of the twentieth century, some feminists believe that coeducation is part of the problem. Comparisons between coed and single-sex high schools for girls reveal that girls who attend single-sex schools have higher levels of academic achievement, higher levels of participation in extracurricular school activities, higher self-esteem, and hold less rigid sexual stereotypes.

Despite research findings that paint troubling pictures of young women's educational experiences, many women have pursued educational experiences that have challenged traditional assumptions about women's roles. Not all women have been silenced by their classroom experiences. On the contrary, women over the past two centuries used their education to challenge the status quo of their social status and gain equal rights. Some, it would seem, left high schools and colleges with high self-confidence and high ambitions. Women involved in education—as students, professors, and administrators—are indebted to generations of feminists who opened school doors and helped transform what they found behind these doors. Each new generation of feminists, in turn, will have to challenge practices and ideas left unexamined by their predecessors.

What direction will these challenges take? There are a number of possibilities. First, feminists who study all levels of education need to do more research to understand how the overt and hidden curriculums can, and in some cases clearly do, lower the self-esteem of girls and women. Second, although more and more women attend college, most continue to opt for professions that are traditionally associated with women's work, such as teaching and nursing. Schooling, of course, can not shoulder all of the responsibility for these trends. Other social practices, such as those associated with popular culture, convey multiple messages that help reproduce traditional gender roles. Feminists in education, therefore, will have to pay more attention to the way educational practices beyond school doors intersect with social forces outside of schools. Their goal, in part, will be to think about how schools can become sites for intervention into cultural practices at large. Finally, the bulk of feminist research over the past century has focused on the way that schools shape femininity. Without an equally sophisticated understanding of how schools prepare young men to adopt masculine roles, however, social change will be uneven.

Chapter 23

Law and Feminism

Mary Childs

Law is an area of professional and academic endeavor that has historically been almost exclusively occupied by men; the influx of women into legal practice and study since the 1970s has been a dramatic change, one associated with new developments of legal thought. As law occupies a central position in the power relations of Western societies, it is not surprising that it has been the focus of feminist critiques as well as the site of many struggles over the meaning and extent of gender equality. Feminists have provided profound and challenging critiques of legal theory and practice at many levels. Old practices and ideas have been reexamined, from the most abstract principles of legal philosophy to the pragmatic details of courtroom practice and professional power structures.

Before an examination of how feminism has transformed and informed the field of law can be clear, law itself must be defined and explored. Law is a system of rules enforced by courts and related institutions. Legal rules are different from other types of rules not by virtue of their content, but in their manner of creation and enforcement. A nation's constitution delineates how laws are to be made, and only rules created through that process will be acknowledged as legal rules. This does not mean that other rules are unimportant: social and cultural rules are central to an ordered society, but they will not be enforced through those mechanisms and structures reserved for legal rules.

What, then, does the academic study of law involve? At one level it involves the study of the substantive laws of a jurisdiction—the rules describing criminal offenses and punishments, or the laws regulating television and radio broadcasting, or the laws concerning marriage and divorce, or those applicable to any other area of human activity. Learning such rules is only part of the study of a law student; she must also understand where they originate, how they come to be recognized as having the force of law, and how they may be changed.

Legal scholars also study the policy arguments behind the drafting of laws, and consider arguments for and against proposed reforms. Linked to this is the examination of how laws operate in practice: whether the impact of a statute is as the legislature intended or not. Work in the area of socio-legal studies brings the insights of the social sciences to the study of law. At the most abstract level of study, legal academics debate the very nature of law; such theories are grouped together in the general category of jurisprudence, or legal philosophy. Legal philosophers discuss the meaning of concepts such as justice and equality and fairness, ideas of central concern to feminists.

The rich and diverse range of feminist work is reflected in the multiplicity of feminist critiques of law. The 1980s and 1990s have seen the introduction of academic journals specifically devoted to issues of law and gender, law and women, or law and feminism; a few of the many titles are the *Yale Journal of Law and Feminism, Feminist Legal Studies,* the *Harvard Women's Law Journal,* and the *Canadian Journal of Women and the Law.* Important articles applying feminist insights to law also have been published in the most prestigious and influential generalist legal journals.

Earliest feminist critiques of law challenged the existence of legal rules treating men and women differently: laws permitting men to vote but denying the same right to women, laws giving women fewer rights to inherit and own property, laws excluding women from university study or entry to certain professions. As well as making political arguments about the position of women, feminists pointed to one of the central principles of Anglo-American legal systems: that like cases should be treated alike. They argued that since men and women are sufficiently alike, it is illogical and unjust to treat them differently.

As explicitly sex-based laws were repealed, critiques extended to legal rules that contained no direct reference to sex but nonetheless affected men and women differently. For instance, laws giving fewer employment rights to part-time workers tend to disadvantage women as a group because they are more likely than men to work part-time. Feminist scholars have raised awareness of the way in which superficially neutral laws, when superimposed upon a lived inequality, may have very unequal effects. Feminists did not stop at criticizing existing laws, however; they have also attempted to use laws for their own purposes. Thus in the United Kingdom and Canada, governments have legislated to prohibit sex-based discrimination in employment and/or in the provision of services to the public; European community states have also introduced schemes to ensure that male and female employees are paid equally for work of equal value. Feminist legal scholars have provided strong arguments supporting the need for such legislation, as well as debating the most effective wording, conceptual structure, and enforcement regimes for such laws.

Other feminist scholars have argued that some areas of law are shaped by the fact that the vast majority of those involved in litigation and lawmaking have been male. For example, criminal law is generally applicable to both men and women (with the exception of some sexual offenses), but historically men have outnumbered women in the statistics of those convicted of criminal offenses. Critics have argued that this has shaped the definition of both offenses and defenses, which reflect ways of thinking and behaving traditionally seen as "masculine." Thus, the partial defense of provocation (which in many jurisdictions will reduce what would otherwise be murder to the lesser crime of manslaughter) rests upon a notion that the accused is less culpable because the killing was done while in a state of "sudden and temporary loss of self-control" as a result of some provoking event or words. In the early years of this defense, only physical violence would be considered sufficient provocation, with two exceptions: the discovery by a husband that his wife had been unfaithful, or by a father that another man had seduced his son. No equivalent exceptions protected wronged wives and mothers. Furthermore, the emphasis on a "sudden" reaction tended to benefit men who lashed out in anger during a fight, while failing to extend similar protection to women who, it is claimed, are more likely to experience a "slow burn" reaction to provocation.

Provocation is not the only criminal defense alleged to be neutral on its face but applied in a way that may produce outcomes disadvantageous to women. Another example is the law relating to self-defense, which has been described as based upon a barroom brawl model; someone who claims they used force in self-defense must show they used no more force than necessary in the circumstances to avert the threatened harm. Women who kill abusive partners have had difficulty establishing this defense when the killing took place during a lull between violent episodes; the idea that they could just walk out and thus avoid the threatened violence has been used against them. In some jurisdictions, courts have accepted feminist arguments about gender bias in the interpretation of this defense, and have admitted evidence of "battered woman syndrome" to enlighten juries as to why abused women might react in a way apparently inconsistent with male-centered notions of appropriate self-defense.

Feminists have consistently drawn attention to the gendered impact of the way rules are enforced and applied. Domestic violence was for many years viewed as a private matter between partners, and not suitable for legal intervention. Thus, police forces often took little action against abusive men other than perhaps intervening to put an end to a particular attack; the violent man was often neither arrested nor charged, despite the fact that a similar attack occurring outside the home on a victim other then a wife or partner would be treated as a criminal assault. Feminists argued that it was not sufficient to have a law making a particular course of conduct illegal if sexist notions about the acceptability of domestic violence meant that the law was not being enforced. Consequently, many police forces established special units to deal with domestic violence.

Similar problems of low investigation and conviction rates applied with respect to the crime of rape. Feminist scholars have paid considerable attention to the gender bias in many areas of rape law: warnings to juries that female complainants were untrustworthy, cross-examinations of victims conducted as attacks on character, apparently low sentences compared to other assaults, rules permitting husbands to rape wives with impunity. Furthermore, feminists argued cogently that the failure of the law to treat rape seriously and protect women is a matter of concern not just for individual victims, but a phenomenon that creates an atmosphere of insecurity for all women.

Another area of law that has developed rapidly in response to feminist work is the law relating to sexual harassment. The term was introduced into the law in the 1970s; until then the practice of subjecting workers or students to unwanted and offensive sexual words or conduct had no legal name. Feminists (notably Catharine MacKinnon) gave it a name and argued that it was neither normal nor merely an isolated phenomenon. They showed that it was a widespread practice of sex discrimination, and pressed for employers to be held responsible should they fail to take appropriate steps to deal with the problem.

Just as the rules of substantive law have been thoroughly criticized, so have the personnel and procedures of the legal system. Feminists have observed that the legal profession and related occupations are overwhelmingly male, from the judiciary to prison guards. Although increasing numbers of women obtain law degrees, they are still underrepresented in the upper ranks of the legal profession. Female lawyers are more likely to be unemployed than their male counterparts and tend to earn less when employed. Feminist lawyers have debated the vexed question of whether the structure of the legal profession and legal practice itself must be changed in order to improve the position of women. This question is of particular importance, of course, in societies where a legal career is the most common route to public office. Changing the composition of the legal professions may also be seen as one possible way of changing the law's attitude to women, through the introduction of more female voices and faces into the upper echelons of practice and of the judiciary, where women may introduce different values and perspectives.

The question of perspective and gender has occupied feminist legal scholars as it has feminists in all disciplines. In the field of law, many thinkers have been influenced by the work of Carol Gilligan, a psychologist whose research into the moral development of boys and girls led her to speculate that there might be very different approaches to problem solving, one most commonly associated with males and the other more commonly found in females. Boys tended to approach certain questions (solving hypothetical moral dilemmas) by considering the application of general rules, and deciding which rule should prevail in the fact pattern given. Girls seemed to be more concerned with personal and social relationships, and more open to the possibility of compromise. This notion of a different voice has not been universally accepted, and the research has been criticized on both theoretical and methodological grounds, but has nonetheless been influential in shaping critiques of law voiced by those who see its rule-based approach as embodying classically masculine approaches to people and problems. This argument suggests that the very idea of the Anglo-American legal system, and, perhaps, of any legal system, is fundamentally gendered in its style of reasoning.

Even feminists who do not take such a radically skeptical position regarding the nature of law may be cautious about the problems of seeking to use law as a tool for social change. Law is a fairly conservative force; reliance on following past precedent tends to support the status quo, and the judiciary who interpret and apply legislation are widely viewed as unrepresentative (they tend to be older, affluent, white males) and often conservative in their political and social outlook. Some feminists see reliance on law as problematic because it places further power in the hands of the state and a system still dominated by traditionally powerful groups. They urge caution in our approach to law, and suggest that feminists should use it only when other strategies are unavailable or ineffective.

This cautious approach to extending the power of law is characteristic of those who oppose one of the most controversial feminist legal endeavors, the attempt to use law to attack pornography. Most feminists share a concern about negative images of women and sexuality in pornographic materials, but there is strong disagreement about whether it is appropriate to use law to address the phenomenon. Some feminist lawyers advocate using law to prohibit access to sexist pornography, or to give its victims a right to seek compensation from producers and distributors. Others argue that enactment of such laws is dangerous because ambiguous wording, such as degrading, humiliating, or exploitative, is likely to be interpreted in a way that protects traditional images and outlaws the images of minority or unconventional sexualities (lesbian feminists have expressed particular concern). Feminist lawyers have been deeply divided over the acceptability and dangers of legal regulation in this area.

Differences of opinion between feminists over the emotive issue of pornography have highlighted the fact that feminist lawyers, as well as other feminists, must be aware of the multiplicity of feminist standpoints and the very real issues that divide as well as unite women. Women whose access to the realm of legal practice and teaching was easiest were those who might be seen as relatively privileged; any claims they might have made to speak for all women have now been strongly challenged by other groups: disabled women, poor women, women of color, and lesbians. Recognition of diversity in legal discourse is often associated with the work of postmodern legal theorists and those associated with the critical legal studies movement, a loose grouping of thinkers whose work challenges and deconstructs traditional legal concepts. In raising awareness of diversity and its effect on one's experience of the law, feminist work has thus complemented and enriched the work of other theorists.

The question arises: where will feminism in law go next? Recent feminist work has looked at the way law constructs bodies, both bodies of knowledge and corporeal bodies. Feminist lawyers are also developing and refining the critiques begun by their predecessors in all areas of legal thought. It is difficult to predict what lies next for feminist legal work but, undoubtedly, it will continue to challenge and inform both mainstream legal work and feminist thought in other disciplines.

Feminism and women's studies have given rise to new analyses and critiques of every aspect of law. The most specific details of courtroom practice have been examined, as have the most general and abstract conceptual frameworks of law. The full effects of the influence of feminism and women's studies on law have yet to be seen, but, clearly, their impact will be pervasive and profound. Law may still be seen as a bastion of middle-class male privilege, but feminist challenges are striking at the very foundations of the fortress.

Chapter 24

Women's Place: Architecture and Feminism

Jeanne Halgren Kilde

In 1873, Eliza Jane Thompson, convinced that alcohol consumption was the root cause of the abuse of women and the break-up of families, led a group of middle-class women into saloons in Hillsboro, Ohio, where they prayed, sang hymns, and urged proprietors to eliminate liquor from their premises. In 1972, at the Houston, Texas, Summit Auditorium, Denise Wells, after standing in line outside the women's restroom for several minutes suffering severe discomfort, ducked into the men's room. In 1994, Shannon Faulkner, convinced that the military education she desired could not be attained at any institution open to women, walked on to the previously all-male Citadel military academy campus to enroll in classes, armed with a U.S. Circuit Court of Appeals ruling.

What links these three incidents, and countless others like them, is that in each one achieving the desired goal necessitated a violation of gendered space. Each of the venues—the saloon, the men's lavatory, and the military training institution—was reserved exclusively for men. Although the motivations that brought these women to challenge male spatial privilege varied, all three found that the spaces themselves limited them, or carried meanings that limited them, and only by placing their bodies into the "off-limits" spaces, by claiming them as women's place, could they achieve their goals.

These incidents aptly demonstrate the power space wields over all of us. We live our lives in built environments—landscapes consisting of buildings and spaces that have been created by human hands, hearts, and minds. More than simply settings for our everyday activities, these environments constantly affect our lives. They carry meanings and associations, many of which are about gender. They help us define who we are as women and men. They teach us where our place in the world is—and where it isn't. Although the study of architecture has long acknowledged the importance of built space in conveying meanings to society, it has been feminist scholars who have urged architectural history and architectural practice toward a fuller understanding of how the built environment affects women and the construction of gender.

When we think of the built environment, we rarely consider it a product of women's efforts. Yet numerous examples demonstrate that throughout history women have played major roles in the creation of the built environment, often shouldering primary responsibility for sheltering families. For instance, in many African cultures women traditionally have been responsible for building their families' mud and dung rondavels or round houses. During the nineteenth century, Lakota and Cheyenne women cured buffalo and deer hides to use in tipi construction, and they both erected and broke down the structures as their bands migrated. Hopi, Moki, and Zuni women in the American southwest constructed pueblos from adobe. Furthermore, scholars speculate that women of ancient Greece designed and built the clay buildings of the cities of Minoa and Thera. Non-Western women have proven perfectly capable of and, in fact, responsible for building. In contrast, Western society has historically relegated women to passivity with respect to the built environment (they don't produce it; they simply exist within it). Feminist scholars, including historians, anthropologists, archeologists, sociologists, architectural historians, and architects, are investigating why and how this has happened. They are also examining the ramifications of the erasure of women's actual contributions to the built environment from the historical record.

French philosopher Simone De Beauvoir was among the first feminists to raise these questions. In her landmark study *The Second Sex* (1957), she posits that defining the relationship between women and the built environment was an essential strategy in the patriarchal suppression of women's freedom. Since ancient times, concepts of female inferiority and male dominance have carried a spatial component. Females have been associated with "nature" or the "natural" landscape, which is seen as fertile, passive, and awaiting human hands to transform it. Males, in contrast, have been associated with "civilization," or landscapes that have been cultivated or otherwise "improved" from their natural state. The power of these gendered associations is revealed in language. Rape metaphors, often used to describe violent transformation of the land, linguistically suggest male action performed on a passive female. Because "civilizing" is granted a much higher degree of cultural significance than the untransformed natural environment, these gender associations help to maintain the lower status of women in society vis-á-vis men.

Modern Western society has applied a similar gender dichotomy to the sociopolitical economy. During the early nineteenth century the shift to a capitalist market economy changed the nature of men's and women's labor. Whereas a century earlier women had worked alongside their husbands, raising foodstuffs, running artisan shops, or providing services, in the nineteenth century, a growing middle class sent men out of the home to work for wages and left women in the home to maintain it and take care of family members. To justify this new economic situation, society distinguished ideologically between a public sphere of politics, economics, and business that thrived on the masculine values of individualism and competition and a private sphere that functioned on the feminine values of domesticity and nurturance. These ideological spheres were then mapped onto physical spaces: masculine places included city streets and commercial areas while the private feminine place was the home.

Under this ideological model, upper- and middle-class women particularly were considered distinctly out of place in masculine public space. Perceived as delicate and submissive, women could easily be endangered on the rough streets, so they were advised to observe rigid behavior restrictions when in public. They were never to appear unescorted nor speak to men on the street; they were to wear clothing that covered their bodies from head to toe, walk at a brisk pace, and avoid the eyes of strangers. Not surprisingly, many women rebelled. They did go into the streets alone, to work, shop, and pursue political and social agendas. Society responded by creating semi-public female spaces such as women's colleges, tea rooms in downtown cities, and "ladies parlors" in public libraries to mitigate the public evils. In contrast to these middle-class women, working-class women, both black and white, had no choice but to enter the public streets, factories, and businesses to earn a living. Society was not forgiving of these women's trespasses into male-oriented public spaces, however, and women who appeared alone in public were often considered sexually available simply due to their presence on the street.

During the nineteenth century, then, the private home was deemed women's true place. Yet even within the home, as rooms became increasingly specialized, families created gendered rooms, reserving studies and libraries for men, and kitchens, parlors, and boudoirs for women. Eager to control whatever spatial factors might be at their disposal, however, middle-class women set about improving their lives by improving their homes. In *A Treatise on Domestic Economy* (1841), Catherine Beecher evaluated domestic spaces from the standpoint of their impact on everyday tasks. Sensitive to the amount of time and labor required to keep houses clean, to wash dishes and clothing, to prepare meals, and to monitor children, Beecher advocated creating more efficient workplaces by eliminating basement kitchens that kept women running up and down stairs all day; placing water pumps, sinks, and drainpipes inside kitchens to eliminate trips to outdoor wells; and developing house plans with convenient room and stair arrangements. Such efforts brought women into the realm of architectural design but not necessarily in ways that altered patriarchal power. Not a feminist, Beecher firmly believed that the domestic roles of homemaker, wife, and mother perfectly suited women (although she never took them on herself), and by performing these roles well, women could significantly improve society.

By the turn of the century, however, social reformers reassessed the single-family home from a distinctly feminist perspective and concluded that too often it significantly hindered women's full participation in society. The continuous work needed to maintain a middle-class home isolated adult women and afforded little time to devote to personal needs or to the social and political life of the community. Critics such as Charlotte Perkins Gilman urged the development of cooperative housekeeping arrangements to alleviate women's isolation and workload. She advocated the creation of feminist apartment hotels that, while providing separate family apartments, eliminated private kitchens, dining rooms, and laundries in favor of communal ones and provided community child care facilities. Although rarely acted upon through much of the twentieth century, these ideas re-emerged in the 1960s when journalist Betty Friedan explored the powerful domestic ideology of the post-World War II era. In *The Feminine Mystique* (1963), Friedan argued that many college-educated women of her generation felt frustrated with the popular belief that women's fulfillment lay in motherhood and home-making, and that they, like Gilman, found the home not a liberating haven in which modern technology eased the burdens of housekeeping but a trap that consumed their time. Friedan argued that the then-popular open-plan ranch and split-level houses, with their huge kitchens that opened into family rooms and family rooms that opened into formal living rooms, left women no personal space at all. The whole house had become a kitchen, so to speak, one huge room in which children constantly played and thus needed constant monitoring and cleaning.

Either explicitly or implicitly, the approaches and authors discussed thus far have assumed that men and women are identified with specific spaces and that women have a special connection to domestic space. More recent studies, however, have challenged this model of the gender/space relationship because identifying such gendered space in the contemporary built environment is difficult. Do we consider our own homes women's place? Are our kitchens feminine space? Sociologist and urban planner Daphne Spain says no, arguing that gender distinctions within modern homes have essentially disappeared. Yet our relationship to the built environment remains strongly affected by our gender identity. For instance, architect and urban planner Leslie Kanes Weisman points out that although women now occupy public spaces and buildings with impunity, their presence is often restricted to daylight hours due to fear of assault at night. In addition, Spain shows that business office arrangements which assign closed-door, private space to managers and easily transgressed, open-plan secretarial pool or reception space to lower status workers tend to support the sexual disparity still characteristic in business hiring and promotion. Consequently, the relationship between gender and space seems more complicated than the separate spheres model can account for, and feminist scholars continue to seek ways to understand and evaluate it.

One alternative model builds upon a biological understanding of gender construction. Theorizing that reproduction lies at the heart of human existence and that differences in reproductive roles constitute the most fundamental level of male/female identity, some argue that masculine buildings imitate the "projective" male reproductive role and feminine buildings imitate the "recessive" female role. Masculine skyscrapers (phallic symbols on the landscape that literally display male power) are complemented by feminine cavelike enclosures. Drawing upon psychological research showing that when given building blocks boys tend to build towers while girls build enclosures, some theorists have argued that not only do buildings mimic masculine and feminine traits, but that sexual identity infuses the architectural designs created by individuals. Thus, women architects necessarily bring a preference for recessive spaces to their drawing boards while men bring one for projections.

Many feminists, however, consider this "essentialist" idea that biology determines human behavior (and building design) profoundly wrongheaded, arguing that like the nature/civilization dichotomy, it is another socially constructed means of limiting women's participation in society. Even the critics of essentialism, however, generally agree that women and men are socialized into gender-specific sets of values and that these values then inform building design. Women's life experiences and education make them favor community, cooperation, interdependence, and organicism over patriarchal values of individualism, rationalism, competition, and hierarchy. Consequently, they tend to imbue their buildings with these values. Architect Margrit Kennedy, for instance, advocates a "feminist" architecture that purposively reproduces "feminine" principles drawn from these values, among them user-orientation (designs that explicitly aid users rather than demonstrate an architect's brilliance), organic organization (spaces with natural flows and appearances in tune with nature rather than formal spaces with monumental appearances) and flexibility (multi-functional spaces rather than specialized ones). In a similar vein, architect Kimberley Jones's design for the Gloucester, Massachusetts, House of Justice intentionally challenges the individuality, monumentality, and conformity of patriarchal architecture. Consisting of two semicircular courtrooms placed back-to-back like turtle shells, her building opens outward suggesting community. As these examples demonstrate, the biological-essentialist model of gender and space is intimately linked with the model of socially constructed gender values.

Attempting to refocus the discussion, some scholars are looking more carefully at precisely how the built environment actually functions with respect to ideological understandings of gender. Weisman, for instance, argues that the built environment articulates and maintains masculine privilege. Most housing in America, she argues, assumes an idealistic model of two-parent, male-headed families in which wives work full-time in the home taking care of house and children, a model that only accounts for some 7 percent of the U.S. population. The intractability of this housing model helps to maintain stereotypes that devalue women's paid employment outside the home and that identify women only as wives and mothers rather than autonomous citizens. The domicile remains a male refuge and a female workplace, a reality to which Weisman traces domestic abuse as well as the inequality of women's and men's domestic workloads.

Such studies have inevitably led to examinations of how women have resisted the limiting gender ideologies embedded in the built environment. For instance, historians Patricia Cline Cohen and Sarah Deutsch, respectively, have shown that women regularly used reputedly dangerous public transportation (canal boats and railroads) and walked through all areas of large cities alone during the eighteenth and nineteenth centuries, refusing to succumb to the fear of public danger that society so strongly emphasized. Furthermore, historian Dolores Hayden has recovered the feminist housing plans of several turn-of-the-century architects, homes intentionally designed to expand women's choices rather than limit them to domestic work.

My own study of the late-nineteenth-century religious campground, Chautauqua, in New York State, argues that its informal forest setting aided middle-class women as they redefined proper feminine behavior. By ignoring strictures for dress and behavior, donning the working-class uniform of a simple skirt and shirtwaist, refusing to wear hats, wandering the grounds alone, shouting to one another unreservedly, and even talking to strangers, Chautauqua women flouted the spatially defined (i.e., public) standards for women's behavior. Soon, their challenges extended to tests of the ideology of "women's sphere" as they engaged in such supposedly masculine activities as delivering public lectures, attending college-level classes, and pursuing suffrage and temperance legislation. By providing women with a place in which they could feel comfortable engaging in behavior that was actually quite radical, Chautauqua itself played an important role in these gender challenges. At this camp, women understood that they need not abide by the same ideas about feminine behavior (in other words, gender roles) that they did in the outside world. This case study, then, illustrates how built space itself, in this case a specific space, can function as a salient factor in the actual construction of gender.

The effect of such feminist ideas on the actual construction of new buildings has been irregular, however, and not without controversy. Many architects fear that feminist concerns diminish women architects' status and discourages patrons from commissioning buildings from them. In this highly competitive profession dependent upon customers who finance both planning and construction, veering too far from traditional designs can be suicide for one's career. However, one particularly significant result of the modern feminist movement is that the number of women going into architecture has risen profoundly. Whereas in the 1960s only a handful of women pursued architectural degrees, by 1995 about a third of all students in American university architecture programs were women. As more women have entered the field, they have made the profession more responsive to their needs and interests, developing strong organizations devoted to raising the visibility of women in the profession and providing professional support for women. These groups have sponsored conferences devoted to issues of importance to women architects, organized archives of materials, and combated sexual discrimination and sexual harassment on the job and in educational institutions. Yet women have met with obstacles. The American Institute of Architects, the flagship professional organization of all architects, still can only boast about 9 percent female membership.

Ordinary citizens, however, are becoming aware of the influence space has upon their lives, and women are translating this knowledge into efforts to claim spaces previously denied them and to make spaces more responsive to their needs. From "Take Back the Night" marches organized in cities throughout the United States to efforts to degender military educational institutions such as the Virginia Military Institute, women are refusing to accept barriers that previously kept them out of specific spaces. Public outrage over the lavatory trial of Denise Wells (she was acquitted and the original $200 fine was dropped) resulted in regulations to increase the number of women's toilets in public buildings. Recent years have also brought the placement of diaper-changing tables in both women's and men's rooms; the installation of lighting, emergency phones, and security cameras in parking lots; and the incorporation of other amenities into our built environments to make life easier for both women and men. Thus, although women's studies has not yet transformed the field of architecture, it has certainly contributed an awareness of gender as a critical element in understanding the built environment. As we learn more about this dynamic relationship, we will be better able to generate new visions of space that more effectively satisfy human needs. With growing numbers of women architects, women are sure to increasingly define their own place in the built environment.

BIBLIOGRAPHY

Beecher, Catherine. *A Treatise on Domestic Economy*. New York: Schocken Books, 1997. [c. 1841].

Cohen, Patricia Cline. "Safety and Danger: Women on American Public Transport. 1750-1850." In Dorothy O. Helly and Susan M. Reverby (Eds.), *Gendered Domains: Rethinking Public and Private in Women's History* (pp. 109-122). Ithaca, NY: Cornell University Press, 1992.

De Beauvoir, Simone. In H.M. Parshley (Ed. and trans.), *The Second Sex* (p. 450). New York: Alfred A. Knopf, 1957.

Deutsch, Sarah. "Reconceiving the City: Women, Space, and Power in Boston. 1870-1910." *Gender and History 6* (August 1994): 202-223.

Friedan, Betty. *The Feminine Mystique*. New York: Norton, 1963.

Kennedy, Margrit. "Gyn/Ecology: On the Relationship Between Women/Nature/Space." Paper delivered at the Annual Meeting of the Finnish Association of Women Architects. Helsinki, March 1981.

Kilde, Jeanne Halgren. "The 'Predominance of the Feminine' at Chautauqua: Rethinking the Gender-Space Relationship in Victorian America." *Signs 24* (Winter 1994): 449-486.

Weisman, Leslie Kanes. *Discriminating by Design: A Feminist Critique of the Man-Made Environment*. Urbana, IL: University of Chicago Press, 1992.

Chapter 25

The Impact of Feminism on the Library Science Profession

Amy Begg DeGroff

Feminism, a theory of social, political, and economic equality among the sexes, has had a limited impact on the library science profession. Despite library science's tradition of being a female-dominated profession, masculine styles of leadership and inequality in the structure and pay scales of libraries abound. Feminism, which rejects hierarchy and encourages cooperation and collaboration, would greatly benefit the library science profession, were it to be adopted uniformly by librarians and the library community.

Library science is a field that encompasses the work done by librarians and library technicians. The field includes the science of selecting materials for use by patrons, cataloging materials so that they are accessible, retrieving materials for research needs, and preserving materials for the future use of patrons.

Librarianship is often perceived as a traditionally female-intensive profession. Historically, however, this has not been the case. Initially, the library profession was dominated by men. At the first American Libraries Association (ALA) convention in 1876, only thirteen of the 104 attendees were women. Women quickly moved into the field, however, and by 1910, nearly 80 percent of all library workers in the United States were women; only the nursing and teaching professions consisted of a higher percentage of female members.

During the late-nineteenth and early twentieth centuries, library work was viewed as appropriate for women, since it involved sedentary, quiet work and required limited physical strength. This profession absorbed many college-educated, unmarried, self-supporting Gibson Girls who were entering the working world. (Gibson Girls refers to drawings by Charles Dana Gibson; the Gibson Girl was athletic and independent, while remaining dignified and feminine. She was featured in sketches in serial publications from about 1890 to 1910.) While these women were in public roles, they were still in feminine roles: the library profession was conducted in a safe, confined atmosphere, much like a home environment, and the service aspect of the job embodied domestic virtues. Few of these women developed careers; most left their positions after marriage. However, in spite of the limited time many women remained in the library world, they did have an impact on the profession. Women, whether based on sociological factors or biological realities, generally have a leadership style that is often described as being more interactive. For the most part, women encourage contributions from all members of a group and reject the hierarchical structure often imposed on the workplace. This cooperative leadership style was reflected in the library organization. The library community was collaboratively run and power within the library was shared among all workers whose main motivation was the diffusion of knowledge and the empowerment of their patrons.

From 1900 to 1920, Europeans steadily migrated to America and foreign-born residents made up 13 percent of America's population. The majority of these immigrants settled in American cities, living in communities populated by people from their own countries. They turned to local organizations for assistance in adapting to American life, such as churches and settlement houses. In addition, immigrants turned to public libraries for education and job training. By offering immigrants assistance in learning to read, furthering their education, enhancing the education of their children, and providing social outlets, American public libraries were vital to immigrants' orientation into American culture.

Women librarians were actively involved in the changes instituted by their libraries. For instance, changes in Baltimore's Enoch Pratt Free Library collection and staff development were brought about by the efforts of Mrs. Bloch, a professional librarian, who was appointed custodian of Station Eleven in 1904. Located in Baltimore's east side, Station Eleven was at the center of the Jewish community, which encompassed three square miles in downtown Baltimore. This community, approximately 10 percent of the city's entire mileage, included many Russian Jewish immigrants, who, by 1920, made up 27 percent of the total foreign-born population, and 4 percent of the city's total population. Station Eleven flourished, due mostly to the efforts and skill of Mrs. Bloch. According to the 1905 Annual Report, she spoke English, German, Russian, Yiddish, and Hebrew, and she worked hard to make the immigrants feel comfortable and welcome. In their native languages, she was able to explain to them the many privileges offered to them by the Pratt Library.

Mrs. Bloch's efforts were not directed from library administration. She implemented changes in her branch based on her own observations of her patron's needs and interests. Mrs. Bloch was a successful, effective librarian who changed the services offered by and the collection in the Enoch Pratt Free Library during her tenure. She was an early feminist who made the library a relevant part of the lives of immigrant residents of Baltimore. In her 1906 Annual Report, Mrs. Bloch explained that " . . . we have an opportunity to teach the half acclimated foreigner to think American thoughts and so become Americans in spirit, which is of more benefit to them, and in the end to the people among whom they are destined to live, than all other means used to Americanize foreigners put together" (Enoch Pratt Free Public Library, 1906).

Mrs. Bloch was effective at attracting her patrons to the Station, as her circulation records demonstrate. For example, in 1904 the library was only open fourteen days (due to construction), had 121 registered patrons, and circulated 666 volumes (Enoch Pratt Free Public Library, 1904). Station Eleven was the busiest branch library in the Baltimore system. Mrs. Bloch aggressively recruited volunteers who did not speak English as their first language, so that she could use their language skills to the benefit of all her library users. Mrs. Bloch was a visionary who moved beyond the role of a librarian as a sedentary, virtuous keeper of books and assured that her library and work changed people's lives.

In the early decades of the twentieth century, library science offered professional opportunities for educated women. Although perceived as an appropriate work environment for women, because of its domestic and tranquil atmosphere, women such as Mrs. Bloch found ways to help others and to make their own careers more exciting and rewarding. However, in the 1970s, at the height of the feminist movement, men were receiving coveted leadership positions in libraries. Indeed, as the feminist movement enjoyed its heyday, female librarians were underrepresented in management. In 1979, in eighty major public libraries, seventy-one were headed by men. Research libraries regarded women's ability to lead in much the same fashion. According to the 1983 fiscal year report of the Association of Research Libraries (ARL, 1983), of the eighty-one research libraries included in ARL, men headed sixty-six (Yates, 1979).

The feminist movement of the 1960s and 1970s worked to increase professional and personal opportunities for all women and urged women to look beyond women's work and to strive for "higher" goals. Traditional career paths for women were portrayed as less than ideal. The feminist movement urged women to strive toward higher-status professions, such as medical science or law. The image of a librarian was consigned to the options formerly available to women, rather than an ideal position. Librarians became concerned (and remain concerned to this day) with the perception of their field as a woman's field. Librarians collectively have spent and continue to spend a considerable amount of energy establishing their field as a viable profession, much like the legal or medical professions. These efforts are exerted through societies such as the American Libraries Association, through library education programs, and, informally, in collegial relationships in libraries.

The library science community has worked to be respected as a profession by embracing a definition given in the guidelines of the trait theory, which holds that a profession must include, but is not limited to, the following: the requirement of a higher degree; a unique body of abstract knowledge; a code of ethics for practitioners; an orientation toward service; autonomy in the practice of work; and the association of members through which control is exercised over who is authorized to practice and how much practice is to be conducted (Harris, 1992). The library community adopted the trait theory as a means of proving the value of librarians, and in order to equate them with other professionals, such as medical doctors and lawyers, thereby rejecting their roots as a feminine profession. To fully understand the trait theory, one needs only to apply it to the medical and legal professions. Medical doctors and lawyers obtain higher degrees, pursue a unique body of knowledge, work within and strive to maintain a code of ethics, provide a service, and associate with like professionals in organizations such as the American Medical Association and the American Bar Association.

The trait theory is rooted in masculine leadership styles and focuses on issues of control and hierarchy. An association of members and a code of ethics each require a hierarchical structure for their development and implementation. Likewise, autonomy in the practice of work implies limited collaborative work processes or team-oriented work environments. In keeping with the trait theory and in an attempt to be perceived as professionals, the library science profession has placed a great deal of emphasis on hierarchy. Hierarchy exists not only in the administrative structure of the organization, but also in the profession as a whole. The greatest dividing line, and the single most significant factor in determining someone's place in the hierarchy, is the level of education, which affects the distribution of power and responsibility within the library setting. Most mid- and high-level library positions, which require a master's degree in library science (MLS), are described as "professional" and the job duties and compensation reflect the professional status of the employee. Professional librarians are expected to perform collection development (book selection) and are often responsible for the orientation of new patrons and for training library users on using resources within the library. Less prestigious paraprofessionals perform support tasks within the library. They are charged with managing circulation, interlibrary loans, and collection management tasks, such as coordinating binding, serial management, and book stack maintenance. However, as the profession adopts technology into its daily work life, and suffers from severe budget cuts and staff reductions, the lines between professional and paraprofessional positions have blurred. Computers perform many collection management tasks formerly handled by paraprofessionals while paraprofessional staff interact with patrons and library users on a daily basis. The hierarchy and division of labor, once so vital to the structure of a library, are now irrelevant.

In an effort to resolve these issues, librarians have started exploring alternative leadership styles. An option to the masculine standards and definitions of professionalism, which would still maintain library science as a professional field, is to adopt feminist leadership styles and incorporate these styles into the culture of the library community. Feminist leadership styles reject hierarchy and advocate a cooperative, circular approach toward management. Rather than emphasize the difference in the education of employees, as the current hierarchical structure of the profession does, a feminist approach looks at the positive contributions by each member of the team. This change in approach is really a return to the roots of librarianship, as embodied by Mrs. Bloch of Enoch Pratt Station Eleven, who implemented change when and where she felt it was appropriate, without waiting for the hierarchy of her organization to impose change from above.

Some professional librarians have implemented this more collaborative leadership model. Joseph Boisse, University Librarian at the University of California at Santa Barbara, suggests a team approach to running a library. Each team focuses on a different user service, including acquisitions, automated systems, collection development and research consultation and reference. The structure of each team would be different, based on the members' wishes, but, regardless, hierarchy would be rejected and each member would contribute ideas and work equally (Boisse, 1996).

Another area where the library community could adopt a feminist perspective to the benefit of all is pay equity and equitable promotion. According to 1995 salary figures, men entering the library profession earn 5.3 percent more than women beginning comparable library jobs. In 1976, the disparity in salaries was 2.2 percent. Although it is inconceivable that anyone's pay would be based on their gender, it is even more disturbing to see this type of gender inequality in a field that traditionally offered women professional opportunities when other doors were closed to them. Furthermore, the situation is getting worse, not better (Hildenbrand, 1997).

Despite the predominance of women in the profession, men still succeed in receiving higher positions than women. For instance, the

Associated Research Libraries 1994 survey of research libraries examined the salaries of men and women university librarians with the same number of years of experience. Out of all university librarians who have been in the field for over thirty-five years, women make up nearly 60 percent of the total, while earning 67.23 percent of what their male counterparts make (Association of Research Libraries, 1995).

Gender should not be a factor in the salary or promotion of library personnel. The library community must remain vocal and vigilant about this issue. The library community has grassroots organizations that can work to bring attention to these inequities. The Feminist Task Force (a subgroup within the American Libraries Association) is an active group that holds conferences on issues of women in librarianship. This group needs to vocalize the disparity in compensation between men and women performing comparable jobs and should work to equalize the field to ensure that the management of the library profession is representative of the profession as a whole.

The library profession also could benefit from a return to its roots as a female profession and the adoption of some feminist principles. Enoch Pratt's librarian at Station Eleven, Mrs. Bloch, is a solid example of an early library feminist. She did what needed to be done for her patrons regardless of whether it had been decreed to her from above. Her patrons' needs and interests guided her decisions. Feminist leadership and cooperative management was her style and it served her well. Feminist leadership and cooperative management styles could also well serve today's and the futures' library community.

BIBLIOGRAPHY

American Libraries Association. *ALA Survey of Librarian Salaries.* Chicago: Office of Research and Office of Library Personnel Resources, American Libraries Association, 1979.

Association of Research Libraries. *ARL Annual Salary Survey: Table 19.* Washington, DC: Association of Research Libraries, 1983.

Association of Research Libraries. *ARL Annual Salary Survey: Table 19.* Washington, DC: Association of Research Libraries, 1995, 38.

Boisse, Joseph A. "Adjusting the Horizontal Hold: Flattening the Organization." *Library Administration and Management* 10(2) (1996): 77-81.

Campbell, Jerry. "Building an Effectiveness Pyramid for Leading Successful Organizational Transformation." *Library Administration and Management* 10(2) (1996): 82-86.

Enoch Pratt Free Public Library, *Enoch Pratt Free Library Annual Report.* 1904.

Enoch Pratt Free Public Library, *Enoch Pratt Free Library Annual Report.* 1906.

Enoch Pratt Free Public Library, *Enoch Pratt Free Library Annual Report.* 1908.

Enoch Pratt Free Public Library, *Enoch Pratt Free Library Annual Report.* 1909.

Harris, Roma M. *Librarianship: The Erosion of a Woman's Profession.* Norwood, NJ: Ablex Publishing Corporation, 1992.

Hildenbrand, Suzanne. "Still Not Equal: Closing the Library Gender Gap." *Library Journal* (March 1, 1997): 44-46.

Pritchard, Sarah. "Backlash, Backwater, or Back to the Drawing Board: Feminist Thinking and Librarianship in the 1990s." *Wilson Library Bulletin* (June 1994): 42-46.

St. Lifer, Evan. "We Are the Library: Support Staff Speak Out." *Library Journal* (November 1, 1995): 30-34.

Weibel, Kathleen and Kathleen M. Heim. *The Role of Women in Librarianship: 1876-1976: The Entry, Advancement, and Struggle for Equalization in One Profession.* New York: Oryx Press, 1979.

Yates, Ellen Gaines. "Sexism in the Library." *Library Journal* (December 15, 1979): 2615-2619.

Chapter 26

The Forgotten Discipline: Sport Studies and Physical Education

Dayna Beth Daniels

A couple of summers ago I decided to sit in on a graduate level Education course called Gender and Education. On the first day, the professor asked the students to write down their answers to the following question: How would your life be different if you had been born the other sex? The student complement of this class was fourteen women and five men. We went around the room and read our answers. I do not remember what the men wrote, but twelve of the women indicated that if they had been born male they would have been able to participate more in sports.

If this had been the result of an empirical study, the statistical significance would be obvious. Yet how often, if at all, is girls' and women's involvement in sports and physical activity looked at as an issue of scholarly concern or academic critique in most disciplines, including Women's Studies? Sport is traditionally seen as a male domain. If for no other reason, this should make sport a very important issue of concern for feminist analyses and for investigation in Women's Studies curricula. Learning about why women are excluded or barred from certain human activities ought to be as important as understanding those factors that are central to the lives of most girls and women, in other words, those activities deemed culturally normative and gender-appropriate for females. In the study of women's lives and the power imbalances between the sexes, any factors that are gendered for the purpose of either inclusion or exclusion ought to be high on our inventory of inquiry. Sport and physical activity involvement are among our most gendered cultural forms.

In this chapter, I will explore two primary questions: (1) should women's studies programs include materials and critical analyses of sport and physical activity involvement as they impact on the lives of girls and women; and, if indeed they should, (2) does women's studies still overlook sport and physical activity involvement of girls and women as an area of inquiry and potential empowerment?

In order to answer the first question, an examination of women's studies programs' philosophies and motivations must first be explored. The primary force in the development of women's studies was the invisibility of girls and women in traditional disciplines. Women's perspectives and experiences often were not presented except as footnotes or were presented only when a woman did something that was considered extraordinary. Women's studies was founded to not only correct the omissions related to women, but to provide woman-centered philosophy and theoretical frameworks to use as tools in this endeavor. But, as part of the academic structure, women's studies, considered radical due to its feminist base and women-centered approach, still often suffers from certain traditional biases that exist within postsecondary institutions. When women's studies courses were first developed, the issues that obviously were of greatest concern to girls and women became the foundation of the courses, and eventually the programs, in women's studies.

What makes women's studies so unique and exciting is the examination of issues concerning women from an interdisciplinary approach; in other words, issues that interest and affect women are explored from a variety of perspectives. The connections made among different views often do not happen within typical disciplinary research or course work. One of the most critical aspects of this interdisciplinary nature is to investigate new relationships and create new perspectives on old ideas that might radically change their importance in the lives of girls and women. Women's bodies lie at the center of these interdisciplinary intersections. How women's bodies are socially constructed, how women's lives are affected by these constructions, and how women can be empowered through this knowledge is one of the foundations of women's studies because it helps to define the power relations that exist between women and men.

The centrality of sport in the lives of boys and men has much to do with this power imbalance. From their earliest days, males are taught, through sport, that their bodies are important, experiencing from an early age both bodily pleasure and pain. They are also introduced to male sport figures who become for many boys role models, from whom they learn about masculinity and sexuality. Likewise, boys are taught that sport is a special domain that belongs to males only; females trespass only occasionally across the hallowed ground. The absence of materials on women in sport in women's studies has less to do with what we know about the importance of exercise and physical activity in the lives of girls and women and much more to do with the cultural positioning of sport as male/masculine. If we accept that there are cultural and power imbalances between women and men, and that sport is an obvious site of these imbalances, then the study of sport and its relationship to the construction of cultural dichotomies such as masculine/feminine, active/passive, and central/marginal becomes more important in any disciplinary inquiry into women.

Another dichotomy that permeates intellectual discourse is what is known as the mind/body split. This dichotomy separates what is considered to be intellectual (read: mind/male/important) from what is considered natural (read: body/female/less important). This hierarchical dichotomy has existed in Western culture and education since the time of early Greek civilization. But this mind/body split also presents an ambiguity that confirms the need to study sport and physical activity as it relates to women. Ironically, although the mind/body split essentially has become a male (intellect)/female (body) split, sport and its consequent development of the body are seen to be male. Why is this one factor of the body so closely related to males and protected as a male preserve when almost every other intellectual pursuit associates the body with the feminine? Investigating this paradox of the mind/body split may reveal some very interesting insights into the relationship between women's low self-esteem and poor body image and the lack of emphasis on sports for women and girls.

Recent research tells us that girls who are inactive and nonparticipatory in sport have lower self-esteem and poor body image (Pope, 1999). Existing trends, especially among adolescent girls, when self-esteem often plummets, are to drop out of sports if previously active or become even more physically inactive, or to go to the opposite end of the spectrum and become involved in extreme eating behaviors and excessive or addictive exercise regimens (Rhea, 1998). The issues of self-esteem, body image, and disordered eating are central areas of study in women's studies courses. Understanding the relationships between sport and physical activity to these areas will provide important information and potential solutions to overcoming the perpetual self-surveillance (Bartkey, 1988) and quest for the perfect (unattainable) body that occupies, to the point of pathology, the thoughts and energies of so many girls and women.

Unfortunately, an interest in sports and physical activity in the lives of women and girls, and an awareness of the harmful effect that the omission of sports in girls' lives has on body image, did not surface until the late 1960s, paralleling the rise of the third wave of feminism. Physical education researchers, who bravely called themselves feminist as they worked in a field that was considered male, actively conducted research on females. The research followed the various feminist frameworks that were also developing. Liberal, Marxist, socialist, and radical feminist perspectives were taken up by various scholars who were interested in explaining the inequalities in sport and offering solutions to remedy the problems. Research relating to women and sport came in a broad range of areas relating to the body including femininity, sexuality, and reproduction. Concerns relating to girls' and women's ideas relative to competition, contact sports, winning and losing, same-sex versus mixed programs, coaching, and leadership for girls' and women's sport were investigated with the goal in sight for increasing the participation in sport at all levels for girls and women and for making sport a more woman-centered activity. The underlying goal of all of this feminist research was to show that the benefits, and the hazards, of sport participation were the same for girls and women as for boys and men. The difficult part has been getting this idea accepted!

Dispelling myths about females and female bodies, what they can and ought not to do, what they ought to look like and how girls and women are supposed to behave is an important focus in feminist sport studies research. Threats to the reproductive capabilities of females were often cited in the past as reason why involvement of girls and women in physical activity needed to be limited and restricted (Cahn, 1998; Lenskyj, 1991; Sayers, 1982). It has been strongly, and often erroneously, believed that any activity which might compromise the reproductive capability of a female must be avoided. Since the middle of the 1880s, prevailing medical attitudes supported the idea that certain physical activities were detrimental to the one true purpose of womanhood. Genteel movements and graceful rhythmic activities, such as gymnastics or dance, which maintained a young girl's health so that she would be strong enough to endure childbirth, were encouraged. Rough and tumble tomboy activity was seen as inappropriate and a threat to reproductive health. There was no medical research to support these claims. The fact that working-class women labored at extremely physically demanding jobs and had no more problems with childbirth than upper-class women was never looked at as evidence to disprove these beliefs. Even though there is much evidence today to support the overall benefits of physical activity participation, many myths, such as the belief that girls ought to curtail physical activity during their periods, live on. The suggestion that childbearing might not even be women's primary reason for existence is an idea that many dismiss out of hand as radical. The overlying message is that sport participation by girls and women could endanger their roles as wives and mothers. In other words, if a woman is unable to have children or chooses not to have children, she will not be able to get a man.

Attention to femininity and how sport fits into contemporary notions of femininity have also been a focus of feminist sport research. Just as there are human characteristics that are generally considered to be masculine, there are also characteristics that are labeled feminine. Graceful, caring, emotional, dependent, and quiet are some of the qualities that usually are attributed to females. Generally, these are not factors that are considered important to the successful participation in sports. Although activities such as gymnastics, synchronized swimming, figure skating, and dance require great strength, power, and endurance, these factors are often underplayed due to the artistic qualities that these athletes must also display. These feminine sports are deemed gender appropriate for females. In an attempt to preserve the masculine definition of sport, boys and men who choose to participate in these girl sports are often labeled as "sissy" or gay.

This is one mechanism for maintaining a separation between what real men do and what women do. If women's sporting activities are not considered to be real sports, then masculinity and femininity are not threatened.

One consequence of this is that girls and women who choose to participate in sports that are traditionally considered to be male sports are often accused of being unfeminine. Contemporary standards of femininity are displayed everywhere, in magazines, on television, on billboards and posters; these visual images display the ideal feminine woman and are pushed onto girls and women. This ideal includes an extremely slim, made-up woman with beautiful hair and clothes, and a girlish, almost prepubescent, figure. Although a more muscular physique is acceptable today within the range of appropriate feminine presentation, too much muscle, often the amount needed to be a successful athlete, is seen as masculine and, therefore, not attractive. The hyperfeminine package is sold to women as the road to success for women—the road to sexual appeal—the road to the perfect man. The message here is that for women to be considered sexy and appealing to men, they must be feminine. If women athletes are not feminine, they will miss out on all the wonderful promises that this false image of women promotes. Most important, they will not be attractive to the opposite sex.

Challenging the sexuality of a girl or woman can be very threatening. Often the sexuality of an athlete is questioned if she is perceived to be less than feminine. In many sporting environments, it is often accepted that if a woman is not feminine, she must be masculine. If a woman is masculine, she must be lesbian. Sexual labeling of women athletes is a homophobic reaction to heterosexist practice that has taken place in sports for nearly a century (Cahn, 1994). Whether or not a woman is lesbian or heterosexual ought to be unrelated to her choice to participate in sports. The fear of being labeled lesbian has deterred many young women from pursuing participation in certain sports or sport-related careers. Team sports, contact sports, sports that involve power such as weightlifting or shot-putting, or sports that have exclusively male professional opportunities are those sports that are central to the masculine ideal. The argument is often put forward that if women want to do these masculine activities, they must be masculine or want to be men. Although this is false of both women athletes and lesbians in general, it has been a successfully constructed barrier to women's involvement in most sports. The real deterrent for many women is that if they are seen as masculine or lesbian they will not get a man.

These myths demonstrate that the real issues are not reproduction, femininity, or women's sexuality, but male accessibility to and patriarchal control of female bodies. This theme weaves its thread though most of the issues discussed in women's studies classes. Women's health concerns, women's unpaid labor in the home, sexuality, unequal pay scales for work of equal value, media representations of women, harassment and violence, eating disorders, women's access to pensions and civil rights, and women's responsibilities as caregivers to children and the elderly all can be analyzed from the perspective of male control of women's bodies.

The same issues emerge in physical education and sport studies. What makes the study of sport, and women and sport, an important area to study in women's studies classes is twofold. First, it is on the playgrounds and sport fields where males learn to be men and where boys and men begin to acquire their beliefs about men, women, and the relationships between them. Contemporary gender relations can be illustrated and understood by using sport as a foundation for successful examples. Second, sport is more than just play. It is an enterprise from which girls and women are systematically excluded. The importance placed on sport in North American culture means that the effects of this exclusion reach well beyond the playing fields, courts, arenas, and other sporting venues.

We must be aware that sport and sport-related industries are responsible for billions of dollars being spent and made every year in North America (Hall et al., 1991; Coakley, 1998). Sport-related business employs thousands of workers in all kinds of jobs including professional athletes, sports medicine personnel, coaches, researchers, media writers, broadcasters, producers, manufactures of sporting goods, and sales personnel. Governments pass legislation that affects sport at both the amateur and professional levels. Through all of this, women are virtually invisible and silenced. In many cases, women have little or no access to the social benefits that can come from involvement in sport, which go well beyond personal wellness.

Obviously, then, the study of sport and physical activity in women's studies courses is important. Sport is much more than just an activity; sport is a microcosm of North American society. How women are treated in sport, how their bodies are portrayed and controlled and how certain aspects of sport are closed to women are all reflections of women's struggles in society in general. Yet the question remains: do women's studies programs leave sport and physical activity out of their courses? A brief examination of eight popular textbooks for introductory courses in women's studies reveals that 100 percent of these texts include material on health, body image, and sexuality. Most include material on disordered eating and violence against women. Only one of these texts includes any material on sports or athletics. It is an interesting omission considering all that we know about the relationship between exercise and health, self-esteem, body image, and personal safety.

A perusal of women's studies textbooks is not a definitive study on either the inclusion or exclusion of materials on sport in women's studies classes, but it is one marker among many. A review of the conference proceedings from women's studies association meetings in both the United States and Canada reveals an absence of presentations and research papers in this area. Women's studies associations' membership directories are fairly devoid of scholars who list sport or physical activity as a research interest or area of expertise. My personal experiences* in attempting to discuss this issue at professional meetings related to women's studies is my strongest evidence that this "male preserve of sport" is little understood as an important site for empowerment and personal understanding for all females. Although this evidence is anecdotal, professional experience of fifteen

*For example, a few years ago I had a paper relating to women's bodies in sport accepted at a national women's studies conference. There were three papers in this session, which was scheduled at 8:00 a.m. on the Saturday morning of the conference. By 8:15, there were only three people in the room: myself, one of the other presenters, and a conference participant who admitted that she was in the wrong room, but was too embarrassed to get up to leave. Later in the day when the other presenter and I challenged the conference organizers about the timing of our session, their response was: "Well, we knew no one would show up for a session on sport so why waste a prime time slot." This was also the feeling of the third presenter, which is why she did not even bother to get up so early on a Saturday! This is a fairly typical example of the relationship between women's studies and sport studies by numerous academics.

years in women's studies and twenty-five years in sport studies convinces me that there is support for this supposition.

A growing number of courses are offered in North American universities that deal with women and sport, some of which are included as options in women's studies programs. Yet the very fact that we have courses called "Women and Sport" is an indicator that girls and women are still treated as a special case or problematic within sport studies. Separate courses are needed to make up the shortfall of material in core courses and options within the fields of sports studies. Women and Sport, even in many women's studies programs, is still rare; the traditional focus of many sport studies programs include girls and women as an "add women and stir" methodology.

The importance of sport as a social institution or cultural form is often overlooked by all academic disciplines except physical education and sport studies departments. There are many reasons why this limits the education of students and faculty alike. Even though sport is considered a male domain and, therefore, might be seen as central to studies in a patriarchal society, its apparent focus on the body rather than the mind disqualifies it as a legitimate study by many. The importance of the study of sport and physical activity in women's studies can be argued for exactly the same reasons. The fact that sport is considered to be a male domain that functions to maintain many of the social inequities between the sexes is reason enough for women to be as knowledgeable as possible about this social system.

BIBLIOGRAPHY

Bartkey, Sandra Lee. "Foucault, Femininity, and the Modernization of Patriarchal Power." In Irene Diamond and Lee Quinby (Eds.), *Feminism and Foucault: Reflections on Resistance* (pp. 61-86). Boston: Northeastern University Press, 1988.

Cahn, Susan K. *Coming on Strong: Gender and Sexuality in Twentieth-Century Women's Sports*. New York: Free Press, 1994.

__________. "From the 'Muscle Moll' to the 'Butch' Ballplayer: Mannishness, Lesbianism, and Homophobia in U.S. Women's Sports". In Rose Weitz (Ed.), *The Politics of Women's Bodies: Sexuality, Appearance and Behavior* (pp. 67-81). New York: Oxford University Press, 1998.

Coakley, Jay J. *Sport in Society: Issues and Controversies,* Sixth Edition. Boston: Irwin/McGraw-Hill, 1998.

Hall, Ann M., Trevor Slack, Garry Smith, and David Whitson. *Sport in Canadian Society*. Toronto: McClellend and Stewart, 1991.

Lenskyj, Helen J. *Out of Bounds: Women, Sport, and Sexuality*. Toronto: The Women's Press, 1991.

Pope, Meredith. "Gender Gap." *Girls and Women in Sport (GWS) News* 26 (1999): 3.

Rhea, Deborah J. "Physical Activity and Body Image of Female Adolescents: Moving Toward the 21st Century." *Journal of Physical Education, Recreation, and Dance (JOPERD)* 69 (1998): 27-31.

Sayers, Janet. *Biological Politics: Feminist and Anti-feminist Perspectives*. London: Tavistock, 1982.

Theberge, Nancy. "Sport and Women's Empowerment." *Women's Studies International Forum* 10 (1987): 387-393.

Index

Order Your Own Copy of This Important Book for Your Personal Library!

TRANSFORMING THE DISCIPLINES
A Women's Studies Primer

_______ in hardbound at $59.95 (ISBN: 1-56023-959-X)
_______ in softbound at $24.95 (ISBN: 1-56023-960-3)

COST OF BOOKS______

OUTSIDE USA/CANADA/ MEXICO: ADD 20%____

POSTAGE & HANDLING________
(US: $4.00 for first book & $1.50 for each additional book)
Outside US: $5.00 for first book & $2.00 for each additional book)

SUBTOTAL________

in Canada: add 7% GST____

STATE TAX____
(NY, OH & MIN residents, please add appropriate local sales tax)

FINAL TOTAL____
(If paying in Canadian funds, convert using the current exchange rate, UNESCO coupons welcome.)

❑ **BILL ME LATER:** ($5 service charge will be added)
(Bill-me option is good on US/Canada/Mexico orders only; not good to jobbers, wholesalers, or subscription agencies.)

❑ Check here if billing address is different from shipping address and attach purchase order and billing address information.

Signature______________________

❑ **PAYMENT ENCLOSED:** $______________

❑ **PLEASE CHARGE TO MY CREDIT CARD.**

❑ Visa ❑ MasterCard ❑ AmEx ❑ Discover
❑ Diner's Club ❑ Eurocard ❑ JCB

Account # ______________________

Exp. Date______________________

Signature______________________

Prices in US dollars and subject to change without notice.

NAME______________________
INSTITUTION______________________
ADDRESS______________________
CITY______________________
STATE/ZIP______________________
COUNTRY______________ COUNTY (NY residents only)______________
TEL______________ FAX______________
E-MAIL______________

May we use your e-mail address for confirmations and other types of information? ❑ Yes ❑ No
We appreciate receiving your e-mail address and fax number. Haworth would like to e-mail or fax special discount offers to you, as a preferred customer. **We will never share, rent, or exchange your e-mail address or fax number.** We regard such actions as an invasion of your privacy.

Order From Your Local Bookstore or Directly From

The Haworth Press, Inc.

10 Alice Street, Binghamton, New York 13904-1580 • USA
TELEPHONE: 1-800-HAWORTH (1-800-429-6784) / Outside US/Canada: (607) 722-5857
FAX: 1-800-895-0582 / Outside US/Canada: (607) 722-6362
E-mail: getinfo@haworthpressinc.com

PLEASE PHOTOCOPY THIS FORM FOR YOUR PERSONAL USE.

www.HaworthPress.com

BOF00